The Rochford
Book of Houseplants

By Thomas Rochford and Richard Gorer

*

THE ROCHFORD
BOOK OF FLOWERING POT PLANTS
ROCHFORD'S HOUSEPLANTS FOR EVERYONE

Aphelandra squarrosa Louisae

THE ROCHFORD
BOOK
OF HOUSEPLANTS

THOMAS ROCHFORD
AND
RICHARD GORER

with paintings by
Cynthia Newsome-Taylor

FABER AND FABER
3 Queen Square
London

First published in 1961
by Faber and Faber Limited
3 Queen Square London WC1
Second Edition 1963
Reprinted 1965 and 1967
This new and revised edition 1973
Printed in Great Britain by
Latimer Trend & Company Ltd Plymouth

ISBN 0 571 04807 2

Contents

Contents

Illustrations

IN COLOUR

MONOCHROME

7

Illustrations

8

Illustrations

9

Illustrations

Illustrations

11

Preface to the Third Edition

D uring the last ten years some considerable changes
have come over the houseplant scene, and these have
been thought sufficient to warrant a revision of our
original work. Some of the changes are fairly radical. It is now
somewhat unusual to find houses without some sort of central
heating, which means that a number of plants that might have
expected a rather restricted sale when this book first appeared
can now become available to many more would-be growers. The
spread of North Sea gas has meant that the perils of gas fumes
on plants has now been considerably reduced; the fumes of this
gas being, so far as has been ascertained, more or less innocuous
to most plants. The references to oil fumes in our pages do not
refer to fumes from oil-burning boilers, but to fumes from
paraffin heaters. No fumes should escape from oil-burning
boilers and so no fumes should worry plants from these. A less
desirable phenomenon of the last ten years has been the increasing shortage of good loam, which has led to the formulation of
loamless composts (usually referred to as soilless composts).
These are excellent for short-lived pot plants, but their use with
houseplants poses a number of problems, which are discussed
on page 50. Another mark of the times has been the disappearance
of the clay pot and its replacement with plastic containers. These
have many advantages, being much lighter, not liable to break
if knocked over and they also seem to encourage a more
balanced growth of roots. Against this, being non-porous, the
soil contained therein takes longer to dry out, which means that
watering tends to be at longer intervals, but which also means
that if a plant has been overwatered—and this is the great killer

13

of houseplants—it is that much more difficult to rectify this fault. It is also more difficult for the beginner to know when a plant needs watering. It is no good tapping the side of a plastic pot and it is only experience which will teach you when to water and when to wait, even though the surface may appear dry.

One great advantage of a new edition has been the opportunity to correct some of the mistakes that disfigured our original book and it has also enabled us to rearrange the two Miscellaneous chapters. Originally we had just shoved the various families in as they occurred to us when we were writing, so that there was no way, apart from consulting the index, of guessing where any family might occur. There are two accepted systems of botanical classification; that of Bentham and Hooker and that of Engler. Modern botanists seem to have decided that the Englerian system is the better, so we have now arranged the last two chapters in the Englerian order, with the dicotyledons in the first chapter and the conifers and monocotyledons in the second.

Another phenomenon of the last ten years has been the increasing interest in Victoriana, as we move further away from that period. This has been reflected in house decoration, with the resulting resurgence of interest in ferns and palms. In our first edition we had one palm and one fern, but now, owing to the increased and increasing interest in these plants, we have added a chapter to deal with these. We should confess that in doing this we have tried to foresee the future and, after consulting Victorian books, have described a few plants, notably among the palms, which are not available at the time of writing, but which proved their suitability for home decoration some hundred years ago.

The number of houseplants available continues to fluctuate as new plants are introduced, while difficult plants, which have proved unsuitable have disappeared from the catalogues. In this edition we have added such plants as have proved their worth during the past ten years and also some which are being cultivated now, but have yet to prove their capabilities. In the case of the ivies, this has resulted in an extremely long list of cultivars.

Preface to the Third Edition

But, although we have added all the novelties, we have not deleted many plants which were grown when this book first appeared, but which have since been discontinued and may well be hard to obtain, if not impossible. For example we described 40 different Begonias, but most houseplant nurseries will now only supply about 6 of these, although many others are obtainable from greenhouse nurseries. However the scene is constantly changing and since many of the plants that we described may make a comeback, we have left them all in. The only deletions are three plants, which are really flowering pot plants and which do not agree with the first rule for a houseplant, that it should look attractive all the year round. These deletions are *Bougainvillea, Jasminum* and *Gardenia.*

There always seems to be a considerable brouhaha about the correct Latin names for the various species. We should always remember that plants are given names, so that people know what they are talking about. Most people will know what you mean when you speak of *Beloperone guttata*, but will be completely baffled by references to *Justicia brandegeana*, which is apparently the correct name for the Shrimp plant. Without going to excessive lengths we have tried to give the correct names in some place in our descriptions, but if the plant is better known under an incorrect name, it will probably be the better-known name which heads our description. Names are given by botanists not by the Almighty and the former should remember not to get ideas above their station. The correct botanical name is the earliest published one, not a revelation from Mount Sinai. The only important thing is for the reader to know to what plant we are referring.

We have been much helped in revising this book by Professor E. J. Corner of Cambridge and by the Director of the R.H.S. gardens at Wisley, Mr. Christopher Brickell, but our greatest debt of gratitude is owed to Mr. Desmond Paul, the Secretary to the House of Rochford, without whom, it is safe to say, this new edition would never have been accomplished.

Introduction

―――――――

This book is intended to be a work of reference, rather than a book for continuous reading, which will explain, though it may not excuse, the frequent iteration of details that we have considered important. This has been done deliberately, as we found that a single mention would often pass unnoticed.

We have tried to include all houseplants grown at the present time but it should be borne in mind that new introductions are continually being made and that other plants have not been found sufficiently popular for nurserymen to continue growing them. We have not been able to do anything in foreseeing future introductions, but we have described many plants that are not now easily obtainable. This fact has been mentioned from time to time, but not invariably, and we should perhaps issue a warning that quite a few of the plants described may be temporarily unobtainable. Some, such as *Sparrmannia* and *Oplismenus*, have been found to be unrewarding commercially, while others, such as the less familiar *Philodendrons*, are in very short supply at the moment; this situation will become progressively easier.

The question of which plants to include and which to exclude has troubled us somewhat. Alfred Byrd Graf in his monumental *Exotica* was able to list 4,000 plants, which, by inference, could be grown in the American home. Apart from the fact that Americans keep their houses considerably warmer than we do, he had included some species that would no doubt be unsuitable for our English home (for example the orchid *Phalaenopsis*, which is not an easy plant in the greenhouse) and many that are temporarily unobtainable over here. All the plants that we mention have been grown at Turnford and the vast majority tested for room conditions (in the case of some of the rarer *Philoden-*

drons, such as *gloriosum* and *leichtlinii*, stocks have so far been too small to allow of this), and as a result many plants that would seem perfectly suitable as houseplants have had to be discarded. Even so there are some plants such as *Sonerila*, *Piper ornatum* and *Fittonia argyroneura*, which are by no means easy and we have hesitated before including them. As, however, the successful cultivation of difficult plants is a challenge that many enthusiasts like to meet, we have left them in, accompanied by words of warning.

It is perhaps as well, at this point, to explain that the minimum winter temperatures that we have given must be regarded as applying only to well-rooted, healthy plants. These will survive conditions that will prove fatal to plants that are sickly or not well rooted. From the health point of view the terrestrial parts of a plant are just as important as the aerial ones, and the purchaser of houseplants is strongly recommended to make sure of healthy roots before purchasing. As one of us is a professional grower it would be unwise to labour this point, but it cannot be left unmentioned.

The correct naming of houseplants is far from straightforward; apart from the general flux in taxonomy, to which we have drawn attention in our first chapter, many houseplants are sold under names that any botanist would dismiss as invalid. We have done our best to give the correct names, as at present established, as a correct name seemed preferable to one that was incorrect, even if popularly held. In this matter we have been helped in particular by Mr. L. J. Stenning, Curator of Kew Gardens and Mr. Maurice Mason of King's Lynn, who has made so many fascinating introductions. We have also made full use of the *R.H.S. Dictionary of Gardening* and the aforementioned *Exotica* of Mr. Graf. Monographs on separate families have generally proved unobtainable or written in unfamiliar languages and have not been consulted as frequently as might be wished. We were, however, able to obtain the volumes of Engler's *Pflanzenreich* dealing with the *Philodendrons*, and, though this dates from 1913, it has not yet been superseded. By far the most difficult problem for us has been the selection of suitable language for describing the various plants. We are not writing for professional botanists and it could only be confusing to most readers to find a leaf described as, for example, suborbicular, apex cuspidate. On the other hand it is by no means easy to find colloquial equivalents. Whether we have really made things easier by saying 'lance-shaped' instead of 'lanceolate' or 'shaped like a spear-head' instead of 'hastate' is a problem that has much exercised us. Our aim has been to cut down technical jargon to a minimum. We have tried to avoid botanists' shorthand without falling into gush and to steer a middle course between the two extremes that may be exemplified in the following quotations; both, incidentally, describing the same plant.

1. 'A perennial herb with a short erect stock and stout fibrous roots Lvs 2–4 (–8) cm, confined to a basal rosette, obovate-spathulate, broad and rounded at the end, crenate-toothed, narrowed abruptly into a short broad stalk, sparsely hairy. Scapes 3–12 (–20) cm, naked hairy. Head 16–25 mm diam; bracts oblong, blunt, green or black tipped, hairy. Ray-florets numerous, narrow, spreading, white or pink, disk bright yellow.' (Quoted from the invaluable *Flora of the British Isles* by Clapham, Tutin and Warburg).

2. 'Stalk single-flowered; leaves inversely egg-shaped, narrowing at the base, the margin having rounded notches; root perennial. Who does not love the daisy, the little red-tipped daisy, so like Hope and Faith in its constant up-looking; so cheerful in aspect, that, as the poet has said "It smiles even in times unkind"? To our latest days the Daisy will have a charm, while it can remind us that it was the first flower which we gathered in unlimited abundance; the flower which in childhood we linked into wreaths, when we "prinked our hair with daisies"; the flower on whose clustering numbers we were wont to tread and shout, "Spring is come for we can set our foot on nine daisies". Poets have sung its praises from oldest times, from Chaucer who called it the "eye of day", and Ben Jonson who wrote of "sweet daie's eyes", down to the latest poets of our own period; for its beauty and early memories have ever appealed to the heart and imagination,' etc.,

Introduction

etc. for three pages. (From *The Flowering Plants of Great Britain* by Anne Pratt, edition of 1891. This is in many ways a most useful book and this extract is not altogether typical.)

We have tried to be as factual as the first extract, but in a language more suited to amateurs than specialists, and we have tried to avoid the rhapsodic discursiveness of the second. Our whole object has been to help the houseplant grower to cultivate his plants to the best advantage and to draw his attention to other houseplants, when he wishes to extend his collection. Our aim, like our text, is modest, but not so modest as the authors feel on contemplating the gap between their intentions and their achievement.

Turnford Hall Nurseries,
1.10.59.

NOTE

All the temperatures given in this book are in terms of Fahrenheit, but for those who wish to know the Centigrade equivalents there is a conversion table to be found in Appendix 5, page 285, prepared from information kindly supplied by the Meteorological Office.

CHAPTER I

On Latin Names

————◆◆◆◆◆◆◆◆ ◆◆◆◆◆◆————

S ince the houseplant grower will find himself dealing with long and difficult names such as *Philodendron scandens* and *Pittosporum eugenioides* at an early stage, it might be as well to consider the reasons for these inharmonious names, before we start considering the plants. The main reason for giving plants scientific names is, curious as it may seem to the novice, for the sake of clarity. In England there is a poisonous wild flower known as Hemlock, but if you speak of hemlock to an American he will think of a large conifer. If, instead of speaking of hemlock, we refer to *Conium maculatum* and *Tsuga canadensis*, this particular confusion does not arise, though it will be replaced by complete incomprehension in the mind of a novice. This lack of comprehension can easily be overcome.

All plants are given two scientific names, which are generally, though not invariably, Greek or Latin in origin. The first of these names is the *generic* name. *Genus* is the Latin for 'kind' and the generic name literally means the kind of plant it is. All plants in a genus have similar botanical characteristics, though not necessarily similar physical appearances. The creeping Harebell and the stiff upright Canterbury Bell, both belong to the genus *Campanula*. The generic name may be a description of the plant (*Campanula* means a little bell, referring to the shape of the flowers) or it may commemorate the discoverer or a friend of his (*Dahlia* is named after a Swedish botanist, Dr. Andreas Dahl).

The generic name is always written with a capital letter. After the generic name comes an adjective, usually latinized, which is

21

called either the specific epithet or the trivial name. This describes to what species the plant belongs. All plants in a species should be identical. Occasionally, however, there is a slight difference in a species. For example, a plant that normally has red flowers may produce a plant with white flowers, or a plant with green leaves may produce variegated leaves. Such plants are known as varieties and are given a third or varietal name. This name is usually descriptive of the variation, but occasionally commemorates the discoverer of the variety. White heather, for example, is *Calluna vulgaris* var. *alba,* but there is a variegated Hibiscus which is called *Hibiscus rosa-sinensis* var. *Cooperi.* The specific epithet, according to recommended usage, should be written with a small initial letter, even when it commemorates a name, but a capital is allowed in the varietal name when a person is referred to.[1] Varieties are regarded as arising spontaneously and are originally found in a wild state. By breeding and selection other forms of species, differing in size or colour from the usual form, may be produced. These are known as cultivars and are given names in the language of the country in which they are raised. For example, there is a pale pink form of *Anemone hupehensis* which was raised in Germany and is called *A. hupehensis* 'Kriemhilde'.

In more technical botanical books you may sometimes see names or initials after the scientific name. For example, you may see *Philodendron scandens* Koch & Sellow. These names refer to the botanists who first described the plant. This description, which must be in Latin, is known as a diagnosis, and in this case it means that the plant was first described by the botanists C. Koch and H. Sellow. It sometimes happens that a botanist diagnoses a plant, for the first time as he thinks, when it has previously been done by another botanist. In this case the first diagnosis is regarded as being the valid one. This simple rule has recently been productive of such confusion as to have done away with much of the reason for scientific names. There has been a re-examination of the works and herbaria of the older botanists, and as a result there has been a great preoccupa-

---

[1] See last paragraph of this chapter.

tion with the renaming of plants, which will eventually die down, but is at the moment creating considerable confusion. In the course of a few years the Arum lily, while keeping its specific epithet *aethiopica* has had its generic name changed from *Arum* to *Calla*, then to *Richardia*, and has finally come to rest as *Zantedeschia*. Even more confusing is the case of the popular Japonica, which was at one time known as *Pyrus japonica* (the Japanese pear) then, more sensibly, as *Cydonia japonica* (the Japanese quince) but is now known as *Chaenomeles speciosa*. Nor is this the only source of confusion. From time to time botanists undertake a critical examination of a genus. With better equipment, to say nothing of the ambition of seeing Jones or Smith after a new specific epithet, they tend to multiply the number of species and, on occasion, to create several new genera. The old genus of *Aralia* has been practically denuded of species, which have been re-distributed under such genera as *Polyscias, Elaeodendron, Delarbrea, Pseudopanax, Dizygotheca, Fatsia, Kalopanax, Panax, Oreopanax* and *Schefflera*. As can easily be imagined, the writing of any botanical name at the moment is fraught with some danger, and though we have done our best to give the latest names, we cannot guarantee that they will not have changed in the interval between writing and printing.

The various genera are divided among families. These are distinguished by the endings *ae* or *aceae*. All plants in a family have a certain number of botanical characteristics that are present in every member of the family and not found in other families. For example the daisy family, the *Compositae*, are all characterized by a flower head that is composed of numerous florets. This may consist of ray and disk florets, as in the daisy, ray florets alone, as in the dandelion, or of disk florets alone, as in groundsel. Plants in a family may be of different forms, so long as they have the family characteristics. To return to the *Compositae*: there will be such plants as the annual groundsel, the herbaceous perennial, such as Michaelmas daisy, shrubs such as *Olearia*, tuberous plants such as the Dahlia and Jerusalem artichoke, or plants with succulent fleshy leaves such as

On Latin Names

Kleinia. Sometimes the determining factor is not the flower but the fruit. The *Leguminosae* not only include all the plants with pea-shaped flowers, but also the fluffy balls of the mimosas and wattles and the round flowers of such tropical trees as the Flamboyant. Here the determining factor is the typical pea-pod, which is usually extremely evident, though in some small plants such as clover and medick a magnifying glass may be necessary. Some people recommend splitting this family into *Papilionaceae* for the plants with pea-like flowers and *Caesalpineae* and *Mimosaceae* for the rest.

From the point of view of the houseplant grower the botanical families may be disregarded, but it is useful to be able to recognize the generic and specific names. When we come to describe the plants individually, we have given, where possible, the derivation of the generic names and the translation of the specific epithet. This will not make the names much easier to learn, but may well show them to be less a concatenation of meaningless syllables than would at first appear.

Note: The latest edition of the *Code of Nomenclature* would not allow capital letters even for varietal names. There are, however, undoubted advantages in having them, if only to distinguish varietal names from specific epithets, and in the following pages we have given capitals to varietal names, while all specific epithets are written with a small initial letter.

CHAPTER II

Houseplants in the House

———◆———

The main point of difference between a houseplant and any
other form of plant decoration is its permanence in the
home. A floral arrangement, even if mainly composed of
defoliated sprays of rose hips, will eventually fade or shrivel;
a flowering plant will be retired when the flowering is over;
but a houseplant can be regarded as much as a fixture as a
painting or a piece of sculpture. This analogy, though it is
valid, cannot be pressed too far. Paintings and sculpture
require no attention other than an occasional dusting and
cleaning: houseplants need constant attention. Painting and
sculpture remain as they were when purchased: houseplants
will grow larger, or, even worse, may die. In spite of these
and other differences, houseplants may be regarded, like
paintings and sculpture, as permanent embellishments of the
home.

Bearing this in mind, it is possible to draw up a list of qualities
that a good houseplant should possess. First, the plant must be
robust. By this we do not mean that it should be absolutely
hardy and tolerant of frost, but that it should be able to thrive
in the somewhat difficult conditions of a room. Rooms are
shady and capriciously ventilated; they may be warmer at night
than during the day, a condition contrary to the plant's natural
rhythm; rooms may be draughty and will certainly contain
an atmosphere far drier than most plants demand. All these
disadvantages can be mitigated to a certain extent, but they
exist, and a delicate plant would quickly succumb under such

25

conditions. Such a plant, whatever its qualities, would be useless as a houseplant.

Second, if we are to look at the plant all through the year, it should be evergreen. It is true that there are one or two house-plants, notably *Dioscorea discolor* and *Sedum sieboldii,* which offend against this canon and die down during the winter, but they are exceptional. The *Dioscorea* is so beautiful that it is desirable in spite of its annual habit, while the *Sedum* has so short a resting season and is so easy to grow, that it can be admitted without much demur.

Our robust evergreen plant must also be attractive. Since flowers are somewhat ephemeral, the beauty must be sought in the leaves and habit of the plant. The leaves can attract either through their shape or through their colour, preferably through both. If the plant also grows in an attractive shape, so much the better. *Ficus benjamina* is an attractive houseplant chiefly owing to its appealing 'weeping willow' habit. The leaves, though a pleasant colour, are in no way outstanding, and if it grew up a single unbranched stem like *F. elastica* it would not be at all favoured. Growing as it does, with numerous drooping branches, it gives a charming effect.

VARIEGATION

Many leaves not particularly attractive in themselves may be-come so as the result of variegation. Variegation is a curious phenomenon in which portions of the leaf lose their chlorophyll (the chemical giving the green colour to leaves) and become white, ivory or cream, while the other portions of the leaf remain green. Variegation is not always a healthy sign, as it may be due to a virus infection as in *Hedera helix* 'Lutzii', and even where no virus is present, variegated plants will generally be found to be more delicate and slower growing than the unvariegated type. The slowness of growth may be in part due to the fact that the uncoloured portions of the leaves are devoid of chlorophyll, and so do not contribute in any way to the feeding of the plant. The overall effective leaf area of a variegated plant is less than the corresponding area of an unvariegated type. Why variegated plants should be more delicate than the unvariegated types is more obscure. Variegation is not always constant. The variegated *Tradescantias* and *Ficus pumila* are liable to revert to the normal green-leafed types. This reversion is usually permanent, but in some other plants such as the variety *quadricolor* of *Zebrina pendula* there would appear to be a connexion between temperature and the variegation. During cold periods the plant will revert to the usual *Zebrina* leaf, but during the summer, when hot conditions prevail, the variegation will reappear. It is also possible that it is not heat but more intense light that will bring back this variegation, or maybe a combination of the two. Certainly bright light is essential to variegated leaves and if, for example, the variegated *Ficus australis* is stood in heavy shade, when making its new growth, the young leaves will emerge without any sign of variegation. Transfer the plant to a well-lit situation and the variegation will gradually spread through the leaves. Too bright a light may cause a white variegation to turn yellow, but such brightness is rare in England and need not be too seriously considered.

In some plants variegation is innate. Such a plant is *Ficus parcellii*, a native of the Philippines. It is not particularly handsome and is not suitable as a houseplant, but its botanical interest makes it noteworthy.

There are other variations from the usual green colour to be found among plants, and of these the most common is a deep purple colour all over the leaf; the well-known Copper Beech is a conspicuous example of this. This purple coloration, which is superimposed over the chlorophyll, is apparently a protection for the leaves against sun scorch and is usually found in plants that grow in exposed positions. Often, if these plants are put in shady positions, much of the purple colour will disappear. A *Tradescantia* was once brought back from the West Indies with a purple flush on the upper side of the leaf and a bright crimson underside. In our greenhouses in a somewhat shady position it developed leaves of a bright green with no suggestion of purple: exposed to the sun it developed a purple flush on the underside of the leaf only, and this was far removed from the brilliant crimson that the tropical sun had produced. In some plants this purple colour is only temporary and confined to the young growths, disappearing as the leaves mature. This phenomenon is most spectacular in the popular garden shrub *Pieris forrestii*, where the new growths are bright scarlet, but is also found in many roses and even in plants such as Phlox.

It is generally safe to assume that a purple leaf is a sign that the plant should be given as much light as possible. An exception is to be found in the purple-leaved forms of *Begonia rex*, which like shade, though they will take more light than the green- and silver-leaved varieties.

In addition to leaves that are all one colour, there are many that are basically green (or, in the case of *Cissus discolor*, basically purple) but are marked with other colours. Prominent among these are the *Marantaceae* whose leaves are often ornamented with patterns of red, white or maroon. The reason for these coloured markings on the leaves is somewhat obscure. It is possible that the main object is the attraction of insects to fertilize the flowers. For the most part, plants with coloured leaves have small, inconspicuous flowers. Among the most brilliantly coloured leaves are species of *Acalypha*, *Codiaeum* and the *Marantaceae*, and in every case the flowers are inconspicuous. Against this must be set the fact that other species have equally inconspicuous flowers, but no coloration in the leaves. Among the Bromeliads there are some species that normally have a green leaf, but the inner leaves of the rosette turn a brilliant colour before and during flowering. This coloration is certainly due to a desire to attract insects for pollination. In other cases this is possible, but cannot be regarded as certain, but there must be some reason for plants to deviate from the normal green colouring.

A leaf can be brilliant without the green portion being infringed upon. The red veins of *Fittonia verschaffeltii* and the white veins of *Aphelandra squarrosa Louisae* give a striking appearance to a normally green leaf.

Leaves can, of course, be fascinating without any help of colouring. The large exotic-looking leaves of *Ficus decora* are neither unusual in colour nor in shape, nor, indeed, is the plant graceful in habit. Yet the plant is deservedly the most popular of the *Ficus* grown as houseplants, and among the most popular houseplants of any genus. In this case it would seem that the attraction lies in the size and texture of the leaves. The shiny glossy surface attracts in a way that the matt surface of the leaves of *F. benghalensis*, similar though they are in shape and colour, does not; though the branching habit of *benghalensis* gives a different type of attraction. Beauty is an elusive quality to try to define.

QUALITIES ESSENTIAL IN HOUSEPLANTS

An ability to thrive in shady conditions is an evident requisite for houseplants. Compared to the amount of light received in an open position out of doors, even the most brightly lit room is comparatively shady. Window sills may be well lit, but the interior of the room will have the light as diffused as it is under forest conditions in the open. It is not always desirable or convenient to place plants on the window sills; indeed, in the case of tall growing specimens it is particularly undesirable, and so the majority of houseplants are plants that grow naturally in woodland conditions. In this category many climbing plants are included, but it must be borne in mind that a plant climbs so that it may emerge from the shade into the light. Some plants, indeed, notably many of the *Philodendrons* and *Scindapsus*, produce one form of leaf when they are climbing and a different, much larger leaf when they have emerged into the light. This phenomenon may also be observed in the common ivy of our hedgerows, which will produce the usual dark green ivy leaf while climbing, but when about to flower produces a rounder, glossy and brighter green leaf. Another climber, *Ficus pumila*, shows a similar phenomenon, in that the fruiting branches are stouter and with larger leaves than the thin small-leaved trailing stems of the young plant; but in this case emergence to light does not seem necessary and it is purely a question of the size and age of the plant. Once it is large enough it will start to produce fruiting leaves and branches.

Houseplants in the House

We do not require our houseplants to grow too quickly. We can control the habit and rate of growth ourselves in many ways. If a plant is growing too tall it can be 'stopped': that is to say the growing point is removed. With many plants this will encourage the growth of sideshoots and give a more rounded and bushy-looking plant. Some plants, however, such as *Hedera canariensis*, will not 'break' after stopping, but will just produce another growing point (though if it is a large plant and is pruned back hard it will produce more than one shoot). No plant will break satisfactorily if it has not a large healthy root system. But in spite of pruning and stopping we do not require in our homes a plant such as *Rosa brunonii* which is capable of making thirty feet of growth in a season. Both the plant and its rate of growth should be manageable.

Let us recapitulate the qualities that we have decided the houseplant should possess. It should have a robust constitution, capable of surviving abrupt fluctuations of temperature and preferably fairly tolerant of gas and oil fumes[1]; it should be evergreen; it must be attractive to look at either by reason of its habit, the shape of its leaves or the colour of its leaves or by any combination of these qualities; it would be agreeable if it had attractive flowers, though this is not essential; it should be used to shady conditions and it must not be too vigorous a grower. It would be splendid if we could add to this that it should be very hardy and survive under low temperatures, but at this request we come up against a difficulty. For reasons that we will examine shortly, temperate climes produce very few plants that will satisfy our requirements. There are naturally the various forms of ivy, but they are exceptional.

Apart from the ivy there are very few evergreens from temperate climes that are also shade-lovers. A plant such as the golden Privet, which might be thought an admirable subject for room work, requires far more light than we can supply. The growths would be spindly and etiolated and we get far better results from

[1] One of the side benefits of North Sea gas is that the fumes are considerably less harmful to growing plants. Probably even *Begonias* would tolerate these fumes.

planting the shrub out of doors. There are a few exceptions. The Castor Oil plant, *Fatsia japonica,* and its hybrid with ivy × *Fatshedera lizei,* will thrive equally well in the room or in the garden. The Loquat, *Eriobotrya japonica,* although it has a bad habit of browning at the tips of the leaves, will grow happily indoors and rather unhappily out of doors. *Pittosporum eugenioides* from New Zealand will tolerate a little frost and grows happily indoors, while from China comes *Aspidistra lurida* with its iron constitution. In temperate climates, with clearly defined seasons and marked differences in temperature, it is not particularly advantageous for the plant to be evergreen. Apart from some conifers which are specially adapted with their needle-like leaves, there is a risk that gales would uproot a plant in full leaf and that snow would break it. Such a risk is particularly present in the case of trees and as a result most temperate-climate trees are deciduous.

If the trees are deciduous it is likely that the undergrowth will also be deciduous, as otherwise the plants would get buried each year under the falling leaves, and the plants would be suffocated. Ivy and other creeping plants such as Yellow Pimpernel have adapted themselves to these conditions, but the majority of plants prefer to drop their leaves during the winter.

ATMOSPHERE

In the tropics different conditions obtain. There is little fluctuation of temperature and the plant growth is regulated not by temperature, but by the presence or absence of rain. Some tropical regions have a dry season and a wet season and the plants here show a rhythm corresponding to seasonal growth. Other parts have no such clearly defined periods and yet others have nearly continuous rain. In regions where rain arrives fortuitously the plants must be prepared to make their growth rapidly, when the water is there; while in those districts where the rain is constant, so will plant growth be. For these conditions it is to the plant's advantage to be evergreen so that it can make its new growth as soon as conditions are favourable and then rest when the soil becomes too dry and make further growth when the next rain comes. This does not appear to be essential for all plants. Deciduous trees and herbs exist all through the tropics, but the majority of wild plants are evergreen. This is the reason why most of our houseplants originate from the tropics. Incidentally the tropics have not yet been very thoroughly explored from the houseplant point of view. The vast majority of houseplants come either from Malaysia or from tropical South America. Africa, Australia and Melanesia seem to have been overlooked by collectors. It is possible, but not very likely, that there are no houseplants there; anyone travelling in those parts might well keep his eyes open.

We naturally think of the tropics as being very hot, and at sea level they generally are, but in the mountains the temperature is considerably lower, and the higher you go the lower it falls. Even as low as 2,000 feet above the sea the night temperature may occasionally fall as low as 45°, though this is not usual. It is in the mountains with their higher rainfall, in the regions where the clouds descend, that plant growth is most exuberant. Often the coastal plains are dry and full of cactus, while the mountains are tree-covered and full of the most varied vegetation. The plants from these regions will tolerate temperatures far lower than the average temperatures of the tropics would imply. High temperatures, though beneficial, are not essential for tropical plants, but for the majority a moist atmosphere is. Apart from deserts, most of the tropics have a far higher rainfall than Great Britain, and in parts of India over 300 inches a year is the average. As a result the atmosphere is far moister than our own and considerably more saturated than anything to be found in our rooms. We cannot damp down our rooms as we damp down a greenhouse to give a moist buoyant atmosphere, so we have to search for other ways to give the plants favourable conditions.

From the plant's point of view conditions are worst in the winter. Any form of artificial heating will dry the atmosphere in a room. Gas would appear to be the worst offender and hot-water radiators the least harmful. In any case we need a dry atmosphere to have a warm room and this, though delightful for us, is bad for our plants. Under these circumstances we have to try and create moist microclimates for the plants. One of the simplest ways of doing this is to put the plant pot into a container that is too large for it and fill the extra space with some absorbent material such as peat, sphagnum moss, sand or vermiculite. This can be kept permanently moist and will bathe the plant in water vapour, while the soil ball can be watered separately when required. It is for this reason that the metal, wall-mounting pot-holders that are offered for sale are not very suitable for plants from the tropics. They are also uneconomic, as sooner or later you will have to pot the plant on and either have to buy another plant or another holder. A certain amount of moist air can be provided by keeping water in the drip tin, though care must be taken to see that the bottom of the pot is not in contact with this water. A fine syringe such as a scent spray will be of great advantage in providing a moist atmosphere and will also help to keep the leaves clear of dust. But in spite of syringeing, dust is liable to accumulate on the leaves and this occurs so gradually that you do not become aware of it. It is therefore best to sponge all the leaves at regular two- or four-weekly intervals. For this purpose a small piece of cotton wool is suitable. Milk or flat beer will give an enhanced glossiness, but water is perfectly adequate. Olive oil gives a particularly brilliant sheen, but is not recommended as it clogs the leaf pores. Leaves should be cleaned on both sides, as the underside of the leaf is very important to the plant. Newly expanded leaves are soft and easily torn and should be handled with great care or left until they are mature. Smooth leaves are easier to clean than hairy leaves, and care should be taken that little liquid is left on the latter.

The position of the houseplant must depend a great deal on your personal taste, but the requirements of the plant must be taken into account. As we have already noted, purple-leaved plants require strong light, and in shade the purple will be less noticeable and may disappear. Variegated plants need light, but the variegated *Ficus Doescheri* will have its ivory variegation turned yellow if the light is too strong (an unlikely contingency in Great Britain).

Houseplants in the House

Although a moist atmosphere is essential for the majority of houseplants there are some that do not require it and others which are more or less indifferent. These can be placed wherever it is not desirable to supply a moist atmosphere. Plants that like dry conditions are *Sansevieria, Chlorophytum, Aichryson, Pittosporum, Rubus, Sedum, Eriobotrya, Setcreasea purpurea, Grevillea* and *Aspidistra*; those that will thrive under these conditions (though a moist atmosphere is better) include all the *Araliaceae* (except *Dizygotheca*) *Ficus decora, benjamina, lucida, nitida* and most others except *pumila*, most *Tradescantias* and their allies, *Philodendron scandens* and *bipinnatifidum, Citrus, Pilea, Neanthe, Carex morrowii* and *Ardisia*. These can be placed anywhere where light and temperature conditions are favourable. Generally speaking, plants that require a dry atmosphere also require as much light as possible.

Placing plants on the mantelpiece above an open fire is equivalent to signing their death warrant. No plant can survive the fierce heat and the dry fume-laden atmosphere. A constant cold draught will also kill a plant rapidly, though warning is usually given by leaves dropping. If these two pitfalls are avoided a plant can be found to suit any position in the house. It is, of course, essential to bear in mind the light and temperature requirements of the plant. If the site is very shady the choice will be restricted to such plants as *Philodendron scandens, Ficus pumila, F. radicans*, most *Begonias*, the unvariegated *Peperomias* and the *Marantaceae*. For a normal well-lit room that does not receive too much direct sunlight the choice is limited only by the temperature. Strong light will be appreciated by all plants with coloured leaves with the exception of *Begonias* and the *Marantaceae*. Although most of the *Ficus* will grow happily in strong light, it is advisable to move them to a shady position when the new growth starts appearing. In the shade the new leaves will grow to nearly twice the size that they will attain if they expand in sunshine. (*Ficus decora* would appear to be an exception to this.) All young growth is very liable to scorch and if the sun is very strong it is always worth while to move the plants to shadier positions, if young leaves are unfolding.

34

Houseplants in the House

At the moment of writing the question of artificial light is not particularly apposite, but manufacturers are apparently developing an electric bulb that will emit sufficient infra-red and ultra-violet rays to encourage plant growth. As tropical plants are accustomed to a twelve-hour day and a twelve-hour night our climate is liable to upset their natural growth rhythm, and it will be interesting to see if the results are beneficial or not. We would imagine that decided benefits would accrue in the winter, but what will happen in the summer appears doubtful.

Provided it is not too cold, fresh air is extremely beneficial to all plants and the lack of it may have serious results. In the winter it is natural to air the sitting-room at bedtime or at night, but remember that the fire may be going out and your plants may get unpleasantly chilled.

CONTAINERS

When we come to consider containers, we shall find that it is generally best to keep the plants in flower pots, as they are then much easier to manage and to examine, but it is possible to plant them out in bowls of peaty soil. Flower pots, though indubitably useful, are not particularly ornamental and so their presence is usually disguised by a second container. As we have seen, this is particularly advantageous for plants requiring a moist atmosphere as this can be best provided by surrounding the plant by some material that can be kept damp.

For groups of plants few containers are better than a trough, which can be made either of pottery or of wood. If the latter material is employed, it is necessary to have a metal lining fitted to obviate any risk of water leaking from the trough. As it is undesirable that the bottom of the pots should be in contact with any water that may drain out of the pots after watering, put a layer of pebbles or clinkers at the base of the trough and either stand the pots directly on this drainage bed, or place a strip of perforated zinc on the bed and stand the pots on it. The depth of the drainage bed should not be less than an inch. The intervening spaces can be filled with peat and topped with moss to give a more attractive appearance.

Houseplants in the House

Many people exercise their ingenuity by adapting such things as old oil lamps, tea caddies, primitive electric fittings and similar objects to hold houseplants, often with very pleasing results. For this type of holder, the old-fashioned soap dish with a perforated top makes a satisfactory stand for the plants. These will generally have to be selected from those that will tolerate a dry atmosphere as there is usually little room or facility for the provision of additional moisture in such conversions. There are numerous commercially produced holders adapted both for placing on flat surfaces and for mounting on walls. These are often very decorative but are made to hold one size of pot only, and so have at intervals either to receive fresh plants or to be replaced by other holders adapted to a larger-size pot. If the wall-mounting holders are purchased, it is as well to bear in mind that the holder with a pot inside is quite weighty and will require to be securely fixed. A flimsily built partition wall may not be able to support the Rawlplug.

PLACING

Although the main function of houseplants is decoration, they can on occasion be given a more practical use. For example, in many modern houses there is a large room that can be divided, by means of screens or folding doors, into two rooms. This division can also be done with houseplants. You will require troughs, capable of holding a 7-inch pot, mounted on castors so that they can be easily moved. To these troughs are fixed strips of metal trellis, which can be obtained from most horticultural sundriesmen. Up this trellis are trained such climbers as *Hedera canariensis, Cissus antarctica, Rhoicissus* or *Tetrastigma*.

The placing of houseplants depends on three factors: taste, the conditions of light and shade, and the temperature available during the winter. The first condition is not one that concerns us, though it is of course of great importance. We have already said something about the second and will be saying more when we come to discuss the plants individually. With regard to minimum temperatures we have divided houseplants into three groups, which we term hardy, delicate and tender. These categories correspond to the cold house, intermediate, and warm house divisions of greenhouse plants.

TEMPERATURE

'Hardy' houseplants are those that will thrive at a temperature of 45° during the winter, and will not blench at an occasional drop to 40°. Plants that like these cool winter conditions will not thrive so happily if the temperature is too high during the winter. Such plants as the ivies, × *Fatshedera*, *Pittosporum* and others from the temperate zones do not like to be too warm in the winter. On the other hand, tropical plants such as *Peperomia* and *Tradescantia*, though they will survive happily at low temperatures, will not be discomforted by higher temperatures.

'Delicate' houseplants should ideally not be exposed to a temperature lower than 55°, though no harm will accrue at 50°.

'Tender' houseplants should not be allowed to fall below 60°; 65° is the ideal temperature, and higher temperatures will be welcomed. Although tender houseplants will not be happy under conditions that suit delicate plants, the delicate plants will for the most part thrive under semi-stove conditions. There are a few plants, notably *Philodendron scandens*, *P. bipinnatifidum* and *Monstera pertusa* '*Borsigiana*' which will grow happily under hardy, delicate and tender conditions.

With all these categories a drop in temperature for a short time will do no harm, provided the plant is not too wet, and a more prolonged one will for many plants cause a check in growth and perhaps leaf damage, but will not destroy the plant. We have had the experience with an electrically heated greenhouse, of the temperature, owing to a power cut, dropping to as low as 36° for some six hours, and rising only slowly to 50°. The damage was far less than would have been expected. The plants that died were *Philodendron melanochryson*, *Calathea ornata* and *Fittonia argyroneura*. These deaths were immediate; *Pellionia pulchra* and *Scindapsus* 'Marble Queen' died subsequently. *Calathea mackoyana* and *Fittonia verschaffeltii* suffered considerable damage but later recovered. The *Ctenanthes* and *Marantas* were untouched apart from slight leaf scorch in *Maranta leuconeura Massangeana*. No damage affected *Philodendron scandens, cordatum* or *imbe*; *erubescens* showed leaf scorch and subsequently dropped a few leaves. *Scindapsus aureus* and *argyraeum* appeared unaffected; *Monstera* showed slight leaf scorch. Of the *Dracaenas* present, *godseffiana* was badly scorched, *sanderiana* showed no damage at the time, but has since grown rather slowly and some root damage must be suspected, *Cordyline terminalis* showed only very slight leaf scorch. Of the *Aphelandras*, *Louisae* showed no damage, while *leopoldii* dropped all its leaves, but grew away subsequently. The only *Ficus* to show immediate damage was *religiosa*, though later some leaves fell from *lyrata*; surprisingly, no damage was shown by *nekbudu*. The only *Peperomia* damaged was *sandersii*, but *scandens* was not among the plants and would very likely have been damaged. *Hoya carnosa variegata* and *bella* were undamaged. No damage was shown by *Elettaria*, *Rhoeo* appeared unhurt, but subsequently dropped leaves, *Dichorisandra reginae* suffered severe leaf scorch and has made little subsequent growth. *Setcreasea purpurea* sustained no damage, but *striata*, though showing little leaf damage, has made slow growth since. There was only one *Begonia* present and that showed no damage. Of the vine family only *Cissus capensis* and *Tetrastigma* were in the house and neither showed any ill effects. Unfortunately there were no Bromeliads, no *Aglaonema* and no *Dieffenbachia*; it does not seem likely that the latter would have survived. *Spathiphyllum* showed very slight leaf scorch.

Of course the longer the low temperature had been prolonged, the more damage would have been done, but the relatively small amount of actual losses was very surprising. It is rare that any room in a house drops to as low a temperature as was experienced by these plants, and it would seem not improbable that many delicate houseplants would survive under 'hardy' conditions and that semi-stove plants would tolerate a constant temperature as low as 50°.

There is, however, a marked difference between plants that survive and plants that are thriving and it is the latter condition that we want to obtain. How this can best be achieved we shall be examining in the next chapter.

CHAPTER III

The General Care of Houseplants

The conditions that cause healthy plant growth are many and diverse. The soil must contain the right chemicals, the right bacteria and the right amount of water. It must also be of the right texture, so that the roots can penetrate and grow easily; and it must also be well aerated. The atmosphere must be at the right temperature, must contain the right amount of water and must not be too agitated. No plants can grow in a perpetual gale. Fortunately for the plants as well as ourselves none of these conditions is critical and a wide variation is possible. Some plants are more exigent than others and these are usually rare in the wild state. Little is really known as to why some plants are rare, but it seems probable that they require conditions and perhaps certain trace elements that are only found in special places. In fact they have adapted themselves too well to their environment and cannot survive if this is changed. With the majority of plants these special considerations do not apply, and if we provide an approximation to their requirements they will grow happily.

SOIL AND AIR

The two most important aspects in plant growing are soil and air. If the soil is not right the roots cannot grow and if the air is not right the leaves will not develop. The aspects of the soil to which we must pay most attention are the texture, the amount of water it contains and its chemical constituents. Of these the texture is perhaps the most important. It is easy enough to add chemicals, and watering is of course a continuous process, of which we shall have much to say later, but unless the texture is suitable, the presence of water and chemicals will not make their full effect. Now, as we have seen, the majority of houseplants are inhabitants of woodlands in the wild. The characteristic of woodland soil is a light texture caused by the presence of a large amount of humus as a result of the decaying leaves. This humus is continually being added to, though, in cases where the majority of the trees are evergreen, this process is slow and gradual. Woodland plants are generally shallow rooting as the tree roots are already occupying the soil at any depth, and the smaller root system of the woodland plants cannot compete with them for nourishment at the lower levels. This shallow-rooting system means that the plants may often have their roots dried out and that they absorb water from the atmosphere in large amounts.

Many of the *Peperomias* grow as much on the trunks of the trees as in the ground and so absorb almost all the water they require through their leaves, the amount that their roots can take up being very limited.

Rainfall in the tropics varies, naturally, from one region to another, but that in the Brazilian jungles, from which so many of the houseplants come, is 56 inches a year, nearly twice that of Great Britain. The *Anthuriums*, which one might imagine were remarkably suitable for houseplants, come principally from a warm region of Colombia with an average rainfall of 390 inches per year. As a result they require so saturated an atmosphere that they are quite unsuited, with one or two exceptions, to room culture.

The temperatures in the tropics range from 52° in Brazil to 66° in Malaya, so that giving the plants the correct temperature is not difficult. These temperatures are the mean minima and lower temperatures are occasionally experienced, though the average is of course ten degrees or more higher. Even so there is not much difficulty in providing suitable temperatures for tropical houseplants. Providing a suitable atmosphere is far more difficult, though just as essential. We have already mentioned the advantage of surrounding the pot with some moist absorbent material, and during cold spells this may well be moistened with nearly boiling water (in which case the greatest care must be taken to see that it does not come in contact with the plant) so that the plant gets its bath of water vapour. During warm spells syringeing the leaves once or twice a day is very beneficial.

WATERING

The rhythm of growth of tropical plants differs from that of plants accustomed to clearly defined seasons. We are used to plants that start their growth in the spring, flower and fruit during the summer, cease growing in the autumn and rest during the winter. In the tropics growth is either continuous or limited by dry and wet seasons. The amount of daylight remains constant and there is no seasonal variation in temperature. In adapting tropical plants to our rooms the temperature will probably have to be the controlling factor. After the temperature has dropped to a certain level, which varies from plant to plant, they will not make any growth. They do not come to any harm, either at this temperature or at a lower one, but they cease making any growth until the temperature rises. If a plant is not growing, it will not take up water from the soil, and so it is advisable when low temperatures are to be expected, to give the plant the equivalent of a dry season. A saturated soil encourages the growth of the fungi and bacteria that cause root-rot; and once infection has started, damage is certain and the death of the plant only too frequent. It therefore is wise during the winter to keep watering down to a minimum.

What this minimum is, must be a matter for empirical observation; it can only be learned by experience. No houseplant is liable to be damaged by drying out occasionally; though *Ficus pumila* is an exception to this rule and so, to a lesser degree, is *Aphelandra Louisae*. Apart from these it is safer to withhold water during the winter until the plants flag. When water is given, it is less of a shock to the plant if it is tepid; very cold water will lower the soil temperature and may damage the roots. It should, perhaps, be mentioned here that plants may flag as a result of damage to the roots through overwatering. If the plant is flagging and the soil is damp, do not, if you value your plants, water them more but let them dry out. We shall be coming back to this subject later.

On occasion a pot may appear dry on the surface and yet be moist lower down. Where clay pots are still in use, tapping the side with your knuckle will enable you to find out the condition of the soil. If it is dry you will get a ringing sound, while if the soil is still moist the sound will be a dull thud. However clay pots are tending to be replaced by plastic pots and with loamy composts it is not easy to establish whether the soil is still moist or no, except by turning the soil ball out and looking. Since the plastic pots are not in themselves porous, they will retain moisture longer than clay pots, so that watering should be less frequently called for. It is sometimes possible to judge by the weight of the pot and this is the only way for composts with a lot of peat, such as the so-called soilless composts. These will feel very light when dry and heavy when moist.

The plant itself will give you some idea of its requirements. Thick fleshy succulent leaves are a clear indication that the plant is used to prolonged dry periods. A plant like *Sansevieria* can go for months without water and so can many of the *Peperomias*, while plants like *Begonia* or *Maranta* will need water more frequently. Even with these plants the winter is their most vulnerable period and the amount of water they will need will be very little, unless you keep your rooms at a high temperature. If you have a good heating system and can keep a high tempera-ture in your rooms, growth will probably not cease altogether and the application of water, though probably less than during the summer, will be regularly called for. If there are no signs of growth give the plants water only when they flag and this water, as we said, should be tepid. Water should be given when the room is beginning to warm up, so that most of it can be ab-sorbed before it starts to cool off. (This of course applies to rooms where a fire is lit and later allowed to die out.)

Once the winter is over, it will be necessary to start the plant in growth again. This can usually be left until late April, but a

43

warm early spring will cause growth to start earlier. When the soil has been left dry for a long period it is liable to shrink and the first thorough spring watering is best given by placing the pot in a bucket of water and leaving it there until bubbles cease to rise. It should then be removed and the soil firmed down around the edge of the pot with the thumbs, so that no gaps are seen. If, at any time when you are watering, the water appears to run straight through the pot, it is probable that the soil has shrunk and is not getting properly moistened. The bucket will generally overcome this. Occasionally the soil may become so parched that it will not absorb water at all. In this case it is best to stab the surface with a knitting needle and make several small holes before plunging in a bucket of water.

After this soaking watch the plant to see if growth is starting. If buds unfurl and new leaves appear the matter is beyond question, but some plants such as the large-leaved *Ficus* make considerable root growth before any change is noticed in the aerial parts of the plant. To inspect the roots, invert the pot and strike the edge gently on some flat surface, such as a potting bench or draining board, holding one hand over the top of the pot, with the plant between your fingers. The soil ball should come out easily from the pot and can be replaced without disturbing the plant. New roots are easily recognizable by their white tips, and if these are in evidence it may be assumed that growth has started. Once growth has started water is supplied whenever necessary. This is never a regular interval, such as once a week, but is dependent on various factors such as the temperature, the amount of roots relative to the amount of soil, and the size of the plant. Regular inspection is the only safe way of regulating watering. Water is most conveniently supplied by a can with a narrow spout and is applied to the top of the pot. (Rain water is preferable, but not essential.) There should always be a space between the surface of the soil and the rim of the pot varying from $\frac{3}{4}$ inch in a 3-inch pot to 2 inches for a 6-inch pot, and when watering, you should fill the pot to the brim. Anything less will not penetrate the soil ball and the lower roots will be dried out.

The General Care of Houseplants

FEEDING

When growth is well started, it is advisable to feed the plants. There are numerous proprietary foods on sale; the most convenient, perhaps, are those in the form of pills, which are inserted in the soil and dissolve rather slowly, taking approximately three weeks. Other feeds such as Fisons or the John Innes Liquid Feed are dissolved in water and have a more rapid action, though care must be taken that none of this solution touches the leaves, as otherwise damage may result. Other feeds, such as the old favourite 'Clays', are in powder form and are placed on top of the soil and watered in. Whatever form of feeding is used, it is as well to bear certain points in mind. It is a waste of time to feed plants that have not got a vigorous root system. If a plant is sickly or if it has recently been repotted and the roots have not yet penetrated the new soil, feeding is not only unnecessary but may even be harmful. Feeding should never be started until there are signs of root growth. If there is no root action the food will be wasted and detrimental to the plant. Always observe the directions as to the amount and frequency of application of the feed, and do not imagine that a double dose will do twice as much good; the converse is more likely to be the case. Epiphytes such as the majority of Bromeliads use their roots principally as anchorage and absorb very little nourishment that way. They do appear to respond to feeding, but this should be given through the cup or vase, and is taken up by the leaves.

Arguably the most convenient way of feeding your plants is by means of a foliar feed. This is a mixture of chemicals, which is dissolved in a given quantity of water and then sprayed on to the leaves. The chemicals are in a very fine suspension and do not mark the leaves in any way, while the plant gets immediate benefit from this spraying. For the houseplant grower there are, possibly, some disadvantages. These foliar feeds are made up in packets, which are usually based on a gallon of water and it is very unlikely that you will use up all this in one application to your plants. There is, however, no objection to storing what

45

liquid remains in some container in a dark place until the next application is required. The most usual dose is once a fortnight and this can be applied from the beginning of May until the end of September. The plants are not growing very vigorously for the period October–April and feeding should be either suspended or reduced drastically during these months. It may well be inconvenient to spray your plants in their permanent situations. It is just as satisfactory to immerse the plant in the solution (taking care, however, that only the leaves are wetted) or, alternatively, the plants can all be moved to some situation convenient for syringeing and then brought back again. A few plants, such as *Senecio macroglossus*, *Sansevieria* and some of the large-leaved *Ficus*, do not retain water on their leaves and for these foliar feeds are obviously unsuitable, but for the majority of house plants they have much to commend them.

Although in this country we tend to purchase proprietary feeds, on the Continent they frequently make up their own. This is done by mixing one part (by weight) of potassium nitrate with one part of calcium phosphate and two parts of ammonium sulphate (e.g. 4 oz. of each of the first two and 8 oz. of the ammonium sulphate) together and storing them in a container that can be kept absolutely dry. The chemicals are dissolved in water at about an ounce to the gallon and watered on to the soil ball. This should not be done when the plants are very dry, as the chemicals could damage the roots. Indeed all feeds applied to the soil should be given when the soil is still moist.

Once growth is completed and there is no further sign of new leaves emerging, feeding should stop and watering will be needed less frequently, and as winter approaches will practically cease. Plants from the tropics may not show any signs of growth completion, but with the advent of October it is wise to withhold water as much as possible, so as to stop further growth and encourage the growth that has already been made, to ripen. Under these conditions you do not water the plant when it appears dry, but only when it flags.

The frequency with which water is given during the growing season depends not only on the root action of the plant, but also on the size of the pot in which it is growing. Most houseplants are sold in 3-inch or 3½-inch pots, and these tend to dry out more rapidly than larger plants in 5-inch pots. With the majority of houseplants a larger specimen, though initially more expensive, is easier to manage.

If strong sunlight falls on newly expanded leaves it may scorch them and this should be avoided if possible. Protection can be given, with great advantage to the plant, by spraying the leaves with a fine spray. A scent spray is particularly useful as no harm accrues if some of the water goes elsewhere. This spray is not a substitute for sponging the leaves, as it is not sufficiently copious to remove the dust.

'Stopping' and Repotting

In order to make a shapely plant, it is often necessary to 'stop' the plant. This should never be done unless the plant is strongly rooted and making growth. 'Stopping' entails pinching out the growing point and, in some cases, removing a portion of the stem if this should be etiolated or in any way unsightly. Some of the ivies and *Philodendron scandens* tend during the winter to make growth that is small-leaved and looks sickly. In the spring the plant can be cut back to the first good leaf. Stopping encourages the growth of sideshoots and the formation of a bushy plant. The sideshoots are sometimes stopped in their turn and the process can continue for some time. Stopping gives the plant a temporary check and watering should be done with some care, until the new growth is seen. Some plants such as the self-branching ivies will produce sideshoots without being stopped, but stopping will encourage more vigorous growth and is recommended. Stopping is best done in late spring, but it is as well to make sure that the roots are active, before removing any growing points.

As most houseplants grow they eventually produce so many roots that they become potbound and have to be moved into larger pots. This is not necessary with all of them. The epiphytal Bromeliads, as we have already noted, do not have a large root system and this is chiefly used as an anchorage. In the same way many of the *Peperomias* seem to depend far more on a moist atmosphere than on any soil mixture. When found in the wild they are usually rooted in moss at the base of trees and seldom grow in soil. The climbing *Philodendrons* throw roots from every leaf joint and do not appear to make a particularly large root system in any one place, though some potting on will eventually be necessary. Most of the other houseplants will eventually need putting into larger size pots. The usual sequence is from a 3-inch pot to a 5-inch pot, and then progressively into pots an inch wider in diameter. The 4-inch pot is for some reason little used. If you have no facilities for potting on the plants yourself, a local nurseryman will usually be pleased to do it for you. For those who wish to do it themselves, this is the usual procedure.

Plants are only potted on during the growing season, as otherwise there would be no root action to penetrate the fresh soil. The plant to be potted on must have its soil ball in a dry, but not dust-dry condition. This is because the plant is watered after repotting, and if the ball was already wet there would be the risk of overwatering, and also the risk that the new and old soil would not amalgamate. The potting soil should be in a similar condition; neither dust-dry nor wet and sticky, but crumbly and easy to handle. It should not stick to your hands. The pot into which the plant is to be moved should be thoroughly clean inside. Special pot brushes are manufactured for nursery work, but a handful of newspaper is quite as effective. If you have purchased new clay pots, they should be soaked in water for twenty-four hours before using, as they are very absorbent and would otherwise take all the water from the soil. With the John Innes compost, which we describe later, it is advisable to place a crock over the drainage hole at the bottom of the pot; with the various Turnford mixtures this is not necessary, as they are all very open in texture. Place sufficient soil in the pot to bring the level of the plant, when stood thereon, about an inch or more below the rim of the pot. This must be effected by trial and error. When this has been achieved, place the plant which has been removed from its old pot on this soil in the centre of the new pot,

48

1. A mixed collection of Bromeliads growing on a tree and on the ground

2. Ficus elastica decora, Philodendron scandens, Hederas in variety, Dracaena terminalis tricolor

3. Philodendron bipinnatifidum, Neoregelia marechatii,
N. carolinae tricolor

4. Aralia elegantissima, Sansevieria trifasciata Laurentii, Dracaena deremensis, Aechmea fasciata

5. Philodendron scandens, Dieffenbachia picta Jenmanii, Aglaonema robelinii

6. Philodendron bipinnatifidum

7. Philodendron erubescens

8. Philodendron elegans

9. Philodendron imbe

10. Philodendron laciniatum

11. Philodendron melanochryson, P. laciniatum, P. ilsemanni

12. Philodendron hastatum

13. Philodendron wendlandii

14. Philodendron melanochryson, Anthurium scherzerianum

15. Anthurium crystallinum, Aglaonema commutatum

16. Aglaonema treubii, Ctenanthe lubbersiana, Aglaonema 'pseudo-bracteatum'

and fill up with soil all round until you have reached the level of the old plant. This soil should be firmed down with the thumbs, but not pressed too hard and the final result should be a level soil surface. Finish off with tapping the pot on the bench to settle the soil and then give the newly potted plant a good watering. It will be some time before any further watering is needed, as the roots have to penetrate the new soil. Care should be taken not to fill the pot too full, as otherwise water will not penetrate the whole of the soil ball.

The majority of houseplants are woodland plants used to growing in an open-textured, friable and rather shallow soil. Others such as *Ficus* and *Pittosporum* are trees. Now one of the oldest beliefs in gardening is that hard-wooded plants should be given hard potting; that is to say that the soil should be rammed hard with a wooden rammer. This process enables one to get more soil in a pot, but this will not be well aerated and the young roots will find difficulty in penetrating this impacted mass. It is as well, here, to take natural conditions as your guide. The young trees will not be deeply rooted and it is only at a certain depth that the soil becomes impacted and close-textured. It follows therefore that any ramming should be done only when the plant is comparatively large and only then if you do not wish it to grow too vigorously. If plants such as *Ficus* and *Pittosporum* have reached a size when they will have to be moved into an 8-inch pot, the arguments for using the rammer are cogent, but for pots of smaller size, thumb pressure will give a sufficiently firm texture. The encouragement of vigorous root growth is, of course, of prime importance in the production of healthy specimens, and a well-aerated open-textured mixture appears to encourage root growth far more rapidly than a close-textured hard soil.

SOIL MIXTURES

Different mixtures of soil are required for houseplants, as will be detailed in later chapters, but quite a few will grow in the John Innes compost, which is usually abbreviated to JIP. This can be bought ready made up from most horticultural sundriesmen, but if you wish to make it yourself this is the formula. Loam, peat and sharp sand are mixed in the proportions of 7:3:2. The loam should be sifted and the peat should be sifted and moistened. With some of the sand should be mixed 4 oz. of John Innes Base and ¾ oz. ground chalk for every bushel of the mixture and the sand and chemicals are mixed in with the loam and peat. The John Innes Base is usually bought ready mixed but the formula is two parts hoof and horn, two parts superphosphate and one part sulphate of potash; the parts are by weight. This mixture is known as JIP 1. For 5-inch pots it is best to double the quantity of chemicals, thereby making JIP 2 and for 6-inch and larger pots the chemicals are trebled and the resultant mixture is known as JIP 3. The composition of the loam is of prime importance for this mixture, as ordinary garden soil is not really good enough. Rotted turves are recommended and a high humus content (humus is produced by rotting vegetation) is essential.

Although the John Innes composts and the various other mixtures given throughout this book are to be preferred, there is such a shortage of good loam that scientists have devised composts based mainly on peat. These are loosely referred to as soilless mixtures, but since both peat and sand are soil ingredients, they would more accurately be referred to as loamless composts. Both peat and sand are valueless, so far as plant nutrients are concerned, and so all the essential nourishment has to be added in the form of chemicals, which are very carefully and accurately formulated. These composts are ideal for plants that are only expected to last out a single season, but, since the amount of nourishment contained therein is strictly limited, they are less satisfactory for houseplants, which we hope will survive from year to year. Of course we add chemicals to the other composts, but the loam does provide additional nourishment which is lacking in the loamless mixtures. This means that if you wish to grow houseplants in loamless composts, you must start to feed almost from the moment that you receive the plant. If this is at a dead time of year (between October and April) this is probably inadvisable, but otherwise a

The General Care of Houseplants

fortnightly feed is essential. In this way the level of nourishment is maintained and the plant will continue to thrive. It must also be borne in mind that you cannot mix loamy composts with loamless ones. If your plant is in a loamy compost it must be potted on in a similar loamy compost and vice versa. You cannot take a plant in a loamless compost and add John Innes when you pot it on, so it is as well to be sure what medium your plant is in. The loamless composts are much lighter than the more conventional mixtures and dry out very much quicker.

If in spite of all your efforts the plants do not seem to thrive it is best to call in an expert, but if, for some reason, this is not possible you will have to try and diagnose the trouble yourself. In a later chapter we shall be dealing with some of the commoner pests and fungus diseases, and if you suspect that your troubles are caused by insects or fungus turn to this chapter.

Causes of Disease

The commonest cause of disease in house plants is root-rot caused by overwatering. The leaves will wilt and then yellow and drop off and the plant will feel unsteady in its pot. Once this stage has been reached it is difficult to save the plant and it will be some time before it reaches its former state. This is a case where prevention is far better than cure. To effect a cure, place the plant in as warm a position as possible and let the soil dry out completely. This will take a long time. When the plant is dry, leave it in that condition for at least a fortnight, syringeing the leaves if the plant flags. At the end of this period turn the plant out to see if there are any signs of new roots (they will be whitish in colour). If there are not, try again in another week. When new roots can be seen you may start giving the plant water again, but do it as sparingly as possible until the plant has regained its former condition and until the soil is fairly full of the new roots.

Fear of overwatering may lead to underwatering. If the plant is not making the growth it should (this, of course, can only be learned by experience) or if the leaves seem a very dark green, the plant is probably too dry. It may be that the pot is filled too

51

full. Water the plant and some hours afterwards turn it out and examine the ball. If the water has not penetrated evenly through the soil, and the soil at the bottom is dry, you must either repot, if the plant is in a suitable condition, or else water twice each time you water. (If the water just runs straight through the pot apply the bucket treatment referred to above.) This trouble is easily cured and it is rare that a plant comes to lasting harm through excessive dryness. (Though of course it can be over-done. You cannot go away for a month's holiday and expect to find your houseplants ready to greet you when you return, if they have not been cared for.) There are, however, two excep-tions to this statement: excessive dryness encourages the Red Spider mite, which we deal with in a later chapter, and it may also cause leaves to drop. Plants transpire through their leaves and if they become too dry they will try to preserve what water they still have, by shedding some of their leaves. If apparently healthy leaves are falling from a plant the most probable causes are either dryness or draughts and this can easily be remedied. Plants that are overwatered also lose their leaves, but they generally yellow beforehand and do not look healthy.

As we have already said, many of the tropical plants require a moist atmosphere, particularly when they are growing, and it is as important to provide this as to keep the soil wet.

OTHER CAUSES OF WILTING

In very hot weather some plants may wilt, particularly if they are in direct sunshine, even though their soil is suitably moist. Syringeing the leaves will effect an almost immediate recovery and in any case they will pick up when the temperature falls and the sunlight is removed.

If the plant is not growing well, though apparently neither over- nor under-watered and is free from pests, it is probably starved and will need either repotting or feeding.

Frosting sometimes occurs when plants are left in the window. Its symptoms are unmistakable and the only thing to do is to ensure that it does not re-occur and to see that the plant does not thaw out too quickly. Frost damage is caused by the water in the plant cells freezing and bursting the cell walls. Remove the plant to a cold position (though naturally frost free) and spray it with cold water. Recovery depends on slow thawing, though some plants are more resistant than others.

When you purchase a new plant it will take a little time to acclimatize itself to its new position. If it has come straight from the Nursery, it is probably moving into a colder climate; if it comes from the Florist, it may already have spent some time in colder conditions than it likes. Houseplants are frequently given as Christmas gifts, which means that they are moved under the worst possible conditions. They come from a warm greenhouse to a cold shop, where they may quite probably be watered daily, and they may be received in a state in which damage has been done to the plant, even though it is not visible. It is probably best to put them in the warmest possible position in your house, and if they appear very wet to let them dry out, before giving any water. If they are very dry when received, give them a good watering in tepid water and then leave them to dry out in a warm place, before placing them in their permanent positions. It is advisable to cosset them slightly for the first six weeks, after which time they should have acclimatized themselves. In any case it will take some time to adapt itself and must therefore be kept fairly dry until signs of growth appear. If the plant arrives in the winter there will be no signs of growth in any case and common sense must guide you on watering.

Common sense indeed should be your guide in all aspects of houseplant growing. Observation will teach you more than any printed word can, and the possession of that mythical attribute 'green fingers' is usually to be found associated with affection and keen observation. Plants can, of course, be killed with kindness and as we have said, with perhaps nauseating over-emphasis, too much water is the commonest mistake from which most houseplants suffer. It does not take long before the correct routine becomes second nature and your houseplants become a source of pleasure unalloyed by any anxiety.

CHAPTER IV

Araceae

———————◆◆◆◆◆———————

THE ARUM FAMILY

I n the course of the next eight chapters we intend to give a
catalogue raisonné of the various houseplants known to
us. These have been assembled into their botanical families,
and when there were sufficient we have assigned a chapter to a
family. Where the number of houseplant members of a family
is small they will be found described in one of the two miscellaneous chapters; indeed many of the most popular houseplants
will be found there. The various genera are treated in alphabeti-
cal order, but when one is of more general interest than the
others (such as *Philodendron* in this chapter and *Hedera* in the
next) this genus is put first.

The Arum family contains some 115 genera and over 1,000
species and can be found in practically every country in the
world. In Great Britain it is represented by the common Lords
and Ladies of the hedgerows (*Arum maculatum*); and its best
known member is the Arum lily. The *Araceae* can be distinguished by their very individual inflorescence. The actual
flowers are rarely visible, being very small and clustered at the
base of the *spadix*, a club-like process, which protrudes for
some inches. This is sometimes surrounded, sometimes merely
matched, by the *spathe*, a kind of ornamental leaf, which is often
brightly coloured and serves the same purpose as the petals in
most flowers. In the case of the Arum lily this spathe is pure
white and surrounds the yellow spadix; in the case of *Anthurium*

scherzerianum, both spathe and spadix are bright scarlet and the spadix is quite detached from the spathe. The majority of the houseplant aroids are not, however, grown as flowering plants with two exceptions, but for the sake of their pleasantly coloured and shaped leaves.

The aroids manifest themselves in many different types of plant. Many of the *Philodendrons* are vigorous climbers, *Dieffenbachia* will eventually produce a small trunk, others are ordinary terrestrial herbs. The climbing species of *Philodendron, Scindapsus* and *Syngonium* produce aerial roots at every leaf joint. These roots not only serve as a support to the plant, but also serve to absorb moisture and other nutrients if possible. In the wild state these plants not only climb up trees but also over rocks. In the former case many of the aerial roots will eventually descend to the soil and in the latter they will penetrate any fissures in the rock in search of it. When they are grown in the home they can either be trained on to bark (in the United States 'Bark plants' are very popular) or they can be trained up a stout green wood stake or a wire-netting cylinder that is filled with moss. Whatever method is used it should be borne in mind that water is necessary for the aerial roots; and if this is supplied, you will be rewarded with far larger leaves. For plants that are not too large and vigorous, such as *Philodendron scandens, cordatum, elegans, sagittifolium, micans, melanochryson, Scindapsus aureus,* and *Syngonium podophyllum,* training on bark is by far the most satisfactory. The usual bark employed is cork bark, which is wired around the base with two wire legs protruding which are inserted in the soil at the back of the pot. The plant is first secured to the bark by means of india-rubber bands, but will soon attach itself by its roots. During the growing season this bark should be moistened every day and in hot weather twice a day would not be too much. With the more vigorous species such as *P. erubescens,* some larger support will be necessary, but this too should be kept moist during growth, though in the home there are certain practical difficulties. Naturally all plants with aerial roots appreciate a moist atmosphere, and surrounding the pots with moist moss or peat is very beneficial. Owing to their habit of producing roots along the stem, these climbing aroids do not need very frequent potting on, though if the aerial roots cannot take in nourishment, the plant will produce more roots in the soil.

The majority of aroids have thick fleshy roots which will rot very rapidly if the soil becomes waterlogged. It is therefore necessary to grow them in a very open compost, so that between waterings (which should be thorough) air can penetrate to them. The following mixture will be found generally suitable:

2 parts loam

1½ parts leaf mould. (If unobtainable, peat may be used)

1 part sharp sand

¾ part rotted farmyard manure

   All parts by bulk

1 5-inch pot full of superphosphate to each barrow load.

The loam should be slightly acid: a pH of 5·5 is the ideal and it should be as fibrous as possible. The deep black loam found at the outskirts of woodlands is usually the best if available. The leaf mould should not be too well rotted; it should be possible to recognize the leaf shapes on the potting bench. Leaves that have just fallen are too hard, but one-year-old leaves are very suitable. The sand should be as coarse as possible, almost a fine grit. As sand has no nutritive value, its sole purpose is to improve the texture of the compost and make it more open, thereby encouraging rapid root growth. The ingredients of the compost do not require to be sieved, but any coarse lumps should be crumbled by hand. If the ingredients are too dry, it is advisable to damp it down slightly and leave for twelve hours. On no account must it be used when it feels muddy and clings to the hand.

Genus PHILODENDRON

The name comes from two Greek words meaning fond of trees; many of the species are climbers. They all come from the tropics of South and Central America. In some of them the leaves of the young plants are shaped differently from those that are produced when the plants are fully developed, and in the case of *P.*

melanochryson and *P. andreanum* it would seem that two forms have been diagnosed as two different species. It has also been stated that *P. ilsemannii* is a juvenile form of *P. sagittifolium*, but this seems unlikely.

1. Philodendron scandens (Plate 5)

Scandens is the Latin for 'climbing'. This is one of the most popular of all houseplants, being easy to keep, hardy, and tolerant of gas and oil fumes. Although it thrives best in a damp atmosphere, it will tolerate more dryness than most of the other species. It is a native of the West Indies and the isthmus of Panama. The plant is naturally a vigorous climber, but, as a houseplant, it will benefit from regular stopping to encourage a bushy growth. During the winter it will probably make some rather weak growth and this should be removed in the spring by cutting the growing tip back to the last formed well-developed leaf. If the plant is getting too large and leggy it can be cut back further, but if the plant has got very long it may be simpler to bend the flexible stem in two and tie it in, after stopping. In this case the breaks will come at the base of the plant where they are most needed. *P. scandens* is particularly suitable for training on bark, but can be grown into a tall climbing specimen if required. Like all the climbing members of this genus it produces aerial roots from each leaf joint. The dark green leaves are heart-shaped with a long thin point, and the growing tip is enclosed in two pale green leaf-like sheaths, known as stipules. As the new leaf emerges these open out and soon fall off. The leaf is some 3 to 4 inches long and $2\frac{1}{2}$ inches across, though it will be larger in a well-grown specimen. Flowers are not produced until the plant is very large and there is no record of its flowering in cultivation, although the very similar *P. oxycardium* has been known to produce small purplish arum-like flowers from the leaf axils.

A variegated form, *P. scandens variegatum*, has recently been re-introduced. This has an irregular cream blotch on the lower half of the leaf. It would appear that this is a virus-induced variegation and it is liable to be accompanied by distortion of the leaf shape. Growth is naturally slower than in the type and the plant has not proved, up to date, as satisfactory as might be wished. Rigorous selection may eventually produce an acceptable strain of this variety.

2. Philodendron andreanum

This plant was named in honour of E. F. André who edited the *Revue Horticole* towards the end of the last century, and who was responsible for the diagnosis of several species of South American *Araceae*. It is the juvenile form of this plant that the houseplant grower is most likely to meet with, and this has been long thought to be a separate species and has been called *P. melanochryson*. As it is usually sold under this name, we are deferring our description.

3. Philodendron bipinnatifidum (Plates 6 and 68)

Bipinnatifid is a botanical term, derived from the Latin word *pinna*, a feather. If a leaf is divided into numerous sections, but not into separate leaflets it is described as pinnatifid. If these sections are further divided in two parts the leaf is bipinnatifid. *P. bipinnatifidum*, in spite of its name, is not entirely bipinnatifid. The leaf can be divided into three main sections of which the two bottom parts and the central section are bipinnatifid, while between them is a portion which is only simply pinnatifid. This sounds complicated and it is perhaps simpler to think of the leaf as a broadly based triangle with a very irregular outline. The plant, a native of Brazil, belongs to that section of the genus that contains the non-climbing species. It makes a compact plant with its leaves springing from a central point and borne on round green petioles, which in large specimens will reach a height of two feet. Similarly a mature plant will bear a leaf 2 feet long and 18 inches across. The new leaf is sheathed in the base of the petiole of the last leaf to have unfurled, and as a result all the petioles have a boat-shaped hollow at their base. Growing as it does from one central point the plant cannot be stopped and propagation is by seed only. The seed must be sown in a temperature of 85° for satisfactory germination. The first leaves are heart-shaped, and it is only as the plant ages that the leaves become more and more incised. They attain their mature form about two years after germination. *P. bipinnatifidum*, in spite of its Brazilian homeland, has proved extremely hardy, and in Germany is among the most popular of houseplants. It likes a good open compost with good drainage and should not be allowed to dry out completely, though it dislikes overwatering. This indeed applies to all *Philodendrons*. When repotting this plant it is as well to take care not to break the thick fleshy roots, which smell unpleasantly if broken.

4. Philodendron cordatum

Cordate means heart-shaped and this species has large heart-shaped leaves, eventually reaching a length and breadth of 12 inches. This is a climbing plant, but is slow-growing and will not make an unwieldy specimen too quickly. The leaves are a bright, nearly emerald green, with the midrib and principal veins conspicuously marked. The final point of the leaf is less elongated than in *P. scandens*. As in the previous species the new leaf is protected by the petiole of the preceding leaf and subsequently the base of the petiole shows a large hollow. *P. cordatum* should be treated as delicate, though it has tolerated low temperatures without damage. It is a native of Brazil. It is possible that our plant is wrongly named as it does not correspond exactly with the diagnosis of *cordatum*. It may possibly prove to be *P. pittieri* (named in honour of a plant collector, M. Pittier), a native of Costa Rica.

5. Philodendron × corsonianum

The × denotes that we are dealing with a hybrid plant. Hybridization is usually only possible between plants of the same genus (and not always then) but intergeneric hybrids are known, particularly among orchids, and we shall find one in the next chapter. Although they occasionally occur naturally, they are usually man-induced. Hybrids are frequently more hardy and vigorous than either of their parents, and it may be possible to obtain a plant that combines the beauty of one parent with the hardiness of another. In the case of *P. corsonianum* there is some mystery about its parentage. Engler in his *Pflanzenreich* says that one parent is *P. verrucosum* and the other unknown; the *R.H.S. Dictionary* merely says of unknown parentage (it also calls it *P.* × *corsinianum*). The plant is a climber of some vigour with a large heart-shaped leaf with a lightly crenulated edge some 9 inches long and 7 inches across of a medium green. The petioles and stem are lightly spotted with dark red spots. The plant is reasonably hardy, though a minimum winter temperature of 50° should be aimed at.

6. Philodendron erubescens (Plate 7)

Erubescens means blushing and this species is given the name because of the rosy stipules that enclose the young leaves and the rosy tint of these leaves themselves as they develop. The plant is a vigorous climber, producing roots at each leaf joint. The leaves are shaped like an arrow-head and may reach a foot in length though 7 to 9 inches is more usual. They emerge a rosy pink but as they develop they turn a dark glossy green that gives coppery reflections. Although a native of Colombia it has proved hardy in cultivation, but a warm, moist atmosphere will produce more rapid growth. It is reasonably tolerant of gas and oil fumes and appears equally content in shade or sun. Propagation is by cuttings, and it has been found best to take the top cutting first and wait for the sideshoots to develop in the lower leaf axils, before taking any further cuttings. Cuttings of leaf joints without a growing point are very slow to develop.

'Burgundy' is a selected form of *P. erubescens* with more brilliant colouring and also more vigorous growth. The young stems and the leaf stalks are a rich wine-red, while the young leaves are olive-green with a suggestion of being shot with purple, presumably they pick up reflexions from the purple portions of the plant. Mature leaves are a very dark green indeed with a purple underside.

Although *P. erubescens* is a delightful plant, it is rather large for ordinary dwellings, so hybridists have been trying to get the coloration of *erubescens* with the more compact growth of smaller species. Here comes the plant with the rather ambitious name of **'Red Emerald'** which looks as though it is a cross between *erubescens* and a member of that confusing group which includes *P. hastatum* and *sagittifolium*. This is compact and close-jointed with arrow-head shaped leaves which are up to 7 inches long in young plants and 3 inches across. The young stems and leaf-stalks are a rather dull plum-purple. As the leaves emerge they are a very attractive pale bronze and they mature to a dark olive-green with a very thin purple margin, while the midrib on the underside is also purple. It thus retains many of the characters of *P. erubescens*, although it is not so impressive a plant. It is, however, a plant of manageable dimensions.

7. Philodendron elegans (Plate 8)

The specific epithet explains itself: 'elegant'. The plant is a charming dark-green leaved climber of only moderate vigour and does not make a very large specimen. The leaves may be as much as 21 inches long and 15 inches across, though they are not usually so large. Although the leaf can be seen basically to be divided into three lobes, each lobe is so deeply incised that the general effect is more of a palm leaf than of anything else. The botanists, with their flair for harmonious names, term this type of leaf pinnatisect. *P. elegans* comes from most parts of tropical South America, but presumably from high altitudes as it is not fussy about high temperatures, and is indeed rather easy of cultivation.

8. Philodendron fenzlii

This plant is named in honour of E. Fenzl, who was Director of the Vienna Botanic Gardens in the last century, and is a vigorous climber with dark green leaves divided into three elongated oval lobes. Although this is hardy and vigorous, it appears to have an unholy fascination for all insect pests and has practically dropped out of commerce. It is very similar in appearance to *Syngonium vellozianum*, and as this latter is very much easier to cultivate, it has supplanted *P. fenzlii*.

9. Philodendron gloriosum

The glorious *Philodendron* is a native of Colombia and requires rather warmer treatment than any we have been discussing so far. It is associated with rocks rather than trees in its native haunts and may need some persuasion to grow upwards. The handsome leaves are some 9 inches long and 7 inches across, heart-shaped and of a rich olive-green with an effect of iridescence caused by the very pale almost ivory main veins. The young leaves are enclosed in a purple sheath, and on freshly unfolded leaves the top of the leaf stalk and the underside of the main veins are reddish in colour, fading as they age.

10. Philodendron hastatum (Plate 12)

A hastate leaf is one shaped like a spear-head and to a botanist a spear-head is roughly triangular, rather long and slightly curved at the base, and that is what the leaves of *P. hastatum* are like. The plant comes from southern Brazil, where the winter can be quite chilly and so is well adapted to room conditions. The leaves are very glossy, about 7 inches long and some 4 inches across at the base. The leaf stalks are thick and fleshy, which suggests that the plant can tolerate quite dry conditions at times, although since it has the usual habit of producing aerial roots it must also be used to a damp atmosphere. This is reasonably slow-growing and so remains compact for longer than the other large-leaved climbers in this genus, which has its advantages. As it elongates the length of stem between the leaves tends to become longer, so that any very tall specimens are best pinched back in the spring.

11. Philodendron ilsemannii (Plate 11)

We have been unable to find out who Herr Ilsemann was. This is an extremely beautiful, but extremely slow growing climber with arrow-head shaped leaves borne on round thin stalks. The leaves emerge a beautiful creamy pink in colour and develop to a dark green with white variegation. This variegation is irregular and no two leaves are identical. The leaves are some 8 inches long and 3½ inches across though they may be larger in more mature specimens. In spite of its variegation it is remarkably hardy and one specimen is known to have experienced a temperature of 36° for 12 hours with no ill effects. It requires a certain amount of light as otherwise the variegation will not develop. The plant was not described until 1908, and its country of origin is not given in any of our books of reference. Engler suggests that it may be a juvenile form of *P. sagittifolium*, but this is quite impossible. *P. sagittifolium* has a short oval leaf stalk and the leaves are sheathed in the base of the stalk of the last leaf to emerge. *P. ilsemanni* has the young leaves enclosed in a sheath and long thin round leaf stalks. There may be a change in leaf shape between juvenile and mature forms, but not a change in structure.

12. Philodendron imbe (Plate 9)

What the specific epithet means we cannot say, unless it was the name of the locality where the plant was originally found. It is a native of Brazil. The plant is a vigorous climber with a thick-stem rooting at the leaf joints. Both this and the petioles are covered with purple spots. The bright green leaves are shaped like a long thin arrow-head and may reach 1 foot in length and some 5 inches across. Although found quite high above sea level the plant prefers warm conditions and, given these, will soon make a large specimen, too large for most rooms and, unless a very large specimen is needed, it is best replaced by the very similar looking *P. sagittifolium.*

13. Philodendron lacerum

The specific epithet means torn, referring to the incised margin of the leaf. This plant, which is found all over the West Indies at all elevations, is admirably hardy and prefers a sunny position. It is unfortunately a very large and vigorous plant and is only suitable for large rooms. The leaves are roughly an elongated oval in shape, but the edge is so wavy and crenulated that the basic shape is not apparent. The young leaves are a plain oval in shape and it is only as the plant develops that the leaves get their characteristic shape.

14. Philodendron laciniatum (Plates 10 and 11)

Laciniatum means jagged and again refers to the leaf shape. In this species the leaves are a very dark green and not dissimilar in general outline to *P. bipinnatifidum*. The mature leaf is some 9 inches long and 6½ inches across and can be considered as roughly triangular in shape. At the bottom of the leaf two lobes protrude, which are divided at the ends. The centre portion of the leaf is divided into two or three jagged portions and the centre lobe is shaped like a spear-head. The plant is a climber and a native of Brazil, British and Dutch Guiana and appreciates warm conditions. It makes a shapely plant and is not too vigorous.

15. Philodendron leichtlinii[1]

Named in honour of Max Leichtlin, a famous nurseryman of Baden-Baden at the end of the last century: this *Philodendron* has one of the most curious leaves of all plants. The basic shape is that of a rugby football, but the larger portion of the leaf is absent, and it gives an impression of a green skeleton of a leaf, with numerous holes where we would expect the blade to be. This formation, which is found in a lesser degree in the genus *Monstera*, suggests that the plant grows where gales may be expected. Unfortunately this fascinating plant is extremely difficult to grow, requiring great heat and a saturated atmosphere. It is also slow-growing. A minimum temperature of 70° seems to be what the plant requires and a shady position.

16. Philodendron mamei

This is a creeping species though it may be trained upright. The leaves are large and heart-shaped some 13 inches long and 9 inches across and have a slightly wrinkled surface. The colour is a darkish green, mottled with silver. Where the green petiole joins the leaf it is reddish in colour. The plant is a native of

[1] This should probably be termed *Monstera leichtlinii* as it does not seem to be a *Philodendron* at all. The same applies to *M. pertusa*, which is still called *Philodendron pertusum* in some writings.

Ecuador and likes warm conditions, but will tolerate low temperatures, as it is found quite high up.

17. Philodendron melanochryson (Plates 11 and 14)

The specific epithet is a combination of two Greek words meaning black-gold, referring to the intense colouring of the leaves. It is only comparatively recently that it has been recognized that this is not a true species, but the juvenile form of *P. andreanum*. *Melanochryson* was diagnosed by Linden and André in 1873 and *andreanum* by Devansaye in 1886. As the juvenile leaves have sometimes disappeared in a well-developed adult plant, it might not seem so surprising, were it not that Devansaye's diagnosis included a description of the juvenile leaves. It is doubtful if the houseplant grower will meet the plant in any but its *melanochryson* form. This is a slender climber with heart-shaped leaves some 5 to 6 inches long of a dark velvety green on the surface and a pale purple-pink on the underside. This combination gives the leaves the dark appearance with a gold iridescence that the specific epithet suggests. The adult leaves are shaped like an arrow-head, and may be over 2 feet in length and 10 inches across, and are a dark green with very prominent ivory veins. The plant is a native of Colombia and other districts in the equatorial Andean foothills. Until recently it has been regarded as very difficult to grow successfully in the house. Nowadays it would appear to have adapted itself somewhat, and many florists report that it is fairly easy to keep in good condition. It is essential to make sure that the plant purchased is well rooted. Temperatures lower than 50° are not recommended and a constant 55° to 60° would seem to be the ideal for winter. It is not always easy to tell if the plant needs water, as the leaves grow naturally vertically and look superficially as if they were wilting. It is thus necessary to examine the plant carefully. During the winter there will be little growth and the plant can be kept on the dry side, as the roots are liable to rot if the temperature is too low and the soil too wet. The plant is one of the most handsome of the genus and, indeed, among all houseplants.

18. Philodendron micans

Micans means shining. A brief description of this plant would be to say that it has the leaf shape of *P. scandens* and the colour of *P. melanochryson*. In point of fact the leaf is rather more purple than the last species, but there is a marked similarity. It is a native of Central America and the more southerly West Indies and needs warm and shady conditions. It is of very slender growth and seems to grow as happily as a trailer as a climber. It is sometimes offered under the incorrect name of *P. cuspidatum*.

19. Philodendron radiatum

The specific epithet means ray-like. A vigorous climber similar to *P. elegans*, but with larger and coarser leaves, this plant seems to have been somewhat neglected as a houseplant. The mature leaves are very similar in shape to *P. bipinnatifidum*, but more deeply incised. The growing point is enclosed in two pale pink stipules that give a flower-like effect. In a well-grown specimen the leaves may be as much as 2 feet in length, though half this is more normal. The leaves are carried on long stems and so a certain amount of room is needed for this plant. The countries of origin range from southern Mexico through Central America. This means that the plant should be regarded as delicate, but not excessively so.

20. Philodendron × rubris nervis

This hybrid is probably identical with one named 'Florida' formed by crossing *P. selloum* with *P. squamiferum. Rubris nervis* means 'with red veins'. This is a sturdy terrestrial *Philodendron* with leaves similar to *P. bipinnatifidum*, though rather larger and with the end lobe enlarged to the spear-head shape of *P. squamiferum*. The growing point is enclosed in a cream-coloured sheath. The leaf is a dark shining green and the principal veins show red on the underside of the leaf. This would appear to be a most desirable plant and should prove hardy.

66

21. Philodendron sagittifolium

The arrow-leaved *Philodendron* is very similar in appearance to *P. imbe* and may be only a regional variety. It is found as far north as Mexico and throughout Central America. The leaves, a bright emerald green on emerging, are similar in shape to *P. imbe*, though not quite so large. The stem and petioles lack the red spots of *imbe* and the plant is a slower grower and hardier. It will tolerate quite low temperatures without ill effects and where a compact plant is needed can be thoroughly recommended. For a large specimen *imbe* is more effective but *sagittifolium* is of more conventional dimensions.

22. Philodendron selloum

This plant was probably named in honour of a famous botanist and collector, Sellow. His name is usually latinized as *sellowianum*, so this derivation may not be correct. In its early stages this plant is practically indistinguishable from *P. bipinnatifidum*. As the plant ages, however, it will produce far larger leaves and also a short tree-like trunk, which may eventually reach a height of 5 feet. Plants with trunks as large as this have survived to a great age and there are few in cultivation. The plant comes from the same district as *P. bipinnatifidum* and requires similar treatment.

23. Philodendron sodiroi

Sodiroi's *Philodendron* is a rather tender climber with long heart-shaped leaves, not unlike *P. mamei*. The leaves are decorated with silver spots and the veins show a violet colour on the underside of the leaf. The leaf stalks are also violet in colour and this rare plant should prove a useful introduction.

24. Philodendron squamiferum

Squamiferum means bearing scales. These scales are borne on the climbing stem. This species is said to be almost entirely arboreal; the seeds rooting in cracks in the bark of trees and the stem climbing rapidly to the heights. The large shining leaf is in two shades of green, one dark, the other lighter, in parallel bands. The leaf can be divided into five lobes, of which the bottom two point back to the petiole. These two bottom lobes are slightly jagged. The next two lobes are not dissimilar in shape, but point forward and are not serrated in any way. The centre lobe is elongated and shaped like a spear-head. The veins show red on the underside. The most characteristic thing about this plant is the leaf stalks, which are thickly covered with purple bristles; so thickly that they give a moss-covered effect. The plant is a native of French and Dutch Guiana and also of Brazil and will tolerate quite cool conditions. Owing to its arboreal habit, it requires a certain amount of growing space and will appreciate more light than many of the other species.

25. Philodendron 'Tuxla'

This very attractive plant, found at Tuxla in Mexico and still requiring a proper name, is very similar in appearance to *P. hastatum* and seems to be intermediate between this and *P. sagittifolium*. It produces a short close jointed stem, which appears to break naturally quite early so as to give a bushy plant, which is rather unusual among philodendrons. The leaves are the same shape as those of *P. hastatum*, up to 7 inches long and 3 inches across at the base, bronzy with a purple underside when emerging and this purple underside persists for some time, while the upper surface turns a mid-green and is very glossy. Judging from its provenance it is probably a very good form of *P. sagittifolium* and will require similar treatment: the temperature not falling below 50° during the winter and a moist environment during the spring and summer growing season. The stem is very stiff, so that no support is needed and the growths tend to come at an angle, suggesting that in the wild it is a rock dweller. Although there is no one feature to distinguish the plant, it has an elegance of poise which makes it stand out in any group.

26. Philodendron verrucosum (Plate 112)

The specific epithet means 'covered with warts' and its appositeness is not very clear. This plant is probably the most beautifully leaved of all *Philodendrons*; *melanochryson* being the only rival. Unfortunately it is rather tender and requires a constant temperature of 60° if it is to thrive. It has the usual climbing stem from which spring leaves of a typical 'arum lily' shape, of a shining dark green with nearly black patches between the main veins. On the underside these black patches are a reddish purple. The leaf stalk is thickly covered with green bristles that give it a moss-encrusted appearance. The plant is a native of Colombia and Costa Rica, and is always found growing in thick woods and so can scarcely be too heavily shaded.

27. Philodendron wendlandii[1] (Plate 13)

Wendland was another of the early collectors in South America. This *Philodendron* is a terrestrial species, but unlike *selloum* and *bipinnatifidum* has simple oblong lance-shaped leaves, not unlike those of a *Ficus*. These are said to reach a length of 14 inches in a well-developed specimen. The plant comes from Costa Rica and Panama but has only recently been re-introduced and its tolerance of temperature has not been established. We would imagine it would respond well to delicate treatment, with an ideal minimum temperature of 50°. Another introduction under the name of *P. dubium* appears very similar.

For many people this genus has a peculiar fascination and we may hope for further introductions in the future. Most of the climbing species that remain to be introduced are rather large for houseplant work, but there are a vast number of terrestrial species that should repay further investigation.

Genus ACORUS

The genus *Acorus* contains only two species, one of which, the Sweet Flag, is naturalized around ponds and lakes in the British Isles. Both species look more like rushes than members of the Arum family.

---

[1] In one publication it is suggested that this plant is a hybrid between *P. imbe* and *P. hastatum*, but this sounds highly improbable. How can two climbers produce a non-climber? Perhaps some hybridist gave this name not knowing it was already a good species.

Araceae

1. Acorus gramineus var. variegatus (Plate 17)

Gramineus means grass-like and describes the leaves, which are thin, and variegated cream and green. As the plant will survive out of doors it is one of the hardiest houseplants there are. It is a marsh lover and therefore it is scarcely possible to overwater, though this could be done in the dormant period. It must never be allowed to dry out completely. It is seldom used on its own, but is put in mixed groups. These, however, should be selected with care as not all plants will tolerate as much water as *Acorus* demands. It is propagated by division. It is sometimes known as *Acorus japonicus argenteo-striatus* though, in its wild state, it is not confined to Japan. It is seldom that the leaves exceed 6 inches in height.

Genus AGLAONEMA

The name comes from two Greek words meaning 'shining thread' and its application to the plants of the genus has never been satisfactorily determined. The *R.H.S. Dictionary* suggests that it refers to the stamens, but these are no brighter than those of any other aroid, and its appositeness must remain obscure.

This is a comparatively small genus; Engler lists forty-one species and an additional two which he considers doubtful. All its members are to be found in S.E. Asia from Northern Burma to the Philippines and New Guinea; all districts visited by the monsoons. They are all small plants, with the exception of *A. oblongifolium*, and have oblong lance-shaped leaves on short stalks all arising from a central growing point. As the plant ages it develops a short trunk, marked with circular scars where the old leaves have fallen off. The plants enjoy naturally a warm moist environment, but have been found to tolerate temperatures as low as 48° without ill effect. They will not stand gas or oil fumes and must be kept as dry as possible during cold weather. Propagation is by seeds or cuttings and high temperatures are necessary for rooting or germination. *Aglaonemas* make ideal houseplants as they are nice and compact, and not too difficult to preserve, and should be more widely known.

Araceae

1. Aglaonema commutatum (Plate 15)

Commutatum means 'altered', and its appropriateness here is obscure. This is quite a large plant for an *Aglaonema* with leaves up to 5 inches long and 2 inches across in the typical lance-shaped form, borne on stems some 3 inches long. The colour is a dark green, with thin silver-grey zones on either side of the lateral veins. This pattern is found in several other *Aglaonemas*, notably *robelinii* and *treubii* among those in cultivation, and in several species that do not appear to be obtainable at the moment. *A. commutatum* is a native of Central Malaya and the Celebes.

2. Aglaonema costatum (Plate 19)

Costa is the Latin botanical term for the midrib of a leaf and this species is distinguished by its very prominent midrib, which, in most varieties, is ivory-coloured, making it even more distinct. This is a variable species and the leaves vary from a plain green to a marked ivory variegation. The leaves are more rounded than any of the other houseplant *Aglaonemas* and may attain a length of 8 inches, though this is not frequent, and a width of some 4 inches. The variety in the Turnford collection agrees fairly closely with Engler's variety *maculatum* (spotted). The midrib is a striking ivory and the dark green of the leaf surface is spotted irregularly with small ivory spots. The species is a native of S.W. Malaya.

3. Aglaonema oblongifolium

The oblong-leaved *Aglaonema* is the largest of the genus, and may eventually grow a trunk 3 feet in length. The leaves are said to reach a length of 18 inches, but this has not yet been seen in cultivation, and half that length is more usual; possibly the larger measurement included the leaf stalk. The type has plain dark green leaves, but the variety *Curtisii*, named in honour of the botanist Charles Curtis, has silver-grey bands marking the course of the lateral veins and is a very striking plant. It is a native of S.W. Malaya and Borneo.

71

4. Aglaonema pictum

Pictum, the Latin for 'painted', is a specific epithet that botanists are liable to apply to any variegated leaf. In the present case it is more appropriate than usual; the leaf really does look as if it has been painted. The whole leaf is covered with irregular blotches in three different shades of green: very dark, emerald and so pale as to appear silvery. It is impossible to say what the ground colour is. A variety, *tricolor*, has some yellow in the light greens, but is otherwise similar. The leaves reach a length of 6 inches and a width of 2 inches, and are slightly more rounded than most of the species cultivated as houseplants, though less so than *A. costatum*. The plant is a native of S.W. Malaya, Borneo and Sumatra and will evidently enjoy warmth.

5. Aglaonema 'pseudo-bracteatum' (Plates 16 and 19)

There is a plant in the Turnford collection with this label, but it does not appear to be correct, as no *Aglaonema* has been described under this name. There is a variety *pseudobracteosum* of *A. robelinii*, but it does not seem to be that. The Turnford plant has the usual *Aglaonema* leaf some 9 inches long and $2\frac{1}{2}$ inches across, with a golden zone along the midrib and grey-green markings along the lateral veins. These zones are irregular, but are wider near the midrib and tail off towards the leaf margin. Unlike the majority of *Aglaonemas*, this variegation is present on the underside of the leaf, as well as the surface.

6. Aglaonema robelinii (Plate 5)

Robelin was presumably a botanist, but we have found no details of his career. This is quite a vigorous plant with leaves up to 10 inches long and 5 inches across. It would appear to be a somewhat variable species; the Turnford form has leaves almost entirely silver green but with an irregular dark green margin. The plant is a native of central Malaya.

Probably the very attractive Aglaonema known as 'Silver Queen' should come here as it seems to resemble *A. robelinii* fairly closely. It could, of course, be a hybrid with *A. robelinii* as a parent. In any case it has the usual lance-shaped leaves about 6 inches long and 2 inches across; almost the dimensions of *A. Treubii*, although somewhat different in habit. These are almost entirely a very pale silvery green, with occasional dark green blotches between the lateral veins, while there is a thin margin of dark green around the outside of the leaf. As the leaf ages the dark green blotches tend to increase in number, but the bulk of the leaf always remains silver-green.

7. Aglaonema treubii (Plates 16 and 56)

This species is named in honour of Melchior Treub, who was director of the famous botanic garden at Buitenzorg. The plant has the narrowest leaves of all the species we have been discussing; the average leaf is some 5 inches long, but only 1½ inches across. The ground colour is a rather dark green with irregular grey-green zones along the lateral veins. This is an attractive plant, though not particularly spectacular. It has been found in Celebes and probably elsewhere in Indonesia.

Genus ANTHURIUM

The name comes from two Greek words meaning tail flower, probably with reference to the thin tail-like spadix. This is a large genus of some 500 species, most of which come from the wetter parts of Colombia. Many of the plants have extremely handsome leaves and some species climb like *Philodendrons*; but the extremely hot moist atmosphere that most of them require has not tempted anyone to try them out as houseplants, with the exception of *A. scherzerianum*. Against this we may record seeing *A. crystallinum* in a hotel at Las Palmas, where the atmosphere is remarkably dry, being treated as though it were an aspidistra in an English boarding house and apparently thriving. There is evidently some room for experiment here. At the moment only one species is generally grown as a houseplant, and that for the sake of its flowers rather than its foliage. This is

1. Anthurium scherzerianum (Plate 14)

This was discovered in the late nineteenth century by Herr

Scherzer of Vienna, in Guatemala. Owing to their peculiar shape the flowers are sometimes called 'Painter's Palette'. The plant has long, lance-shaped dark green leaves and bright scarlet flowers that look as if they are made of wax. The spathe is detached from the spadix and though its kinship with the Arum family is evident, it is very dissimilar in shape.

The plants must be given very good drainage; at least an inch-deep layer of crocks should be put on the bottom of the pot and the plants should be potted in a mixture of sphagnum moss and well-rotted leaf mould, with a few small crocks to keep the mixture aerated. As the plants grow, the new roots will appear above the surface and they must be mossed up. During the growing season the plants require to be kept warm and moist, without becoming waterlogged. During the winter they are kept on the dry side, but they should never dry out completely. Propagation is by division and this is best done in January under greenhouse conditions; but specialist growers on the Continent deprecate this and propagate by seed. Under dwelling-house conditions it would probably be risky to try propagation. The plant needs tender conditions and requires a damp atmosphere. Although it is not particularly suitable as a houseplant, it is very popular in Scandinavian countries. In these countries the usual method of heating the rooms is by a continuous burning stove, which is kept going the whole winter. This provides an even temperature of around 60°, which is what the plant appreciates. Fluctuating temperatures it dislikes, though a higher temperature during daylight hours is natural for all plants. The scarlet flowers are, of course, very striking.

2. Anthurium crystallinum (Plate 15)

This is called 'crystalline' because the whole of the leaf surface glistens as though it were covered with fine transparent crystals. The plant is compact, about 10 to 12 inches high, and sends out its leaves from a central growing point. These leaves are heart-shaped, but the lobes are so wide that they meet; and the general effect is oblong-oval. The leaf is a deep velvety green with the principal veins and the midrib picked out in shiny silver. This is some 10 to 12 inches long and 6 inches across.

As can be imagined this is a most striking plant; but it is extremely difficult to keep in good condition in the winter. Even in the greenhouse, yellowing of the leaf edges is hard to avoid. It does not appear to be entirely a matter of heat, though a warm atmosphere is what it has in its native Colombia. It seems to be quite happy at 55°. It does appear to be very sensitive to sudden changes in temperature and these should be guarded against as much as possible. It is evidently only suitable for a room with permanent winter heating. Most of the *Anthuriums* seem to rely more on the atmosphere than the soil medium for their water supply and a moist atmosphere is essential. Even if the plant cannot be kept in good condition in the winter, it is so extremely handsome in the spring and summer that it is worth trying.

Genus CALADIUM (Plate 18)

The name is derived from an Indian name for the plant.

The plants cultivated are mostly by now a hybrid swarm of such species as *C. bicolor, C. picturatum* and *C. schomburgkii*. As the species themselves are very variable and have many different leaf colours, identification is very difficult. The plants originate from South America, mainly Brazil and British Guiana. They are not true houseplants, inasmuch as the leaves die down every winter and reappear in the spring, but they are very ornamental and are often bought in the summer as pot plants. The leaves spring from an underground tuber and are borne on stems from 6 to 12 inches high. The leaves are generally shaped like an arrow-head, though some forms are more circular. They vary in size from 9 inches in length to 2 feet 6 inches in *C. bicolor 'Baraquinii'*. They vary in colour from green with cream or red markings to a bright red, but all are showy and conspicuous. They should be given as much light as possible. They require plenty of water when the leaves are emerging, but less when growth has ceased and can scarcely be too warm. They are not easy to keep alive, unless you have a warm greenhouse. As the leaves begin to fade, water should be withheld and the tubers stored in a temperature of about 60°. The soil in which they are potted should neither be allowed to become dust dry, nor to become too wet, as the tubers will rot should either of these occurrences take place. They should be started into growth at a temperature of 70°, preferably in March, and this temperature should be maintained or increased until the plants are well provided with leaves and the pot is well filled with roots. At this stage they may be brought in a cooler position and, if they are in a greenhouse, brought into the house. They are not easy plants for the amateur and, if finances allow, it is much simpler to purchase fresh plants yearly.

Genus DIEFFENBACHIA

This genus was named after Herr Dieffenbach, the gardener at the imperial palace of Schönbrunn, Vienna in the 1830s. They are similar in growth to *Aglaonemas*, but considerably larger and generally with far more brightly coloured leaves. They are native to South and Central America, though one species also occurs in the West Indies. They need warm moist conditions and will not thrive if the temperature drops below 50°. Ideally it should not drop below 60°. Growth should be kept as continuous as possible, as the individual leaves do not survive for a long period. As the plant ages and the trunk elongates it is liable to turn sideways and eventually grow in a corkscrew-like shape. Although many of the species come from very windy districts, they are very intolerant of draughts. Gas fumes do not appear to be fatal, but oil fumes are. The plants are propagated by cuttings, which require a temperature of 80° while they are rooting. First the growing top is removed and then each ring of the trunk; these rings can be halved, thereby giving two plants from each ring. The plants are extremely poisonous and are commonly known as Dumb Canes, as biting any part of them will prevent speech for several days. As a result of wishful thinking they have also been christened the Mother-in-law Plant! Most of the plants grown are varieties of *Dieffenbachia picta*, but are usually sold as though the varietal name was the specific epithet; e.g. *Dieffenbachia 'Bausei'*, rather than *D. picta* var. *'Bausei'*. Here we have put the various *picta* varieties under *picta*, as there are some other species now being used as house-plants. JIP is suitable both for this and the former genus; they also grow well in a mixture of equal parts of loam, peat and leaf mould with enough sharp sand to give an open texture. They will, of course, thrive in the Turnford aroid mixture.

1. Dieffenbachia amoena (Plate 20)

Amoena is the Latin for 'pleasant' and the pleasant Dieffen-bachia is one of the better ones for room culture, although it requires a winter temperature not lower than 55°. The oval leaves are up to a foot long and some 6 inches across at their widest and are dark green with cream or yellow marbling along the lateral veins.

2. Dieffenbachia arvida (Plate 21)

This is also known as *D. hoffmannii* and the form most usually grown is known as 'Exotica perfection'. *D. arvida* is found in many parts of Central America, but this particular form was found on the banks of the Rio Ysidho in Costa Rica. It is more compact than most of the other species in cultivation, having leaves only some 6 inches long and 3 inches across and the un-usual habit of producing small plantlets from the base during the summer months, creating a bushy plant. It has proved to be the variety that is most accommodating for room work and has more or less supplanted the others as a houseplant. The young leaves resemble a small leaf of *D. amoena*, being dark green with cream marbling, but as the leaf ages the cream tends to spread over most of the leaf surface so that mature leaves are almost entirely cream. A particularly brilliant form with large, oval leaves some 12 inches long and 6 inches wide with very short internodes has been given the name 'Tropic Snow'. Although a winter temperature of 60° is desirable, the plant will survive if it falls as low as 50°, although some care is necessary under these cool conditions and leaves may well be shed prematurely.

3. Dieffenbachia bowmannii (Plate 23)

Named in honour of its introducer David Bowman, who was collecting for Veitch in Brazil in 1866. This is a large plant with oblong-oval leaves some 11 inches long and 4 inches across, mottled in a very dark green and a light yellowish green. The markings are irregular, but the dark green portions are more frequent around the edge of the leaf.

4. Dieffenbachia imperalis

The imperial *Dieffenbachia* has a rather less rounded leaf than the last species, but is equally vigorous. The leaf is 12 inches long and barely 4 inches across, and is of a medium green marked with a few not very large cream blotches. A large specimen can apparently produce leaves 2 feet in length, borne on stems of the same length, but plants of these dimensions have not been seen in cultivation. The plant is a native of Peru.

5. Dieffebachia oerstedii (Plate 19)

Anders Oersted was a nineteenth-century plant collector in South America. This is an extremely dramatic-looking plant with plain dark green leaves, with one solitary ivory stripe down the midrib. The leaves are not quite so large as those of the two previous species, being some 9½ inches long. They are somewhat more rounded than most of the houseplant *Dieffenbachias* and are 4½ inches wide. The plant is a native of Central America, particularly Guatemala and Costa Rica.

6. Dieffenbachia picta

Occasionally we come upon plants that are still apparently in an active stage of evolution and have not yet finally adopted a definite form. Our own British marsh orchids may be numbered among these and so may *D. picta*. This is what is termed a polymorphous species, and at least seventeen varieties have been named. The originally described type, now referred to as var. *typica*, has a long thin lance-shaped leaf some 9 inches long and 3 inches across. The basic colour is a dark green, but most of the space between the lateral veins is coloured cream. The cream markings are irregular, thickest at the centre of the leaf. This was originally found in Brazil.

(*a*) Var. **Jenmanii.** (Plate 5) This is close to the type, but with a narrower leaf and regularly marked cream blotches between the lateral veins.

The variety is named in honour of George Jenman, a curator of the botanical gardens in Jamaica, in the last century.

(*b*) Var. **Roehrsii.** (Plate 22) This is wider leaved than the type, the leaves being 9 inches long and 4½ inches across. Most of the leaf is a pale yellowish green, with the lateral veins showing ivory and the margin of the leaf and midrib a dark green.

(*c*) Var. **memoria.** The leaf is similar in shape to the type, but the colour is silver-grey with a dark green irregular margin. The resemblance to any other *picta* variety is hard to see. The name *memoria* (memory) seems obscure, and it might be a misprint for *nemorum* (woodland) that has now been perpetuated. Most *Dieffenbachias* enjoy a certain amount of light and the unusual coloration of this variety might be due to shady conditions. Its country of origin is unknown.

(*d*) Var. **Bausei.** This plant is apparently not a variety at all, but a hybrid between *D. picta* and *D. weirii* and is of garden origin. The leaf is similar in shape to *Roehrsii,* but not quite so wide, and is of a vivid bright green with dark green blotches and a few silver spots.

Dieffenbachias would make ideal houseplants were they less tender. There is one variable species, *D. seguine*, which has predominantly green leaves, but which is considerably hardier. It is found in the West Indies and Central America at quite considerable heights above sea level. If this species could be hybridized with *picta*, it should be possible to get a plant with the showy leaves of the one species and the hardiness of the other.

Genus MONSTERA

This name means what it looks like, a monster. These South American aroids have thick round stems that give a serpent-like impression, and are characterized by large leaves that are not

79

only deeply serrated but also perforated with large holes. In habit they are very similar to *Philodendrons*, but appear to be creepers rather than climbers. If left to themselves, the stems will grow horizontally and they must be tied to a stake if they are required to make erect plants. The aerial roots are large and thick and require to be trained down the stake into the pot. The serrated and perforated leaf indicates that the plants come from regions where high winds are prevalent. They have proved very hardy in the house, tolerating very low temperatures without any ill-effect, though they need a temperature of 65° before they will make growth. It is best to purchase a sizeable specimen to begin with, as it will increase in size slowly.

1. Monstera deliciosa

It is the pulp surrounding the seeds that is delicious, being juicy and having a pineapple-like flavour. This plant, though perfectly hardy, is far too large for most rooms, with its leaves as much as 4 feet long and 2 feet across. The tough leathery leaves are a dark green, with a deeply incised edge and large holes in the leaf blade. The plant is a native of Mexico.

2. Monstera pertusa (Plate 24)

The specific epithet means 'having slits or holes'. This plant is invariably sold under the name of *M. deliciosa* '*Borsigiana*', but, though the leaves are not dissimilar to *deliciosa* in their serrated edge and perforations, the basic shape is far more rounded. This is a more compact plant than *deliciosa* and far more suited to room work. The leaf reaches 12 inches in length and 10 inches in width. The first leaves are more or less heart-shaped and not broken up in any way, but subsequently they appear more serrated and eventually perforated as well. These curious leaf shapes can be induced, by careful lighting, to throw interesting shadows and *Monsteras* are a favourite with film directors on account of their photogenic properties. Watering needs some care as too much or too little will cause yellowing and browning at the tips. They do not require a very wet soil, but it should not dry out completely. Propagation is by seed or cuttings. The top

17. Acorus gramineus variegatus, Carex morrowii variegata

18. Caladium × candidum

19. Dieffenbachia oerstedii, Aglaonema 'pseudo-bracteatum',
A. costatum

20. Dieffenbachia amoena

21. Dieffenbachia arvida 'Perfection'

22. Dieffenbachia picta Roehrsii

23. Dieffenbachia bowmannii

24. Monstera pertusa 'Borsigiana'

25. *Scindapsus aureus* 'Marble Queen'

26. Spathiphyllum wallisii

27. Syngonium podophyllum 'Emerald Gem'

28. Hedera helix 'Chicago' variegata

29. Hedera helix sagittaefolia

30. Hedera helix 'Glacier', 'Little Diamond', 'Green Ripple'

31. Hedera helix 'Fantasia'

32. Hedera helix cristata

33. Hedera canariensis fol. var., Schefflera actinophylla, Hedera helix 'Nielson'

cutting will root easily, but the leaf-joint cuttings require a very high temperature (90°) and though they soon produce roots are somewhat slow in developing growing points. Seeds also require a high temperature, though 80° is sufficient, and take time to provide a sizeable plant. The place of origin of *M. pertusa* is given simply as tropical America.

A variegated form of this plant turned up in the 60's, with the leaves mottled with cream. This plant is very slow-growing, like most of the variegated forms of aroids, but it is rather striking. It has not been much of a success commercially and is probably not easy to obtain.

Genus SCINDAPSUS

Scindapsus is a Greek name for some unidentified climbing plant. This genus is very similar to *Philodendron* in its habit and method of growth, but is confined to S.E. Asia and the Pacific Islands. The majority of the twenty species are climbers, with rather small heart-shaped leaves in young plants and very large rounder leaves when the plant is of a considerable size. *S. aureus* is a popular climber in warm countries, where it is trained up trees which soon become nearly buried beneath the large adult leaves.

1. Scindapsus aureus

The leaves are an oval oblong and are dark green flecked with yellow. The specific name *aureus* means golden, but it is not an accurate description. Though the plant will grow up an ordinary cane, it will produce considerably larger leaves if grown on bark or moss or green wood. It should be treated in the same way as *Philodendron scandens* and stopped regularly each spring. It does, however, require more light than the *Philodendron*, particularly in the winter, otherwise it may lose its yellow markings. It is surprisingly hardy, but dislikes gas and oil fumes. If it is overwatered it is liable to rot at the leaf joints and the leaves turn an unpleasant brown. It appreciates regular syringeing in the summer. Although it appreciates light it should not receive direct sunlight for any long period. Besides the type there are

F   81 three cultivars, all improvements on the type but somewhat more delicate. Propagation is by cuttings, which should be selected with care as the plants revert quickly.

(*a*) **Scindapsus aureus** 'Giant Leaf'. This is similar in colouring to the type, but as the name implies has a very much larger leaf. In countries where it is possible to grow *Scindapsus* out of doors, it will be found that after the plant has climbed for about ten feet it will start producing much larger leaves that are kidney-shaped. In this cultivar these mature leaves are produced very much earlier, after the plant has grown less than a foot. The leaves are about treble the size of the normal immature leaf.

(*b*) **Scindapsus aureus** 'Golden Queen'. In this cultivar the leaf is almost entirely yellow.

(*c*) **Scindapsus aureus** 'Marble Queen'. (Plate 25) In this cultivar the leaves are almost entirely white and have a netted effect, which is striking.

2. Scindapsus pictus argyraeus

The specific name is Latin and the varietal name is Greek, and the two together mean that the leaves are painted with silver. The description is good. The leaves are more heart-shaped than in *S. aureus* and about 2 inches long. They are olive-green in colour and marked with silver dots. It is a charming little plant, but is not in very abundant supply at the moment. It comes from Borneo and Java. Under houseplant conditions it is a slowish grower and dislikes draughts. It appears to put up with gas and oil fumes. Although given a varietal name it is really the juvenile form of *S. pictus*, but when the plant is mature (and it grows to 40 feet) the silver dots vanish, and their place is taken by pale green dots. It should probably be regarded as delicate, but will tolerate short periods of low temperature without any visible damage. It is at its best in a mixed group. During the growing season it likes to be kept moist.

Genus SPATHIPHYLLUM

The name means that the spathe looks like a leaf, which indeed it does. Many of the species have green spathes.

Araceae

1. Spathiphyllum wallisii (Plate 26)

Named in honour of Gustave Wallis, who introduced the plant from Colombia in 1874. It seems to be identical with a somewhat larger plant which was named slightly earlier as *S. patinii*, and that is probably the correct name for this plant.

This is one of the few houseplants that are grown for the sake of its flowers rather than its leaves. The leaves are a bright shiny green, long and lance-shaped with a thin point at the top. The flowers, which are not unlike *Anthurium* in shape, appear in the spring and again in the late autumn. They are green at first, but later turn white and then, later still, turn green again. It should be treated as delicate, but it is not unreasonable in its requirements. It likes constant shade and the leaves will turn yellowish if exposed to too bright a light. It is a rapid grower and greedy. It is nearly impossible to give it too much feed and it needs frequent repotting. Red Spider is sometimes a serious pest on it. Propagation is by division or by seed, but principally by the former method. This is not a tall plant; the leaves are about 4 inches long and the flower stems about an inch longer. Like so many other houseplants, it is a native of Colombia.

2. Spathiphyllum 'Mauna Loa'

Since Mauna Loa is a Hawaiian beauty spot, this hybrid was presumably raised by one of the Hawaiian nurserymen. It would seem to be the same as the plant described as *S.* × *hybridum* in the *R.H.S. Dictionary* which is a cross between the preceding plant and the much larger *S. cannifolium*. The resultant plant has the compact growth of *S. wallisii*, but the larger flowers of the other parent. It is, in fact, like a very large-flowered *S. wallisii*. Both the leaves and flowers are about 2 inches longer than those of the last species. The plant does require rather warmer conditions than *S. wallisii* and is much less liable to have a second flowering in the autumn, unless some form of additional lighting can be supplied.

It is not very happy about gas fumes, but seems to tolerate oil fumes. During the growing season it will take a lot of water and should not be allowed to dry out in the winter.

Araceae

Genus SYNGONIUM

All that the name means is that the ovaries are joined together. *Syngoniums* are climbing plants, similar in habit to *Philodendron*, from some of which they can be distinguished only by obscure botanical characters, such as the conjoined ovaries. They are found in Central and South America. Some are climbers and others are creepers. They are known as the 'Goosefoot plant', owing to the shape of their leaves, which is not unlike a goose's webbed foot. Two species are cultivated as houseplants, both reasonably hardy. They should be treated in the same way as the climbing *Philodendrons* and be trained on bark or on some mossy stick.

1. Syngonium podophyllum (Plate 27)

Podophyllum means that the leaf is shaped like a foot. The type plant with plain green leaves is not grown as a houseplant, but a form which has been given the varietal name of *albolineatum* (white-lined) and the cultivar name 'Emerald Gem' is very popular. The leaf shape is roughly triangular, or like an arrow-head with a very extended base. The leaf can be divided into three lobes of which the largest central one is some 7 inches long and $2\frac{1}{2}$ inches across and is shaped like a spear-head. The two side lobes are shaped like arrow-heads and are joined to the central lobe. Each side lobe projects for some $3\frac{1}{2}$ inches, so that the base of the leaf is 7 inches across. The side lobes are not more than 1 inch wide. The ground colour of the leaves is dark green, but there are thin pale green zones along the midrib and the lateral veins, giving the leaf a pleasant, partly variegated, effect. As there seems to be no record of this form having been found growing wild, it would appear that the cultivar name should most properly be applied. The type is a native of Central America from Mexico southwards. In America this has been assigned, incorrectly, to the genus *Nephthytis* and is often sold under that name in Great Britain, as the name is more euphonious than *Syngonium*.

2. Syngonium vellozianum

This plant is named in honour of the Brazilian botanist monk, J. de la Concepcion Velloss, who lived from 1742 to 1811. This is a vigorous climber with dark green shiny leaves divided into three spear-head shaped lobes; the central lobe is the largest. The leaves are about an inch longer and wider than those of the previous species, and the side lobes are not joined to the central lobe; so that it is possible to consider the leaf as being formed of three leaflets. This makes its best effect if grown into a large specimen, and, as it is vigorous and does not require great heat, this is not difficult to manage. The plant comes from Southern Brazil. Like *S. podophyllum* it should be treated as 'delicate' but will tolerate an occasional fall in temperature without ill-effects.

As can be seen the Arum family is rich in attractively leaved plants and there seems to be no reason why the list should not be added to. There remain many handsome aroids which might prove very suitable but which require to be re-collected and re-introduced into cultivation. Anyone travelling in S.E. Asia or in South America should keep his eyes open for handsome aroids. It must be borne in mind that often a plant may look rather drab when in the wild state and quite handsome in a pot, and a certain amount of imagination is needed to visualize the difference between a plant in the wild and in cultivation. Similarly a plant that looks a reasonable size in the wild may prove large, and bulky when potted up. Finally, of course, it is necessary to test the plant to see if it will thrive under room conditions. There are, unfortunately, too many plants that we can cultivate in our greenhouses but not in our rooms.

CHAPTER V

Araliaceae

THE IVY FAMILY

The *Araliaceae* are a family of some sixty genera and some seven hundred different species, mainly found in the tropics. It is named after the genus *Aralia*, which has now been so cut down, that the majority of plants once known as *Aralia* are now found in other genera. From the point of view of houseplants, the family is one of the most important owing to the numerous Ivies that have proved themselves so suitable. For the most part they are very hardy, completely tolerant of gas and oil fumes, will put up with considerable neglect, will grow in practically any soil, and do not need frequent repotting. The majority of them are cultivars of *Hedera helix,* the common wild Ivy, though in defiance of correct usage some have been given Latin varietal names. These may well be changed in the future, but the names we are giving are current at the moment. Like some of the aroids, the Ivies produce aerial roots both as a means of support and as a means of nourishment, but it is not necessary, if they are being grown as climbers, to provide them with green wood.

Indeed, the forms of *Hedera helix* are prized for their small leaves for the most part, and it would not be particularly desirable to encourage the growth of larger leaves. On the other hand, the Canary Islands Ivy does possess fine large leaves, but they are not much improved by being grown on green wood. In any case, the Ivies are frequently grown as trailers, or small bushes, or trained in shapes around wires. Their culture presents few

86

difficulties. Most of them are known as self-branching Ivies and require regular stopping every spring and possibly again later in the growing season, if growth is vigorous. A self-branching Ivy will produce sideshoots from practically every leaf joint after stopping. It is this phenomenon indeed which led to the Ivies becoming houseplants. The ordinary wild Ivy would grow in the house, but if it is stopped it will only produce another growing point, or possibly two, if the plant is vigorous. All the *Araliaceae* will grow in JIP, but at Turnford we have found the following formula extremely satisfactory.

2 parts loam
1½ parts leaf mould
1 part sand
¾ part dung
½ part peat.

All parts by bulk. To this mixture a 5-inch pot full of super-phosphate is added to each barrow load. The loam should not be heavy, but open, with plenty of fibre and slightly acid; a pH of 5·5 or 6 is ideal. This mixture is satisfactory for most house-plants.

Genus HEDERA

Hedera is the Latin for Ivy.

1. Hedera helix

Helix is the Latin for a snail or a screw and refers to the way in which the stem twines round trees. *H. helix* is the ordinary wild Ivy, and it might be imagined that its various cultivars would grow out of doors. This, however, is not so. They will tolerate very low temperatures, but not frost.[1] During the spring and summer they require to be kept shaded, but they appreciate more light in winter. If they are being grown as climbers it is probably not convenient to move them, but in that case it may be found

[1] This is not altogether accurate. If placed out of doors at the end of May and allowed to harden in the open air all forms of *H. helix* and even *H. canariensis* will tolerate frost. On the other hand plants that are grown in a room will be soft and liable to damage by frost. As houseplants, therefore, Ivies must be regarded as frost tender.

that the variegated varieties lose their variegation in the winter. If that occurs, the best thing to do is to cut the plant back to the first well variegated leaf in the spring. The *Hederas* do not require a lot of water at any time and, as most other plants, very little in the winter. They do not suffer the attention of many pests, though soft scale is sometimes a nuisance. In the home an occasional sponging will cure this. All the Ivies repay you for the trouble of sponging their leaves at regular intervals: their leaf surfaces are particularly liable to harbour dust. When grown commercially they are usually grown up 20-inch sticks to which they are attached by soft metal rings; others are placed on ledges and grown as trailers.

(*a*) **Hedera helix** 'Pittsburgh'. One of the first of the self-branching Ivies to be introduced, 'Pittsburgh' has small dark green leaves with lighter green veins. The mature leaf is about 1¼ inches long and 1 inch broad, but the central lobe is long and thin so that the shape of the leaves is roughly triangular in appearance, though closer inspection will show that the leaf has five lobes, although the two lowest are inconspicuous. 'Pittsburgh' is a vigorous grower. Like all the *Hederas* it is propagated by cuttings; usually taken in May. They do not require much heat, but sometimes take a surprisingly long time to root.

(*b*) **Hedera helix** 'Chicago'. This is very similar to 'Pittsburgh', but the leaves are somewhat larger, about 2 inches long and 1½ inches across. They emerge a very bright green and remain quite a light green all their life. It is not a very rapid grower. The variegated form 'Chicago variegata' (Plate 28) is an extremely attractive plant, in which the young leaves are almost entirely cream, although as they age the cream is confined to the leaf margin and the centre becomes a light green. This plant needs full light for the variation to develop and during the winter any growth made is liable to be unvariegated and in April these plain green growths should be taken out and the trails stopped back to the first variegated leaf, when it may be expected to break again with variegated leaves. The plant known as 'Harald' is, apparently a variegated sport from Chicago, but in this case the variegation is always confined to the margins of the leaves.

Araliaceae

This is a deep cream when the leaves first unfurl, turning to ivory as they age, while the centre of the leaf is mottled dark and grey-green. Although a sport from 'Chicago' this has lost its self-branching habit and tends to make long trails.

(*c*) **Hedera helix** 'Nielson'. This does not differ a great deal from 'Chicago' but it is closer jointed (i.e. the leaves grow closer together), the leaves are smaller and the colour is slightly darker, though not as dark as 'Pittsburgh'. A charming plant which produces such a profusion of leaves that it never appears straggly. (Plate 33)

(*d*) **Hedera helix** var. *minima*. This is a genuine variety that has appeared outside cultivation. In spite of that it is self-branching. *Minima* means smallest and at one time it had the smallest leaf of any Ivy, but the introduction of 'Maple Queen' has made its varietal name inaccurate. The leaves are much thinner in every way than any of the previous ones we have been describing, the central lobe being very long and thin. It is like 'Nielson' in producing an abundance of leaves and as a result the older ones are liable to be buried and turn yellow. This does not matter as there is such a profusion. There is a variegated form (*H. helix* var. *minima variegata*) in which the margin of the leaves is cream-coloured and the centre greyish. The leaves are more rounded than the type and slightly liable to blemish. This is not, for some reason, an easy plant to grow. Possibly the variegation is caused by a virus.

(*e*) **Hedera helix** 'Maple Queen'. This really is, at the moment, the smallest-leaved Ivy. The resemblance to a Maple or Syca-more leaf is to be noticed in some of the leaves, but not in all; two leaf shapes are present, one very similar to *minima* and the other which is not unlike a Maple in shape. This is another self-branching Ivy and is a vigorous grower.

(*f*) **Hedera helix** 'Little Diamond'. This recent introduction is a variegated Ivy, with very small leaves that are practically without lobes and give the impression of being lance-shaped. The leaf is about an inch in length and $\frac{5}{8}$ inch across, of a dark grey-green with an ivory margin. In time these leaves attain the length of $1\frac{1}{2}$ inches, but they do this very slowly. The Ivy is self-branching and does not appear to be a very fast grower. (Plate 30)

(*g*) **Hedera helix** var. *sagittaefolia*. This is another natural variety. The varietal name means that the leaves are shaped like arrows. In point of fact the name refers only to the central lobe which is very elongated, being double the length of the rest of the leaf. Although this is described as self-branching, it will not produce sideshoots from every leaf joint and it should be allowed to make quite a considerable amount of growth before it is stopped, and then about four inches should be removed. (Plate 29)

(*h*) A new variegated *Hedera sagittaefolia*. This is one of the latest additions to the *Hedera* family. The variegation is very strong in its markings. For a variegated *Hedera* it is quite a quick grower.

(*i*) **Hedera helix** 'Lutzii'. Another small-leafed self-branching Ivy with leaves appearing three, rather than five, lobed and the leaves mottled in varying shades of pale green. The leaves have the typical appearance of a 'mosaic' virus and doubtless this is actually present. The virus does not appear to cause any great diminution in vigour and the plant is a reasonably rapid grower. The name 'Lutzii' may well be changed in the future to something like 'Lutz's Triumph'. (Plate 72)

(*j*) **Hedera helix** 'Golden Jubilee'. This is one of the prettiest of the Ivies and is particularly popular in Sweden. The leaves are small and golden in colour with a wide dark green margin. It is not self-branching and so makes rather a thin plant. It is a very slow grower, particularly when grown in shady conditions. When exposed to a bright light it appears to grow more vigorously and the leaves are more brilliantly coloured. Why 'Golden Jubilee' acts in an opposite manner to most Ivies is obscure. It also appears to appreciate potting-on far earlier than most other Ivies do. The new growth shows a large amount of bare stalk as, under bright conditions, the leaves take their time in expanding to their full size; this, however, they do subsequently. In the winter the gold colour is apt to disappear; in this case cut back to the first coloured leaf in the spring. You will probably only get one growing point to replace it. If two or three plants are put in a pot a more satisfactory effect will be obtained. (Plate 34)

(*k*) **Hedera helix** 'Glacier'. An unusual plant with greyish leaves, with a cream margin which becomes smaller as the leaves age. The general effect is of silvery grey. The stems of the leaves are of an attractive purple tinge. This is not self-branching but is a rapid grower and will produce a sufficiency of sideshoots when large enough. The leaves are not very large, and three-lobed. This is a recent introduction; it is particularly effective as a trailer. (Plate 30)

(*l*) **Hedera helix** 'Green Ripple'. A self-branching Ivy, with remarkably pointed leaves that are suggestive of a vine leaf. The mature leaf is five-lobed and is about 2 inches long and $1\frac{1}{2}$ inches across. The topmost lobe or 'point' of the leaf is 1 inch in length, so the impression is of a long thin leaf. Immature leaves are only three-lobed, the two bottom lobes do not emerge until the leaf is will developed. Young leaves are a bright green and darken with age. (Plate 30)

(*m*) **Hedera helix** var. *marmorata*. Both this and the next variety are sold as varieties of *H. helix* but they are more probably varieties of *H. hibernica*, the Irish Ivy. This has larger leaves than *H. helix*. The Ivy sold as var. *marmorata* has medium-sized leaves variegated dark green and cream. *Marmorata* means marbled and is a good description of the leaves. It is an attractive plant, but a slow grower. Here again the variegation may be due to a virus. The petioles (leaf stalks) are a delicate pink shade. (Plates 36 and 83)

(*n*) **Hedera helix** var. *maculata aurea*. Like the preceding this has medium-size three-lobed leaves which are a fairly light dark green (it must be an Irish Ivy!) mottled with cream. The varietal name means that it is spotted with gold, but this is an over-statement. The petioles are purplish pink and the plant is agreeable, though to some eyes the leaves may suggest a 'mosaic' virus. (Plate 35)

(*o*) **Hedera helix** var. *cristata*. *Cristata* means crested and is given to this variety because the edges of the leaves are fringed like those of parsley. The leaves look nearly round in appearance, but closer inspection shows that they have seven lobes. The leaves are a medium green when young and become very dark as they age. It is not self-branching but, if allowed to reach a good size, will produce sideshoots. Even non-self-branching Ivies appear to benefit from a yearly stopping. (Plate 32)

(*p*) **Hedera helix** var. *nana. Nana* means dwarf and appears to have no application to this plant, which is not particularly dwarf. The leaves, indeed, of the 'Permanent Wave' Ivy, as it is sometimes called, are rather large. They are three- and five-lobed and curiously twisted, making an unusual and effective plant. Again it is not self-branching, but is quite good at producing sideshoots if not stopped too early.

(*q*) **Hedera helix** 'Heisse'. Raised by the nurseryman whose name it bears, this can be succinctly described as a self-branching, upright-growing 'Glacier'. The leaves are about 2 inches long and wide and are five-lobed. They are practically identical in colour with those of 'Glacier' but the cream margin will persist for longer.

(*r*) **Hedera helix** 'Eva'. Also known as 'Little Eva'; this is a slow-growing plant that is not self-branching. It is rather fascinating in that it bears a number of different leaf forms and in the way the leaves change colour as they age. When the leaves first open they are almost entirely ivory, but as they age a central green portion, which is composed of blotches of dark and light green slowly enlarges, so that mature leaves are entirely mottled dark and light green. The most frequently seen leaf shape is three-lobed, with the central lobe at least twice as long as the lateral ones, but sometimes one of these side lobes attains the same dimensions as the central lobe, giving a very odd shape to the leaf; other leaves will be unlobed, to give the same lozenge shape as those of 'Little Diamond'.

(*s*) **Hedera helix** 'Fantasia'. Fairly vigorous non-self-branching Ivy with leaves up to 3 inches long and across. Some leaves are blotched cream and green, while others have a cream margin and a green centre. The leaves are five-lobed. As in most of the variegated Ivies, the cream portion eventually disappears. (Plate 31) Similar to this is 'Anne Marie' with three-lobed leaves up to 3 inches across and 2 inches long. The young leaves have a cream variegation which pales to ivory before it eventually disappears.

(*t*) **Hedera helix** 'Goldchild'. One of the few variegated Ivies to retain their variegation all the time. The young leaves emerge quite a deep yellowish-green with a small central portion composed of blotched dark and light green. As the leaf ages, this central green portion enlarges, but even mature leaves have a wide margin, which has paled to ivory. The leaves can be three- or five-lobed, about 1½ inches long and an inch across, which is not very large. The plant is not self-branching, but has a fairly upright habit. It is very slow-growing.

(*u*) **Hedera helix** 'Mini Green'. This is not self-branching, but maintains an erect habit, although it will trail eventually, if this should be required. The leaves vary in size to some extent, but an average measurement for a mature leaf is an inch long and wide. The leaf is symmetrically five-lobed, giving the impression of half a ten-pointed star, is a rather bright green for an Ivy and, fairly unusually, has a very glossy surface. The leaf is also slightly cupped and has a very wavy edge, which ripples rather more than 'Green Ripple'. The petioles may reach a length of 1½ inches, which seems very long in comparison with the leaf's dimensions and tends to give the whole plant a rather airy appearance, as though the leaves were floating in the air.

(*v*) **Hedera helix** 'Ravenholst'. This is the name under which the plant is sold, but it is difficult to see how it differs from the type of *H. canariensis*, and the fact that the type is never offered makes it even more suspicious. It has the long, almost heart-shaped leaf associated with *H. canariensis* and also the very shiny surface of the leaves. As it ages it develops very large leaves, but it is the very shiny surface that makes it so attractive. Like *H. canariensis* it is more effective as a large specimen. The older leaves turn very dark and the younger, lighter in colour, show off to advantage against them.

In a large nursery the Ivies are continually 'sporting'; that is to say that a cultivar will produce a branch that is different in some way from the usual form. If this 'sport' appears to be an improvement, it is rooted, propagated and in time introduced

93

as a fresh cultivar. Under these circumstances no list of *H. helix* cultivars can hope to be properly exhaustive. They do, however, fall into three main groups: those with small leaves and self-branching, of which 'Chicago' is the type; those with very cut leaves such as *H. sagittaefolia* and 'Green Ripple'; and those with medium-sized leaves such as 'Glacier'. A fourth group is those whose affinity to *H. helix* is doubtful. Any variation is possible in the various groups, but they do not appear to sport out of their groups. The small-leaved ones will not produce a deep-lobed sport, and the deep-lobed ones will not produce minute leaves. The chief sports are on the lines of a change of leaf-shape or a change in variegation pattern. Under greenhouse conditions the change in leaf-shape is more generally from a deeply lobed type to a more solid leaf, rather than the other way about.

2. Hedera canariensis

The specific name tells us that the plant is a native of the Canary Islands (also Madeira and the Azores) and as might be expected they are not quite so hardy as the varieties of *H. helix*. They are still among the hardiest of houseplants, however, and provided they are kept free from frost will grow anywhere. They resent overwatering, particularly in winter, and it is advisable to wait until the leaves flag slightly before watering. Like all the Ivies they resent overpotting. They will spend three or four years in a 3-inch pot and the rest of their lives in a 5-inch. As mentioned above the type is not offered (except perhaps under the pseudonym 'Ravenholst'); but one variety and one cultivar are among the most effective of the Ivies, though they make their best effect when they are large specimens. The *H. canariensis* that grows in the Canary Islands is indistinguishable from any other Ivy. It is a plant with medium-sized bright green leaves. As, however, shade is hard to come by in the Canaries it is probably never seen to its best advantage there.

(*a*) **Hedera canariensis foliis variegatis.** This can be translated as the Canary Ivy with variegated leaves. This is one of the most delightful of variegated plants; the centre of the leaf is dark green and the edges are pale cream, but no two leaves are identical. All the Canary Ivies are slow growers, and it is best to put three rooted cuttings in each pot to make an effective plant. If overwatered the leaves will turn yellow and fall off. Although there is no certainty that the stem will throw more than one growing point, an annual stopping seems to encourage the plant to more vigorous growth, and as it gets larger, more than one growth will be produced. (Plate 33)

(*b*) **Hedera canariensis** 'Golden Leaf'. A complete misnomer; the leaf is not golden at all, but a bright lucent green, with a lighter green patch in the centre, that in some lights looks yellowish. In spite of this it is one of the most effective houseplants, particularly as a large specimen of some 6 feet. A feature is the bright red colour of the stem and leaf stalks. This plant is always delightful but is particularly impressive as a large specimen: it takes some time to reach this height, and, if you are impatient, it is advisable to purchase a large specimen. (Plate 37)

Genus CUSSONIA

A small genus of about twenty species of evergreen shrubs or small trees coming from Africa. The genus was named in honour of the eighteenth-century botanist and physician Pierre Cusson.

1. Cussonia spicata (Plate 39)

Like a large number of houseplants, this will eventually make quite a sizeable plant, a tree up to 20 feet in the wild, and it has, like *Schefflera*, to be reasonably large before it is of much interest. Young plants have dark green leaves, composed of a number of leaflets, varying in number as the plant ages, but all radiating, like a lot of fingers, from the top of the petiole, in the manner of a horse-chestnut leaf. In young plants these are only slightly jagged, but after a few years the leaves become lobed and incised and look very extraordinary as practically every single leaflet has its own individual shape. These leaves are borne on long petioles some 11 inches long and are a rather dark green with a glossy surface. On the underside the very large midrib is a plum purple colour. The individual leaflets may be 10 inches long and are composed of a number of distinct sections. Here is the description of one leaflet. The top 4 inches are composed of a basically diamond-shaped leaf, but with a very incised margin; below this two elongated diamond-shaped sub-leaflets emerge, each about 4 inches long, below this is an inverted triangle, with the base upmost and the tip towards the petiole about 2 inches long and below this is a larger inverted triangle about 4 inches long and wide. However the next leaflet we look at, which is alongside, is quite different, with the larger triangle in the centre, while the lateral leaflets are different still. It will be appreciated that this is a fascinating plant and it also has the advantage, being a native of South Africa, of not requiring very great heat; winter temperatures of 45°–50° being quite sufficient. Ample light is required at all times and the plant will benefit from being stood outside during the period mid-June to September in a lightly shaded situation. If it is kept indoors it should be in a situation where it will receive plenty of fresh air. The plant is propagated from seed and the young plants only start to charac- terize in the third year from seed, which means that the plant has to take up room in the nursery for some time before a saleable plant is produced. This will be reflected in its price. On the other hand it should prove long-lived in the home, although it may eventually become rather large. It can, however, be pruned back to manageable dimensions. Young plants need potting on yearly in April, while older plants (in 6-inch pots or larger) will only need potting on every other year. A compost containing loam is probably essential for this plant.

Genus DIZYGOTHECA

This is one of the new genera which has resulted from the splitting up of *Aralia*.

1. Dizygotheca elegantissima (Plate 34)

Elegantissima means very elegant and is appropriate for the thin spidery leaves. These are shaped somewhat like a horse-chestnut leaf, composed of a number of leaflets radiating out from the top of the petiole. There are from seven to ten of these leaflets and they are up to 3 inches long, but very thin and with small projecting lobes. They are practically maroon in colour, while the petiole itself is almost black, although it is mottled with white. It is so thin that the leaves appear to float in the air. The plant can eventually make quite a sizeable shrub, by which time the leaves have become much coarser; each leaflet then may be an inch across and the lobes are much smaller. At one time this was regarded as extremely difficult to keep in good condition, but plants raised from recent importations of seed have proved to be very much easier. The plant does require moist conditions, as otherwise it is liable to fall a prey to Red Spider. Previously it was thought that the winter temperature should not fall below 60°, but the new plants seem to be quite happy with 50°, although the higher readings are naturally appreciated. Although the atmosphere should always be moist, the soil should be kept on the dry side during the autumn and winter months, so during this time it is advisable to spray the plants occasionally with a fine mist. This is best done around midday.

Genus FATSIA

We had hoped that this was named in commemoration of Fats Waller, but actually *Fatsia* is a phonetic transcription of the Japanese name of the plant.

1. Fatsia japonica

This is also known as *Aralia sieboldii* and is commonly called the Castor Oil plant. The true Castor Oil plant is a member of the Spurge family, but the leaves of the two plants are very similar. *F. japonica* is a shrub with large dark green leaves which are palmate with seven to nine lobes. It is very hardy, indeed it will grow out of doors in a sheltered situation. It is not very effective until it is large enough to go into a 5-inch pot. Cuttings root quite easily, but seed is the best method of pro-pagation. The seed should be sown in a temperature of about 65°.

There is also a variegated variety, but the variegation is restricted to the tips of the leaves and the general effect is most pleasant and unusual. As is customary with variegated plants it is more delicate and slower growing than the type. Propagation is by cuttings.

Genus × FATSHEDERA

The × denotes that we are dealing with a hybrid and *Fatshedera* is what is known as a bi-generic hybrid. That is to say it is formed from the crossing of two genera, in this case *Fatsia* and *Hedera*. The actual cross was the pollen of *Hedera hibernica* on *Fatsia japonica* var. *Moseri*. Bi-generic hybrids are not common except among orchids and when they do take place it is usually between genera with many features in common (e.g. *Heucherella* × between *Heuchera* and *Tierella*). Messrs. Lizé Brothers who had a nursery at Nantes in France must have been gratified at their success. The hybrid first appeared in 1912.

1. × Fatshedera lizei (Plate 37)

This scarcely seems to have made up its mind whether it is a shrub or a climber. It is a tall grower with a thin wiry stem that needs support, and has large dark green leaves with five clearly marked lobes, but they are not so pronounced as in *Fatsia*. The plant is perfectly hardy. It will take rather more water than the *Hederas*.

There are two variants on the most usually seen form. 'Undulata' has the edges of the leaves rather wavy, so that the plant looks somewhat less rigid. More attractive is the variegated form known as 'Silver Prince'. In this the edges of the leaf are a very brilliant white and this maintains itself all through the season, unlike the first variegated sport which appeared. This was liable to brown at the tips during the winter, so that the plant had to be trimmed with nail scissors. Fortunately this is no longer necessary with 'Silver Prince'. (Plate 38)

Genus SCHEFFLERA

Named in honour of a botanist from Danzig, J. C. Scheffler, this is one of the genera resulting from the break-up of *Aralia*.

Araliaceae

1. Schefflera actinophylla (Plate 33)

The specific name means that the leaves look like the rays of the sun. The leaf is divided into a number of leaflets, which increase in number as the plant develops. Young plants have only three leaflets to each leaf, but more mature plants have five or seven. These leaflets are an elongated oval in shape and may reach a length of 7 inches and a width of 2 inches. The plant is native to Indonesia and northern Australia and requires moderately warm conditions, not falling below 50° during the winter, while 55° is to be preferred. The plant is a slow grower, although it can eventually attain tree-like proportions. The leaves are glossy and a mid-green in colour. We are calling the plant *Schefflera*, as it has always been known under that name, but recently a plant flowered and in place of the single spiked inflorescence of *Schefflera*, it produced an umbel of spiked flowers, thereby proving that the plant should correctly be termed *Brassaia*.

CHAPTER VI

Moraceae

THE FICUS

The *Moraceae*, named after the genus *Morus*, the mulberry tree, is a smallish family, comprising some fifty-five genera and about 1,100 species. From the point of view of the houseplant grower only one genus is of interest, the genus *Ficus*. *Ficus* is the Latin name for the fig and the genus includes the fig as well as such plants as the Banyan and Rubber trees. It is a remarkably diverse genus. *Ficus elastica* will form a tree 100 feet high in its native Malaya, while *F. radicans* is a small creeping shrub. As houseplants they may be regarded as one of the most rewarding of all genera. They are easy to keep, being surprisingly tolerant of low temperatures and also of gas and oil fumes, though this should not be overdone. In a comparatively short time they make extremely handsome plants which, if cared for, will continue in beauty practically indefinitely. With the exception of the shade-loving *F. pumila* they grow equally well in light or shade; but it is advisable to let the new growth emerge under shady conditions, when the new leaves will expand more fully: under a bright light the new leaves appear rather small and hard. Provided they are not in a continual draught they will put up with low or high temperatures. In the winter the plants take a decided rest and should be kept on the dry side, though they should not be allowed to dry out altogether. Growth usually restarts about April and then water may be supplied more regularly, though it should never be overdone. Many of

100

the large-leaved species make considerable root growth, before the new leaves start to develop, and it is as well to examine the roots when considering applying additional water. This applies particularly to *lyrata* and *nekbudu* and also to *indica* and *infectoria*.

Overwatering causes yellowing of the leaves and, as for the most part the leaves are thick and leathery, it means that considerable damage has been done before any symptoms have been noticeable. If this has happened, it is safest to let the plant dry out completely and leave for a week, before applying further water. Although tolerant of varying temperatures, *Ficus* are happiest in a constant temperature around 55° to 60°.

Ficus do not like overpotting and are quite happy in a pot that looks far too small for the plant. They will be happy, with additional feeding, in a 5-inch pot until they are about 3 feet high and will grow the next two feet in a 6-inch pot. If you find the plant is growing taller than you require, you can cut off the top section and it will break into two or three branches. This should be done in late April or early May, and is best done where a heated greenhouse is available. If repotting is necessary, late April and May are the best months, as the plant can then occupy the fresh soil during the growing season. If the newest leaves are coming small and wrinkled it is a sign that either repotting or additional feeding is necessary. One of the compound manures that is done up in tabloid form such as Luxigro or Plantoids is perfectly suitable.

Ficus will grow happily in JIP 2 or 3, but the Turnford formula is (all parts by bulk):

2 parts loam
1 part leaf mould
1 part dung
$\frac{1}{2}$ part peat
$\frac{1}{2}$ part sharp sand
2 5-inch pots full of bone meal per barrow load.

Propagation is by seed or by cuttings. Top cuttings are the best, but naturally only one of these is available per plant and on a commercial scale it is necessary to take the leaf joints as well until the stem becomes too woody. To save space in the propagating frame the large leaves are rolled round a small stick and secured by a rubber ring. A temperature of at least 80° is necessary to obtain rooting and though the top cutting will root in a fortnight, the leaf joint cuttings will take from twenty-eight to thirty days. This means that propagation is an expensive business, and as the nurseryman will then have to grow the cuttings on for a year or two to make sizeable plants it will be seen that they are not likely to be cheap.

For some reason the large-leaved *Ficus* are regarded as particularly masculine in appeal and are frequently presented by wives and female relatives to their menfolk to embellish their offices. One would imagine that it was a particularly welcome gift.

Ficus need their leaves cleaned regularly, which benefits the plant as well as enhancing its appearance. A dusty *Ficus* is a sorry sight.

The taxonomy of the genus is in a more confusing state than most of the others, and we have chosen here to give the names under which they are commonly sold, with a note as to what is its correct name at the time of going to press.

1. Ficus elastica (Plate 40)

The India-rubber plant. In the wild this makes a tree up to 100 feet high and is native to tropical east Asia. Until the spread of *Hevea brasiliensis* in the latter half of the nineteenth century, the tree was cultivated for its rubber; this is found in the milky latex which gushes out whenever the plant is wounded. As a house-plant *F. elastica* is seen as a single stem, usually up to 4 feet in height. If the plants get too large, they can be cut back in the spring and the resultant wound dusted with powdered charcoal which will prevent the latex from flowing over the plant. If sufficiently strong the plant will produce several leads in place of the one that has been removed and a branching tree-like plant will be formed. It is, however, best to defer this cutting back until the plant has become too tall for comfort. The most frequent wild form has leaves usually about 7 inches long and 3 inches across and these leaves are shaped elliptically. However this is not usually seen nowadays and the houseplant grower will be offered either the form called 'Decora' or that called 'Robusta'. *F. elastica* 'Decora' has glossy dark green leathery leaves, which are more ronnded than elliptical and which can reach a length of 12 inches and a width of 7 inches. The leaves differ from the type not only in size but also in the fact that the midrib is reddish on the underside, not greenish. In the same way the growing tip at the top of the stem is enclosed in a bright red sheath, while that in the typical form is pale green. When the new growth emerges, this red sheath splits into two and falls off. Sometimes the cane that supports the stem of the plant may prevent this sheath from falling off; if that should happen, remove the sheath yourself, as otherwise it may rot and this rot could spread to the young leaves. It is in May and June (or April in very warm rooms) that the new growth takes place and during this time it is advisable to have the plants in a rather shady situation, as strong sunlight can damage the tender young leaves and may scorch them or inhibit them from achieving a really good size. Otherwise *F. elastica* is somewhat indifferent to the amount of light it receives, although too dark a shade will be resented.

F. elastica 'Robusta' is very similar to 'Decora' but an even larger leafed plant with leaves up to 18 inches long and 9 inches across and shorter internodes. The sheath is not red as in 'Decora', nor is the midrib so marked. The plant needs similar treatment.

There are a number of forms of *F. elastica* with variegated leaves. As so often happens, these are somewhat more tender than the green-leaved forms and are slower growing. They also require to be in well-lit situations as otherwise the variegation is not apparent. Even so the remarks about protecting the young growths from direct sunlight apply to these plants as well as to the green-leaved forms (indeed they apply to all the large leaved *Ficus* species). Incidentally it is only in *F. elastica*, among the large-leaved *Ficus* that variegation has been noted. It occurs naturally in the Philippine *F. parcellii*, but this has thin leaves and is of no use as a houseplant, however interesting it may be to the botanist.

F. elastica 'Doescheri' (Plate 41) has leaves of the dimensions and shape of the typical *F. elastica*, elliptic and not so large as in the selected forms. As they emerge they are light green, tinged with pink and with a cream margin. As the leaves age, the central green portion enlarges and resolves itself into patches of dark and of light green, while the margin turns ivory-coloured and becomes much narrower. For the first year the veins and petioles are a delicate pale pink, which gradually turns green as the leaf ages. In some ways an improvement on this plant is 'Schryveriana' with leaves as large as 'Decora' with a cream margin and the rest of the leaf mottled with cream and dark green, which appear in roughly rectangular shapes. Equally large-leafed is 'Tricolor' with the leaves mottled with yellow, light and dark green, with the yellow mainly at the edge of the leaf. All these variegated forms appreciate warmth, freedom from draughts and ample light. Overwatering will soon cause browning at the leaf edge and this will continue for some time, even though the overwatering may cease immediately. It follows therefore that great care must be taken with watering, particularly in winter. On the other hand if the plant is kept too dry the lower leaves will fall off. If, once a thorough watering has been given, no more is applied until the pot has dried out, no difficulty should be experienced. Cold water on the leaf surface, particularly when the plant is not growing rapidly, will also cause browning. In warm weather or in very hot rooms, syringeing the leaves will be more beneficial than applying water to the soil, although this, of course, cannot be dispensed with entirely.

2. Ficus benghalensis (Plate 42)

The Bengal Fig or Banyan, in its native India, makes a large tree from the branches of which roots descend to become trunk-like in their turn, so that one tree will eventually turn into a copse. There is, of course, no risk of its behaving in this way in

Moraceae

the house. The leaf of the banyan is some 9 inches long and $4\frac{1}{2}$ inches across, oblong oval in shape and pointed at the tip. The new growth, buds and young leaves are covered with hairs, which give a pinkish appearance to the young stems. The hairs eventually disappear from the leaves as they age, but the leaves never obtain the shining appearance of most *Ficus*. The plant is unique among the large-leaved *Ficus* owing to its habit of branching while still juvenile and so making a shapely plant, as opposed to the single stem of *elastica*, *lyrata* and *nekbudu*. The only other large-leaved *Ficus* that will branch while still young is *macrophylla*, and this has to be induced to do so by stopping. *Benghalensis* is extremely hardy, though it will cease growing should the temperature fall below 50°. Above 50° growth is continuous throughout the year. There would appear to be some discrepancy between the *benghalensis* at Turnford and the published diagnosis which assigns to this species smooth unpointed leaves. At Kew our species is labelled *F. monbuttensis*. As, however, the Turnford plants were grown from seed sent from India, it would seem that they should be the correct species.

3. Ficus benjamina (Plate 41)

F. benjamina does not look like a *Ficus* at all with its long thin leaves and numerous side branches. It grows quickly and soon forms a small weeping tree of great grace, equally valuable on its own or in a mixed group. The leaves are about 4 inches long and $1\frac{1}{2}$ inches across, but they curl slightly so that the general effect is of a long narrow leaf. The young leaves are grass green in colour, turning the colour of privet leaves as they age. *Benjamina* likes to be kept rather moister than many of the *Ficus* and will not be happy if the temperature falls below 50°. A certain amount of leaf yellowing and dropping will occur in the winter under any circumstance, though these will be more than replaced during the growing season. This habit does make it more difficult to gauge the correct amount of water to supply during the winter, but fortunately *benjamina* wilts when it is too dry, though it quickly recovers. It is thus possible to prevent overwatering by means of letting the plant dry out occasionally.

105

Moraceae

4. Ficus diversifolia (Plate 43)

This is known as the Mistletoe Fig, from its habit of bearing
small yellowish berries in the leaf axils. *Diversifolia* means 'with
different leaves', as the leaves are an unusual shape for the genus.
Its name has now been changed to *F. deltoidea*, meaning that the
leaves are shaped like the Greek capital D (delta). It is a small
shrub with thick dark green leaves that are nearly circular,
though they taper off slightly at the leaf stalk. It will start to
fruit at a very early age and will produce small red or yellow
berries in the axils of the leaf stalks. It is these fruits that make
the plant so attractive. Although it is a native of India and
Malaya it is surprisingly hardy and will tolerate 45° in the
winter, although 50° is naturally better. It will appreciate a
certain amount of light, but direct sunlight is not necessary,
though it is not harmful. Stopping seems to encourage fruiting
as well as the production of sideshoots, but it should not be
overdone. It will not enjoy either drying out or overwatering
and appreciates a moist atmosphere.

A very large, vigorous form of this plant is sometimes offered
under the name of *F. triangularis*. In this the leaves, which are only
about 2 inches long and an inch across in the form most usually
seen, reach the dimensions of 4 inches by 3 inches, while the
whole plant assumes tree-like proportions, albeit a small tree.
The leaves are also more markedly triangular in shape and it is
possible that the plant is specifically distinct. Even so it is very
close to *F. diversifolia* and requires similar treatment, although
the moister the atmosphere that can be maintained the more
vigorous the growth will be. The leaves are a very dark green
indeed and look most unusual with their triangular shape, although the tree itself is rather graceless in isolation and looks
best when incorporated in a mixed group.

5. Ficus indica

This should, apparently, be known as *F. sundaica* and is a
branching shrub, that can eventually make a large tree. The
leaves are leathery, a dark shining green, oblong oval in shape

tapering off suddenly in a blunt point. The leaves are $4\frac{1}{2}$ inches long and not quite $2\frac{1}{2}$ inches across and are borne on stalks about 1 inch in length. They are not dissimilar in appearance to the popular Portuguese Laurel. Around the margin of the leaf appear a number of minute white dots. These appear to be a feature of the Indian *Ficus* and can be discerned, though with difficulty, on the leaves of *benghalensis* and *infectoria*. In the case of this species they are a feature of the leaf. The plant has proved very hardy in rooms, but is not particularly satisfactory as a houseplant, owing to the long intervals of stem between the leaves, which gives the plant a rather leggy appearance.

6. Ficus infectoria

The specific epithet means 'dyed', though in what sense it is to be taken is not clear. It should, apparently, now be termed *F. virens*. This is another Indian species with elongated leaves, some 5 inches long and 2 inches across with a wavy edge. The leaf is similar in appearance to that of a Holm Oak, though larger and of a lighter green. The trunk is somewhat wrinkled. As the leaves age they become quite hard, but are very soft and delicate when newly emerged. The plant has an indefinable charm, but is not a particularly easy subject, as it is somewhat liable to drop its leaves in the winter. It succeeds best in a warm atmosphere where it can be kept growing.

7. Ficus lucida (Plate 42)

This *Ficus*, which is also known as *nitida* (both epithets mean 'shining'), should properly be known as *F. microcarpa*. It is well known as a shade tree in tropical and subtropical countries, but, as a houseplant, it is akin to *F. benjamina*. The leaves are small and roughly heart-shaped, not more than 2 inches long and about 1 inch across and are produced in large quantities. They are a shining medium green and a large tree is reminiscent, in colour and shape, of a beech. As a houseplant it should make a small shrub, well branched, and should prove very hardy. It will enjoy as much light as it can be given and will not mind dry conditions, though these are not recommended for young plants for fear of Red Spider.

8. Ficus lyrata (Plate 43)

The Banjo or Fiddle-back Fig. This is perhaps the most imposing of all the *Ficus*. The mature leaves are about 12 inches long
and some 9 inches across and are shaped like the body of a
violin. The leaf broadens out from the stem and reaches its
widest at the end. Like *F. panduriformis*, it is a much lighter
green than *elastica*. The midrib and veins are thick and project
on the underside of the leaf, while on the upper side they show
through as cream markings. The leaves are thick and leathery
and can be washed without any risk of damage. The leaf stalk is
very short indeed, and at a superficial glance the leaves appear to
spring directly from the stem. The stem itself is slender and soon
acquires a woody appearance. *Lyrata*, which is sometimes known
as *F. pandurata*, is a native of tropical West Africa. Like all the
large-leaved *Ficus* the stem and leaves contain a white sticky
fluid known as latex, from which rubber is extracted in the case
of *F. elastica*. It is therefore important not to break leaves off
or tear them in any way. *F. lyrata* comes from dry regions and
you will find that if you syringe the leaves, the water will fall
from the leaves down the trunk and collect at the root. It should
not therefore be watered much during the winter, but given
ample in summer when it is making its new growth. It requires
reasonably warm conditions and it is advisable not to let the
temperature fall below 50°. We have, however, known it to be
exposed to lower temperatures, without apparent ill-effect.

9. Ficus macrophylla

This is the Moreton Bay Fig, an Australian *Ficus*. *Macrophylla*
means 'large-leaved' but, in point of fact, the leaves are not so
large as those of *decora*. The plant is similar in appearance to
elastica and has the young leaves enclosed in a long sheath, or
rather two long sheaths, that are a pale green. The leaves are
similar in colour and shape to *elastica* but a little narrower and
more rounded at the base. In order to make a shapely plant it is
necessary to remove the growing point when the plant is about
two years old, and it will then branch out and make a handsome

bush. This is a very hardy *Ficus* and will grow equally well in light or shade. As its English name implies it is a native of Australia.

10. Ficus nekbudu (Plate 44)

The specific name presumably refers to the district where it was first found. There are two *Ficus* from tropical Africa so alike as to be practically indistinguishable, known as *F. nekbudu* and *F. vogelii*. The stem is very much stouter than any of the other *Ficus* and the leaf stalks are long and woody. Both the trunk and the leaf stalks are slightly downy. The leaves, which are about 10 inches long and 5 inches across, are nearly as dark a green as *elastica*, but are more rounded and have a conspicuous creamy midrib and slightly less conspicuous veins. On the underside of the leaf both midrib and veins project, though not so much as in *F. lyrata*. Although from the same climate as *lyrata*. it is considerably harder to maintain in perfect condition. During the winter the leaves are liable to yellow and drop off without any previous warning. As the new growth is vigorous and forms quickly the plant will soon be an object of beauty again, but it may well look rather a sorry spectacle in the late winter. It is possible to preserve all the leaves, but it is not easy. As the plant is very striking it is worth taking a little additional trouble, but in the event of your efforts being unsuccessful, a temporary retirement is all that is necessary. Scale is liable to occur on all the large-leaved *Ficus*, and *nekbudu* appears to have particular attractions. Fortunately, with such large leaves removal is easy; a small blunt stick will dislodge them.

11. Ficus panduriformis (Plate 45)

A *Ficus* of this name has been in the Turnford collection for some years, but its correct name has been a matter for conjecture. It now appears that it should have the tongue-teasing name of *F. cyathistipula*. This epithet means that the stipules —the sheaths that protect the young leaves—are shaped like a wineglass. We would not recommend this as a method of identification. It makes a tall thin tree, with long shiny dark green leaves that reach 12 inches in length and are 4 inches across. The midrib is purplish red on the underside and a creamy green on the top. The principal side-veins are also a conspicuous creamy green. The leaf stalk is short, only about ½ inch long, and is not very stout. The edges of the leaves are slightly waved. It is a rapid grower and one of the hardiest of all *Ficus*.

12. Ficus pumila (Plate 35)

Pumila means small, *repens*, its former specific name, means creeping, and *F. pumila* is a small creeping plant. It is hard indeed to realize that it belongs to the same genus as the massive banyan and rubber trees. *F. pumila* grows rather like an Ivy with numerous thread-like branches that will produce aerial roots to support themselves. The leaves are very small, about 1 inch long, ½ inch across and heart-shaped; and are produced in such profusion that the stems are invisible. A native of China it is extremely hardy, indeed in sheltered places it will survive out of doors. It is equally effective as a trailer or as a climber. It will not stand direct sunlight, but no place is too shady for it. This is one of the few plants that should never be allowed to dry out. Once the leaves shrivel there is a possibility that they will not recover, although of course the plant will eventually produce fresh leaves: but it is much better to keep the plant on the moist side, even in winter. If the plant is allowed to get sufficiently large it will produce fruiting branches, which are straight and stiff and have a larger leaf (from 2 to 4 inches long). This is not an uncommon occurrence when the plant is planted out in the greenhouse, but it has not been recorded, to our knowledge, in the home. The plant has to reach quite considerable dimensions before fruiting. A variegated form of this has been recorded and recently re-introduced. Some of the leaves are variegated with white, others are entirely white, and it is one of the most attractive of variegated plants. Unfortunately this form tended to revert very rapidly to the all green type and it is doubtful if any now survive. We must hope that it will sport again and that the next variegated form will be more stable.

Moraceae

13. Ficus radicans var. **variegata** (Plate 46)

Another small-leaved creeping fig, but this time the variegated form, is that most commonly met with. This again has suffered some name changes and should properly be known either as *F. sagittata* or as *F. heteropleura*. The leaves are larger than those of *F. pumila*, being up to 2½ inches long and an inch across and tapering to a point. The leaf edge is slightly waved. This is an attractive little plant, especially in mixed groups, but it is not easy to keep it in good condition in the winter. A native of the East Indies, it enjoys a warm and moist atmosphere and should not be allowed to dry out. The thin branches, which will trail or climb, are thickly covered with the cream and green leaves, and sideshoots are produced naturally, although stopping will encourage their production.

14. Ficus religiosa

This is the sacred Peepul tree of India. The thin leaves are like those of a poplar or aspen rather than a *Ficus*. They are about 4 inches long and 2½ inches across, and come to a long thin point that is itself nearly 4 inches long. The plant is very fascinating with these long pointed leaves, and more interest is given by the rosy colouring of the principal veins. Unfortunately it is extremely difficult to keep the plant in good condition in the winter. Many of the leaves will become discoloured and will eventually drop off. Like all the thin-leaved *Ficus*, except *pumila*, it requires warm conditions and 55° would seem the safest minimum. It appears to appreciate light and should not be kept too moist, though it must not be allowed to dry out too frequently. It should perhaps be mentioned that, with the exception of *benghalensis*, none of the Indian *Ficus* are easy to obtain.

15. Ficus australis var. **variegata**

There is some mystery about *F. australis*. The name is illegitimate. That is to say that when the plant was first described it was not accompanied by a description of the plant written in Latin (referred to by botanists as a diagnosis) and published in

111

some learned journal. It is a smallish shrub or tree with leaves up to 4 inches in length and $1\frac{1}{2}$ inches across. The shape is oblong and lance-like and the leaves are prettily variegated, with considerably more cream than green. It is possibly a variety of *F. rubiginosa*, the Australian Banyan, but it has no rust-coloured underside to the young leaves which distinguishes *F. rubiginosa*. The leaves are also considerably smaller than *F. rubiginosa*. It is fairly hardy, but like all variegated plants delicate and slow-growing. It can be kept on the dry side in the winter, and stopped in the spring, to encourage sideshoots. It is best, however, to wait until at least one new leaf has been produced before stopping. The leaves have a slightly rough texture.

34. Dizygotheca elegantissima, Hedera helix 'Golden Jubilee'

35. Hedera helix maculata aurea, Ficus pumila

36. Hedera helix marmorata

37. Hedera canariensis 'Golden Leaf', × Fatshedera lizei

38. × Fatshedera lizei 'Silver Prince'

39. Cussonia spicata

40. Ficus elastica decora

41. Ficus elastica Doescheri, F. benjamina

42. Ficus lucida, F. benghalensis

43. Ficus lyrata, F. diversifolia

44. Ficus nekbudu, Cissus antarctica

45. Ficus panduriformis

46. Ficus radicans variegata

47. Cissus antarctica

48. Cissus discolor

49. Cissus sicyoides, Begonia glaucophylla, Zebrina pendula

CHAPTER VII

Vitaceae and Begoniaceae

The Vine family, the *Vitaceae*, comprises some eleven genera and 450 species. Of these only about half a dozen are suitable as houseplants, but they include some of the most popular and easiest to grow; also included is one of the most beautiful, but most difficult of all houseplants. With this exception they are all very accommodating and can be used either as climbers or as trailers. If they are used as climbers they can be trained up sticks or wires into any shape that ingenuity suggests. Regular stopping in the spring is recommended to ensure a bushy growth, rather than a long thin tall single stem.[1]

Propagation is by seeds or by cuttings. Cuttings are taken from ripe wood, as, if the cutting is too soft, it is more liable to rot. After stopping, when sideshoots begin to appear from the leaf joints, is the best time to take cuttings. Take them just below the old leaf and they should root easily.

Repotting should be delayed as long as possible and regular feeding should be given during the growing season. Do not, however, attempt to overfeed them even if they look starved. All feeds are issued with instructions which should be followed carefully. All the vines should be kept on the dry side. *Cissus antarctica* and *Rhoicissus* are tolerant of gas fumes, but the others are not. They will all stand a fair amount of light, but do not enjoy a lot of direct sunshine. JIP is perfectly suitable as a compost, but the Turnford formula is:

[1] This family is nowadays sometimes referred to as *Ampelidaceae*.

H
113

2 parts light loam
1 part well-rotted dung
1½ parts leaf mould
1 part sand
½ part peat
A 5-inch pot of superphosphate and a 5-inch pot of fine bone meal to every barrow load of the mixture.

Genus CISSUS

The derivation is from a Greek word for Ivy; the *Cissus* are climbers.

1. Cissus antarctica (Plates 44 and 47)

The Kangaroo vine. The specific name tells us that it comes from the southern hemisphere and the English name that it comes from Australia. This is the most popular, and, with the exception of *discolor*, the most attractive of the houseplant *Cissus*. It is very hardy, tolerant of gas fumes and immune from most pests, though aphis is occasionally troublesome. In time it will make a very large specimen and plants from 6 to 8 feet high are frequently used when large groups are called for. It is naturally a climber, supporting itself by tendrils. The leaves, which will attain a length of 4 inches and a width of 2 inches, are somewhat reminiscent of an oak leaf in shape and have the same serrated edge. They are a dark green and the petioles are reddish in colour and slightly hairy; the young leaves are a tender yellowish green and provide a pleasant contrast.

2. Cissus capensis

Capensis because it comes from the Cape of Good Hope. This is a hardy and vigorous vine, with round green leaves, crenulated at the edge and not unlike those of the grape vine in appearance. As the young leaves emerge they are slightly hairy and pinky brown in colour; when fully expanded they are a bright green. The older leaves will eventually fall off, but before doing so they will develop 'autumn tints' though not necessarily in the autumn. The plant will break naturally and form a bushy specimen that will trail slightly and will require no support; though it can equally well be trained on to a trellis or something similar. It appears to thrive best in a well-lighted situation and will stand quite low temperatures without any apparent damage. Being a South African plant, it is used to definite seasons and will rest during the winter, when it should, naturally, be kept on the dry side. Growth will start in the spring and then the supply of water will need to be increased.

3. Cissus discolor (Plate 48)

Discolor means of different colours and refers to the remarkable leaves. I suppose if anyone were to draw up a list of plants with the most beautiful leaves, this plant would always figure in the first dozen. It is by no means easy to grow and offends against our requirements for houseplants by shedding many of its leaves in the winter, while those that are retained lose much of their colour. However, it is so beautiful that such disadvantages are overweighed, and anyone able to keep rooms at 55° in the winter and 65° in the summer would be well advised to try *C. discolor*. It is very hard to describe the leaves soberly and we can do no better than borrow the following quotation: 'This beautiful climber cannot be justly rendered, either by the artist's pencil or by the most minute description. The leaves are cordate-lanceolate, the upper side being a vivid metallic green, marbled with white and rich purple and shaded with crimson and peach; the underside is a uniform deep crimson. It is perhaps the most exquisitely coloured variegated plant we have in cultivation.'[1]

Every word in this description is literally correct. When propagating the plant it is best to take a fairly long cutting and this will root at every joint, which can then be potted separately. Layering provides an alternative method. A suitable mixture for cuttings or layers is two parts peat and one part sharp sand.

C. discolor is naturally a climber, but makes a delightful plant in a hanging basket, such as can be seen in the tropical water-lily house at Kew Gardens.

---

[1] *Choice Stove and Greenhouse Ornamental-leaved plants*, B. S. Williams, 1876.

4. Cissus sicyoides (Plate 49)

Sicyoides means that it looks like a *Sicyus*, a member of the cucumber family. A native of South America it is less hardy than *C. antarctica*, but it need not be regarded as delicate. The leaves are compound and come in five sections, each about 2 inches long and 1 inch across, with the middle leaflet slightly larger than the others. The leaves are dark green but the petioles are a bright crimson and bring a touch of colour to the plant. It makes its best effect when it has grown into a fairly large specimen. It is not very tolerant of gas fumes. Like all the *Cissus* it dislikes overwatering and the leaves are quick to yellow if that occurs.

5. Cissus striata

This is the baby among the *Cissus*. The leaves are the same shape as those of *C. sicyoides*, but the individual leaflets scarcely reach 1 inch in length and $\frac{1}{2}$ inch across. These small leaves are produced in great profusion. The mature leaves are dark green with reddish-crimson petioles, while the young growth is pinkish both as to leaves and stem. The plant is best kept as a small specimen, although it can get very sizeable. The plant is native to Chile and will survive outside in the milder parts of the country. It should, therefore, be given rather cool conditions and it will take more water than the other members of this genus, although, as in all pot plants, this should not be overdone. It should be given a shady situation, but this should be well-lit.

Genus RHOICISSUS

Rhoia is Greek for the pomegranate, but in what way *Rhoicissus* resembles a pomegranate we would not like to say.

1. Rhoicissus rhomboidea[1] (Plate 50)

This is a native of Natal, and though some people find it slightly more tender than *Cissus antarctica*, no one could call it a diffi-

---

[1] It has been suggested that this plant is not, in fact, in cultivation at all and that the plant sold under that name is the South American *Cissus rhombifolia*. The main difference between *Rhoicissus* and *Cissus* lies in the flowers, which in

cult plant. The leaf is not unlike the compound-leaved *Cissus*, but is made up of only three leaflets, each of which is stalked; whereas in the *Cissus* the leaflets spring direct from the central disk. The leaves are toothed, dark green and shiny when mature, and will derive benefit from occasional sponging. The young growth is brownish in colour and is slightly hairy. There is a cultivar called 'Jubilee' which has much larger, darker green leaves, set closer together than the type; the centre leaflet is some $4\frac{1}{2}$ inches long and $2\frac{3}{4}$ inches wide, while the type is about an inch shorter in each direction.

Genus TETRASTIGMA

1. Tetrastigma voinierianum

If *Cissus striata* is the baby of the Vines, this plant is the giant. It is large, and vigorous and quite unsuitable for the bijou flatlet, unless you do not intend to live in it yourself. The leaves, composed of five leaflets, resemble very large strawbery leaves in appearance. The centre leaflet on its own may be as much as 6 inches long and 4 inches broad and a fully grown leaf is some 8 inches long and 10 inches across. When an imposing specimen is needed, there are few plants more suitable than *Tetrastigma*. Although a native of South East Asia it is surprisingly hardy; like the other vines it appreciates light in winter and shade in summer. As a small specimen in a 3-inch pot it looks rather grotesque, but it is a vigorous grower and will soon reach the large proportions that its leaf-size needs. An irritating trick that it displays, is for the new growth to snap at an early stage. This does no lasting harm as a new shoot will soon appear. If the new growth is supported, this snapping will not take place: it would appear that the new stem cannot support its own weight. The mature leaves are a dark green, immature leaves are light green with a darker edging and the new growth is covered with a silvery grey indumentum (or fluff). Provided you have a sufficiently large room, this is one of the most attractive and easiest of climbing houseplants.

Rhoicissus have the parts in fives, while in *Cissus* they are in fours, so once our plant has flowered it should be possible to determine this point.

BEGONIACEAE

The Begonia family is not very large, comprising some 450 species distributed among four genera. Of these the genus *Begonia* is by far the most important from the horticultural point of view; the other three genera, *Haplophragma*, *Hillebrandia* and *Symbegonia* are rarely seen. Although they range from small insignificant plants to sizeable shrubs, Begonias are easily recognized by the characteristic shape of the flower and in most cases by the shape of the seed capsule. They are distributed throughout the tropics, though they are absent from Australia, but their chief centres are Central America from Mexico to Brazil and from India to China. They are usually found in woods and hence appreciate shade, though *heracleifolia* is frequently used as a bedding plant in the tropics and will tolerate full sun. Most of the species have leaves of similar shape, though there are considerable differences in size. The usual shape is that of an asymmetric triangle with a rounded base, though, as we shall see, there are divergences. *Begonia* is usually divided into three groups according to the rooting systems. The tuberous begonias are barely represented among houseplants, although they are the most popular as bedding and greenhouse subjects; both the rhizomatous and the fibrous-rooted sections provide admirable houseplants, though the fibrous-rooted types require some attention as otherwise they may become leggy and grow too tall. Although they have a reputation for difficulty, the majority of houseplant begonias will be found easy to cultivate. The one thing they will not tolerate is gas fumes.[1] The presence of a gas fire in the room will kill them in a remarkably short time, and even fumes from an adjoining room will affect the plants, and it is said that they will not grow within a hundred yards of a gasworks. They like a moist buoyant atmosphere, and are therefore more likely to do well if the pots are plunged in peat that can be kept moist in the growing season; and they re-

---

[1] One of the fringe benefits of North Sea gas is that the fumes are far less lethal to plant life and it may prove possible to grow Begonias in houses with gas heating now.

quire very light potting in a very open mixture, as the roots are very small and weak. JIP is not suitable, but a mixture of two parts leaf mould to one part sharp sand is excellent. The Turnford mixture is:

2 parts loam
2 parts peat
1½ parts leaf mould
1 part sand.

Begonias for the most part like a shady position and to be kept on the dry side, though not too dry. Too bright sunlight may scorch the leaves and it is advisable, when watering, not to let the water remain on them. They do not require repotting unless the pot is full of roots. Propagation is usually by leaf cuttings: the leaves are lightly scored on the underside with a sharp knife and laid flat on the propagating medium. Roots and subsequently small plants will spring from the severed main veins of the leaf: a constant temperature of 70° is desirable at this stage. When the plants are large enough to handle, they are potted singly in very small pots with the piece of leaf still adhering. As the plant increases in size it is potted on and is usually sold in a 3-inch pot.

The name of the genus commemorates M. Michel Begon (1638–1710) who was a patron of botany and also a Governor of Canada, when that country was a French possession. There are some 350 species in the genus of which some 150 species have been cultivated. This figure can be augmented by a large number of hybrids. During the latter half of the last century nurserymen in general, and particularly James Veitch and Son in London and the Lemoines at Nancy, created a number of hybrids between the various species and many of these have persisted. As a general rule it was found that the various tuberous begonias could be hybridized among themselves, but not with the two other groups; though James Veitch did manage to get several crosses, they have now all disappeared, as, once they had flowered, they were very difficult to keep alive. Crosses between the other two groups have been successful. Unfortunately, brilliant though these nurserymen were, they did not always record the parentage of their introductions and it is quite possible that we may describe some species as hybrids and vice versa. Matters were not helped by their practice of giving Latin names to their crosses.

Begonias are unusual in having male and female flowers, sometimes on the same spike, sometimes on different spikes. The male flowers frequently, have fewer petals than the females, which can always be distinguished by the seed capsule behind the flower.

Among the most popular of begonias grown for the sake of their leaves are the *rex* group. These are either selected forms of *Begonia rex* or hybridized with *B. diadema*, whose presence can be detected by the jagged edge of the leaf, and with *B. decora*, which brings a red colouring into the leaves. They are all rhizomatous and will occasionally produce a large panicle of dirty white flowers. A well-grown specimen of *B. rex* may have leaves as long as 12 inches, but this is not frequent and 7 to 8 inches is more usual.

Being rhizomatous the plants tend to spread outwards and seldom exceed about 9 inches in height, though a well-grown specimen may be over 12 inches across. The type plant has the usual asymmetric triangular leaf, which is of a dark metallic olive-green, with a silvery green band about 1 inch from the edge of the leaf and running parallel to it. It is rarely seen now in cultivation though the cultivar 'King Henry' is very close to it. Formerly the various cultivars were named and we have used names to help our descriptions, but nowadays they are rarely sold as named plants but just as Rex Begonias, leaving the customer to choose the form he likes.

In the home a temperature of 60° is the ideal to aim at, but it is not essential; though too low a temperature during the winter may induce mildew, which is very difficult to get rid of. In the nursery, lamps that puff out a mixture of colloidal sulphur and steam are used, but this is scarcely practical in the home. A colloidal sulphur dust is possible, but this may scorch the foliage and in any case leaves it coated with sulphur and looking disgusting. If its onset can be detected in time it is best to remove the affected leaves and move the plant to a warmer position. All the *rex* group dislike strong sunlight and should be kept in a shady position. Water should be kept from the leaves, though a fine spray is often beneficial. During the winter they should be kept as dry as possible, though not dust dry; the warmer the room the more water they will take.

1. Begonia rex (Colour Plate I. Plates 51 and 52)

Rex is the Latin for king and this is regarded as the king of begonias. As we have said, many of these plants are crossed with *B. diadema* and *B. decora.* A recent botanical term for a series of hybrid plants coming from the same parentage is the Latin for a flock: *Grex.* It is too tempting not to refer to the plants described below as the *Rex grex.*

(*a*) 'King Henry' ('König Heinrich'). This is fairly near the type of *Begonia rex.* The leaf is smooth-edged and has a very narrow purple band along this edge. Next comes a zone of dark green about 1 inch in depth, with small silver dots thereon, then a much wider zone of silver, and finally, where the leaf stalk joins the leaf, there is a small dark green star-shaped patch. The leaf is about 6 inches long and 4 inches broad.

(*b*) 'Hoar Frost' ('Rauhreif'). The leaf is more pointed than in the former plant and the edge is crenulated. The predominant colour is silver, with irregular zones of dark metallic green along the principal veins and a suspicion of pink along the edge of the leaf. This is a reflection from the underside which has a rosy purple zone round the edge of the leaf and along the principal veins.

(*c*) 'Fairy' (Fée). This is very similar to 'Rauhreif', but has a larger leaf with a much smoother edge. The whole of the underside of the leaf is maroon-crimson.

(*d*) 'Salamander'. This is again similar to 'Rauhreif' and 'Fairy', but the dark green along the principal veins is more extensive and the silver is more split up into dots and blotches.

(*e*) 'Silver Queen'. Larger-leaved than the foregoing and with the leaf almost entirely silver in colour. There are very faint traces of dark green along the veins. The underside of the leaves is a light maroon.

(*f*) 'Heligoland'. The rather jagged leaf suggests the presence of *diadema*. The jagged edge is characterized by a thin purple margin on a dark green zone. Along the principal veins the colouring is silver nearest the edge, but shades into a light plum colour as it approaches the leaf stalk.

(*g*) 'Isolde'. The leaf, though still irregular, is much rounder in shape than any of the former, it is also slightly hairy. The ground colour is a dark lustrous green, with reddish reflections from the underside of the leaf. Between the veins are spots and blotches of silver, edged with purple, and these widen out to make a nearly continuous band, about $\frac{1}{2}$ inch from the leaf edge.

(*h*) 'La Pasqual'. One of the largest leaved. The ground colour is nearly black. About $\frac{1}{2}$ inch from the edge of the leaf but parallel to it, runs a zone of silver shading to purple on each edge about 1 inch in width. There are purple dots on the dark green parts of the leaf and the principal veins bear tiny scarlet hairs. The underside is purple, except under the silver portion.

(*i*) 'Hélène Teupel'. This is probably the most beautiful of the *rex* hybrids. The leaf is very jagged and a dark velvety green, but between the veins are large blotches of silver overlaid with purple giving an iridescent appearance. The whole leaf resembles some gaudy tropical butterfly and is most striking. (The Begonia known as 'Filagree' is very similar if not identical.)

(*j*) 'Friede' ('Peace'). This is very similar to Silver Queen except that all the silver is overlaid with rosy purple. For some reason this is not quite so attractive as it sounds.

(*k*) 'Sperber' ('Superba'?). The ground colour of the leaf is purple with a wide zone of silver just inside the leaf edge.

(*l*) 'Our Queen'. The leaf is slightly jagged and the ground colour is silvery purple, but around the edge and around the leaf stalk it is dark velvety green peppered with tiny silver-purple dots. In this dotted portion a few purple-coloured bristles arise, while around the edge of the leaf there are silver hairs.

There are various other attractive *rex* varieties; one of the most extraordinary is called 'Curly Carnot', in which the midrib is coiled round like a spiral. Other varieties to note are 'Van Eck', 'Pride of St. Albans' and 'Silver Cloud'.

2. Begonia boweri (Plates 54 and 57)

We do not know who Mr. Bower was, after whom the plant is named. This is a small begonia from Mexico with a creeping rhizome. It is only a few inches high and the leaf seldom exceeds 3 inches in length. It is of the typical begonia shape, though more elongated than most of the *rex*. The ground colour is an emerald-green with a narrow maroon-coloured zone around the edge. This zone is not continuous, but is broken up giving a blotched appearance, which is more attractive than the description sounds. *Boweri* should have similar treatment to the *rex* Begonias, though it will tolerate more light. It is not a particularly easy subject. Its propagation is slightly different from that of most begonias: the leaf must be cut off with about an inch of leaf stalk, which is inserted in the propagating medium: the plantlet will be formed at the base of the stalk and particular care must be taken not to insert the stalk too deeply.

3. Begonia imperialis

The Imperial Begonia is another native of Mexico. It was presumably named in honour of Maximilian as it was discovered during his ill-fated reign. It is a low plant with small leaves from 2 to 3 inches in length and more heart-shaped than the species we have been considering. It presents a wrinkled appearance, due to the fact that the leaf is thickly covered with hairs, except along the veins. The ground colour is a very dark green, with a suggestion of black, while along the veins are zones of much lighter green. *Imperialis* is slow growing, but a well-grown specimen is a charming sight. The small white flowers are not particularly decorative; they appear during the summer. There is a rare variety to which the name *smaragdina* has been given. *Smaragdina* means emerald-green and the whole of the leaf is a very vivid green colour.

4. Begonia rajah

One of the few plants for which the specific epithet has not been latinized. This plant is a native of Malaya and is not common. The leaves are rounded and rather thin with bright green colouring along the veins and heavily mottled with red in between. The stems and underneath of the leaves are bristly, while the upper part of the leaves is quite smooth. This plant is difficult and slow growing, requiring a hot steamy atmosphere, which makes it somewhat unsuitable as a houseplant. It is, however, very attractive and could be recommended to those with ample central heating. The leaves are large, some 4 to 5 inches across and about 6 inches long.

5. Begonia masoniana (Colour Plate I. Plate 56)

This handsome plant, until recently known as 'Iron Cross', was brought back from Singapore in 1952 by the well-known collector, Mr. L. Maurice Mason. It was in the collection of the Singapore Botanic Gardens. Although it was originally regarded as a hybrid, with *B. rajah* as a possible parent, it comes true from selfed seeds and is a true species. Mr. Mason thinks that it is probably native of either Malaya or Indo-China, but its habitat has not been defined with any certainty. *Masoniana* has roundish leaves covered with fleshy points that give a moss-covered effect. The leaves are a rather grey-green with a large purple cross-shaped zone in the middle that resembles the German medal. Although usually given warm house treatment it appears hardier than might be thought, though it requires warmer conditions than *B. rex*. It is not a very fast grower.

6. Begonia daedalea

Daedalus constructed the labyrinth, and the specific epithet refers to the maze-like markings on the leaf. This is another rhizomatous begonia from Mexico, but is considerably larger than *boweri* or *imperialis*. The leaves are more elliptical than triangular and end in an elongated point. They reach 6 inches in length and 4½ inches across and are smooth. The ground colour

I. Begonia rex and Begonia masoniana

is medium green with a network of light maroon lines running all over the leaf and occasionally expanding into larger zones, particularly between the veins at the base. The striped hairy stems are some 9 inches long. The underside of the leaf is as striking as the upper. If grown in too shady a position the leaf stalks are liable to get rather too long and make a somewhat floppy plant, and so *daedalea* will enjoy a certain amount of light. It likes treatment similar to *B. rex* or even slightly cooler. Although not unduly difficult to grow, it is a difficult plant to pack and transport, owing to its length of leaf stalk.

7. Begonia 'Perle de Lorraine'

Begonias with the name Lorraine in their titles are almost certain to have been raised originally by Lemoine at Nancy, the capital city of that province. This plant looks very like *B. daedalea*, so far as the leaves are concerned, but is fibrous-rooted, throwing up a single stem, which soon breaks naturally to make a nice bushy plant. The leaves have the usual asymmetric triangular shape of most Begonias, and are dark green with a network of maroon lines running over the leaves. The petioles are less hairy than those of *B. daedalea* and also far less blotched. It is somewhat easier to keep in good condition. The parentage is said to be a cross between the tall fibrous-rooted *B. polyantha* and *B. strigillosa*, which has only recently been reintroduced to cultivation and which is near to *B. daedalea*.

We come now to a group of species and hybrids of which the most typical is *B. haageana*. They are all fibrous-rooted, with tall stems that may tend to become leggy if not stopped and large leaves that are more or less kidney-shaped. All the species are South American and most are Brazilian.

8. Begonia haageana (Plate 53)

This is named in honour of J. N. Haage, a nineteenth-century seedsman. This begonia used to be seen frequently in cottage windows, and will thus enjoy considerably more light than any of the begonias we have been considering hitherto. It is also displayed to better advantage with light behind, as then the red underside of the leaves will shine through to great advantage. It is rather a coarse plant and soon makes a large specimen. It is essential to stop it at regular intervals during the growing season, as otherwise it will become leggy, and once it has grown too tall it will not break from the base. The leaves have one side markedly more curved than the other and end in a sharp elongated point. They are dark green and covered with hairs. A well-developed leaf will be 9 inches long and 5 inches across and is borne on a leaf stalk some 5 inches long. The stems and the underside of the leaves are red and covered with hairs. The flowers are produced in a panicle in the summer and are pinky white in colour. The plant is hardy and easy of culture.

9. Begonia rigida

This begonia does not seem noticeably more rigid than many others of the shrubby fibrous-rooted varieties. It is a smaller plant than *haageana* and slower growing. The leaves are smooth and kidney-shaped, and though a dark green, are lighter than *haageana*. The stem and underside of the leaves are a more vivid red than *haageana*, indeed the underside of the leaf is practically vermilion. The flowers, which are borne in summer, are small and numerous, rose-pink in colour, and borne on a tall stalk some 18 inches long, in a branched cyme. With its smooth leaves, which can be sponged, and its handsome flowers, this makes a desirable houseplant and its more compact size makes it easier to place than some of the plants in this section.

10. Begonia metallica

Although slightly taller growing than the last species, this is still a moderate-sized plant. The leaves are some 5 inches long by 3 inches across and are a bright shiny green. The veins, which show crimson on the underside, are black on the surface of the leaf and give a metallic effect. Although the leaves look smooth they are covered with fine hairs. The stems are green. The pink flowers are borne on short stalks in medium-sized heads in summer, but are not particularly attractive. In time this can make a shrub 4 feet high, but it is not usually a very fast grower.

It will respond to the same treatment as *haageana*, but should be put in a more shady position.

11. Begonia sanguinea

The blood-red begonia is so named from the colour of the underside of the smooth, shining, medium-green, nearly heart-shaped leaves. This will, in time, make a very large specimen and the leaves will reach some 10 inches in length. The small white flowers are produced in spring. This is less hardy than any in this group so far discussed. A form with larger leaves, but without the red underside, has been called 'Lomo alta'.

12. Begonia × Thurstoni

Thurston's begonia is said to be a cross between *B. metallica* and *B. sanguinea*, although doubts have been cast on this parentage and it is possible that it is *metallica* × *rigida*. The leaves are similar in appearance to those of *B. metallica*, but a slightly darker green and lack the black veins. The underside of the leaf is crimson, paling towards the margin and darker along the veins. They are quite large, up to 7 inches long and 4 inches across. The plant bears a handsome panicle of pink flowers in the summer. The plant tends to be rather tall and leggy, with the leaves widely spaced and is useful where a tall specimen is required and is easy of culture.

13. Begonia 'Papa de Chevalier'

This is another *haageana* hybrid, the other parent being *B. duchartrei*. Similar in appearance to *haageana*, it is more bushy and has much larger leaves of a different shape. These leaves may be 12 inches long and 7½ inches across, and are much rounder than *haageana*, though they end in the same elongated point. The red underside is not quite so brilliant as in *haageana*. 'Papa de Chevalier' tends to throw all its leaves straight up, while the other plants we have been discussing tend to fan their leaves out. It is very hardy and easy to grow.

A begonia that belongs to this group, though it is not very nearly related, is

127

14. Begonia manicata

Manicata means that the plant is covered with down, which in the case of this begonia is quite untrue.

The plant has a short rhizome, but throws up a tall stem, so that it gives the appearance of a fibrous-rooted species. The leaves are smooth and light green, with a narrow red margin. As the plant matures, the leaves appear somewhat rounded, though the leaves at the base of the stems are more oval in shape. Along the veins on the underside of the leaf are red bristles which are distributed irregularly. These bristles are also present as rosettes encircling the top of the petioles, which are green spotted with red, and there is quite a tuft of red bristles where the leaf and petiole meet. During the winter *manicata* throws a tall flower spike which carries a large number of small rosy-pink flowers, which are very handsome. It is quite hardy, but requires a warm position in winter, as otherwise the flowers might be destroyed before emergence. We have seen this plant in cottage windows, but the bright green leaves do not suggest that too bright a light is desirable.

We come now to a group of fibrous-rooted begonias, characterized by long thin leaves of various colours, ornamented on the upper surface with white spots. Again Brazil is the principal locality for the species of which the most typical is

15. Begonia maculata (Plate 55)

Maculata is the Latin for spotted. The plant, which has many forms, is typically a much-branched shrub with long thin dark green leaves with a red underside. Between the veins the dark green is spotted with white circular spots of varying size, but in no case very large. The leaves are some 6 inches long, though only 2 inches across, and are slightly hairy. It is a variable species and some varieties have been given separate names. *Wrightii* makes a larger bush than the type and, assuming that the Turnford specimens are correctly named, has smoother-edged leaves and leaves of a brighter green with larger spots. The underside is only flushed purple. It seems more likely that this is an *albo-*

picta hybrid. Another *maculata* variety in the Turnford collection has wider leaves than the type and is more heavily spotted; lacking any varietal name it has been labelled *B. maculata* 'improved'. The flowers of *maculata* can be either pale pink or white and are not particularly conspicuous. The plant is not difficult to keep healthy and will tolerate lowish temperatures, though not for too long a period.

16. Begonia lubbersii

Named in honour of C. Lubbers, who was head gardener at the Brussels Botanic Gardens at the end of the last century. This is a rather slow-growing, shrubby begonia with very unusual leaves. The majority of begonias have the leaf joined to the petiole at the end, but in *B. lubbersii*, the petiole joins the blade at about one-third of its length, thereby dividing the leaf into two unequal boat-shaped ovals, ending with a point at either end. Leaves where the petiole joins the blade at, or near, its centre, are termed peltate. The peltate leaf of *B. lubbersii* is about 6 inches long and 2 inches across, and, as implied above, slightly cupped. It is smooth and dark green with silver spots, while the underside (which is visible, owing to the cupped effect) is flushed with crimson. This is an unusual and attractive plant from South America, which requires rather moist, warm conditions to grow satisfactorily. The winter temperature should not fall below 55°, while 60° is preferable

17. Begonia × corolicta

A hybrid between the showy tall-growing *B. corallina* and the shorter, more branching, *B. albo-picta*, this combines the good qualities of both parents, giving a compact bushy plant with attractive leaves and flowers. The leaves are long and thin, up to 6 inches in length, but only $1\frac{1}{2}$ inches across, smooth and a fairly light green with rather faint white dots on the surface. The red flowers are borne in small racemes from the leaf axils and the plant is in flower for the greater part of the year. It has proved very hardy and adapts itself well to room culture.

18. Begonia × 'Comte de Lesseps'

This fine hybrid, named after the engineer of the Suez Canal, may be the same as Lemoine's cross of 1889 of *B. albo-picta* with *B. olbia* and originally called *B. × argenteo-guttata*. The leaves are less narrow than the preceding hybrid, slightly over 6 inches long and 4 inches across and marked with quite large silver spots, which become more prominent as the leaf ages. The flowers, produced from the leaf axils in racemes, are pale red and quite sizeable. Although the leaves are so large, this does not seem a particularly rapid grower and is not so easy in cultivation as '*corolicta*'. The stems break naturally, early and make a pleasantly shaped bushy plant.

19. Begonia × 'President Carnot'

This magnificent hybrid of *B. coccinea* with either *B. olbia* or *B. maculata* is more at its ease in the greenhouse than the room as it is very tall growing and vigorous. The fine leaves are some 10 inches long and 4 inches in width, very dark green with silver spots on the surface, maroon on the underside. The shape is roughly kidney-shaped, but pointed at the end away from the leaf stalk. Occasionally it will throw a light green leaf, without any red colouring. The scarlet flowers are produced freely, but when well established the plant may reach a height of some 8 feet and would be rather too overpowering for most rooms. It requires reasonably warm conditions, though it is hardier than most text-books would suggest. It is a superb conservatory plant if any of these still survive.

20. Begonia × 'Axel Lange'

Together with 'Abel Carriere' this must be reckoned to be one of the best houseplant begonias. One would imagine, from its name, that it was raised in Germany. The parentage is given as *B. rex* crossed with 'President Carnot' 'and some others'.this suggests to us that the seeds of the *rex*-'President Carnot' cross were sown and 'Axel Lange' was among these seedlings. The plant has the strong, upright growth of 'President Carnot', but this can be stopped to encourage a more bushy plant, if a tall specimen is not required. The stem is so sturdy that no support is needed. The leaves are some 8 inches long and 4 inches across of a dark velvety green, dotted with a large number of rather small silver spots. They remain always slightly cupped, which enables the lustrous crimson-maroon undersides to be displayed. Both the leaves and the stems are hairless, while the margin of the leaf is both shallowly lobed and serrated. The flowers are not produced freely and are not, in any case, particularly attractive, while the leaves remain outstanding.

Our last begonia with spotted leaves has no connexion with any of the foregoing. It is among those collected by Mr. Ghose of Darjeeling and he has called it

21. Begonia rubro-venia picta

This is a rhizomatous begonia and is not easily recognizable as a begonia at all: at first glance one might take it for a *Peperomia*. From the rhizome the plant sends up a short reddish stem from which spring lance-shaped leaves some 4 inches long and $2\frac{1}{2}$ inches across borne at the end of a stalk some 4 inches long. The leaves are practically an emerald-green, but the greater part of the leaf between the main veins is heavily mottled with silver. In the South American species the silver dots are small, but this begonia has as much silver as green. It makes a compact and bushy plant and, like the majority of Mr. Ghose's introductions, is surprisingly hardy.

Our method of dividing the begonias into groups with similar features has no scientific justification. Indeed, apart from isolating the various types of rootstock, the begonias have not been the subject of much investigation. There are, however, so many in cultivation and the forms are so diverse that some sort of rationalization is necessary if the reader is not to be faced with an endless catalogue. The next group is characterized by smooth light green leaves, fibrous roots and, in general, a shrubby appearance.

131

22. Begonia fuchsioides

It is the small oval green leaves and the shrubby habit of this begonia which suggests a fuchsia. The stems are pinkish in colour and the leaves spring directly from the main stem. They are a little over 1 inch long and $\frac{1}{2}$–$\frac{3}{4}$ inch across. The small racemes of pale pink (in some forms, scarlet) flowers are produced freely throughout the summer and autumn, and though they are not outstandingly showy, they are pleasing. The plant is reasonably quick-growing and will take rather more water than the majority of begonias. A fully grown specimen may be as much as 2 feet high and will be a shapely rounded plant.

23. Begonia ulmifolia

The elm-leafed begonia is similar in habit to *fuchsioides* but rather larger in all its parts. The slightly hairy leaves are very similar to those of an elm and are some 2 inches long. The plant is more vigorous than *fuchsioides*, reaching a height of 4 feet in time, and has inconspicuous small white flowers of little decorative value. It is the type of plant that is more useful in a group than as a single specimen.

24. Begonia glaucophylla (Plate 49)

The glaucous-leaved begonia is one of those that possess a short rhizome, although in appearance they are fibrous-rooted. From this rhizome spring thin, rather weak stems bearing oval-shaped leaves some 5 inches long and $2\frac{1}{2}$ inches across. As the new leaves unfurl they are a yellowish green in colour but they darken with age. The flowers are produced in cymes from the leaf axils and are not very large, but a fascinating brick-red. The plant is well adapted for being placed in a hanging container as the long stems will droop naturally. Some forms are described as having white spots on the upper side of the leaves and a purple flush on the underside, but these embellishments are not apparent on any of the Turnford specimens.

25. Begonia × 'Orange-rubra'

This unfortunately named polyglot hybrid (why not orange-red or *aurantia-rubra?*) is said to have *B. dichroa* as one parent, while the other is not given. It has large kidney-shaped leaves with a wavy edge; some 8 inches long and 3 inches across. These emerge a bright grass-green and deepen slightly with age. The stems are green, but the large orange-red flowers are produced at the end of a red stalk and are showy and conspicuous. This makes a pleasant flowering plant and the leaves are sufficiently shapely to lend interest to the plant on the rare occasions when it is not in flower. Fairly warm conditions are needed for this plant.

26. Begonia × 'Corbeille de Feu'

Although the flowers are pretty, the name 'Basket of Flame' is rather too ambitious. This looks like a hybrid between *fuchsioides* and *semperflorens*, the favourite small-flowered bedding begonia. In habit it is shrubby like *fuchsioides* with rather larger and brighter green leaves, while the bright scarlet flowers are produced in cymes from the leaf axils. This makes an agreeable-looking plant, compact and bushy and with colourful flowers. It is perhaps rather quiet in its appeal.

Somewhat similar to the foregoing though sharply differentiated by its leaf colour is

27. Begonia augustae

Another of Mr. L. Maurice Mason's introductions from New Guinea. This has kidney-shaped leaves, with a point at the longer end, of a shining dark olive-green on the upper surface and a rich purple underneath. The leaves, which are some 5 inches long and 2 inches across, constitute the main appeal of the plant as the white flowers are not conspicuous. This makes an excellent houseplant as its smooth leaves are easily sponged and so their shining quality can be maintained. The main stem is green in colour and so provides an effective foil for the dark leaves. It will combine very happily with the previous hybrid. This will tolerate a good deal of light if necessary, though it is equally happy in a shady position. It is vigorous and reasonably hardy.

The next group of begonias consists mainly of plants of Asiatic origin, though *heracleifolia* comes from Mexico. The basic shape of the leaf is nearly circular, but they are all divided to a greater or lesser degree so that a jagged leaf edge is also a characteristic of this group.

28. Begonia heracleifolia (Plates 53 and 54)

Heracleum is the name of a genus of *Umbellifers*, among which is the hogweed that lines so many country roads. *Heracleifolia* signifies that the leaf is like that of an *Heracleum*. This is a rhizomatous begonia with the leaves arising directly from the rhizome. The red bristly petioles are some 9 inches long and end with a tuft of reddish bristles as in *manicata*. The jagged leaves are more or less star-shaped, and indeed one variety of the species has sometimes been referred to as *Begonia stellata*. The leaves are some 7 to 8 inches long and as much across and are covered with fine hairs. The type has dark bronzy-green leaves and throws a tall panicle of small rosy-red flowers on a stem some 2 feet high. The species is variable and the form usually grown as a houseplant is the variety *nigricans*. This has patches of light green along the principal veins and the underside of the darker portions of the leaf are maroon-purple. The flowers are white.

In the tropics *heracleifolia* is frequently used as a bedding plant and can tolerate full sunshine. It is not difficult of culture, but should be kept on the dry side. Although the warmer it is the happier it is, it will remain unmoved through cold periods provided it is kept dry.

29. Begonia cathayana

This begonia, as its name suggests, comes from Cathay, the old name for China. It is a tall fibrous-rooted begonia that will eventually reach a height of some 2 feet. The leaves are similar in shape to *B. rex*, though more symmetrical with a regularly indented edge. The ground colour of the leaves is a rich velvety green with a lighter-coloured zone running parallel to the edge of the leaf, placed about $1\frac{1}{2}$ inches from the edge. The principal veins are a vivid red and the underside of the leaf is coloured bright crimson, except under the lighter green zone. The stems are green, covered with crimson hairs, and the whole plant makes an exceptionally vivid appearance. The stems break naturally to give a nice bushy plant. Great heat is not essential for this magnificent plant, which like a shady position and a moist atmosphere. A well-grown plant will make rather a large specimen and, as it is brittle, it is usually offered as a small plant. This does not really do the plant justice, but if the purchaser can think sufficiently forward he will find few foliage plants are more attractive.

30. Begonia bowringiana

Named in honour of J. C. Bowring, a nineteenth-century orchid cultivator at Windsor. This is one of Mr. Ghose's introductions and is different from an earlier *bowringiana*, which was a synonym of *cathayana*. This plant has a much-branching rhizome from which arise the leaves on 8-inch stems. The leaf is nearly smooth and some 5 inches long and 5 inches across. The outline is jagged, though less so than *heracleifolia*. It is a dark green with a nearly black zone in the centre of the leaf and a dark edge. These dark portions are crimson on the underside and the veins are also coloured on the underside of the leaf. As the young leaves emerge and before they are fully unfurled, they appear nearly scarlet in colour. The green stems are covered sparsely with fine crimson hairs, which fade to green as the leaf ages. This is a vigorous and hardy begonia though not particularly showy. A more conspicuous variety has been termed by Mr. Ghose *B. bowringiana alba*. This throws an upright instead of a creeping stem and the leaves are quite smooth on the surface. The dark portions of the leaves are larger and the lighter portion is a silvery green in colour. The crimson underside of the leaf is more conspicuous. The leaves will bruise easily and turn brown at the edge, but it is an attractive plant in spite of this disadvantage.

31. Begonia laciniata

Laciniata means that the leaves are very cut up in appearance but in this case they are less so than many of the others in this group. This is, like *B. bowringiana*, a rhizomatous begonia with straggling stems, that will turn into rhizomes themselves if encouraged. The leaves are less rounded than in the previous species, being some $3\frac{1}{2}$ inches long and 5 inches across. They are jagged, but less so than *heracleifolia* and *bowringiana*, a dark green on the surface and crimson, fading later to maroon on the underside. The leaves are covered with fine hairs. A variety called by Mr. Ghose *B. laciniata elata* (the tall laciniate begonia) throws an upright stem and has larger leaves of a different shape to the type, being some 7 inches long and 5 inches across. The young leaves are covered with crimson hairs which fade to white as the leaf ages (this also occurs with the type but the fading occurs much earlier). Both these plants are easy to manage and attractive. They will tolerate a certain amount of direct sunshine though this should not be overdone.

32. Begonia sikkimensis

The Sikkim begonia is one of the most surprising of Mr. Ghose's introductions. This is a rhizomatous begonia throwing up from the root leaf stalks some 6 to 7 inches high of a light-green heavily spotted with red. The leaf is divided into six clearly marked sections which are somewhat jagged in their turn. The whole leaf is more cut up than *heracleifolia*. The leaf is bright green with a thin red edge. Coming from Sikkim the plant must be regarded as extremely hardy, and as likely to take a decided rest in winter and require frequent watering during the growing season. In appearance the leaf suggests a paeony rather than a begonia.

33. Begonia luxurians

This is a tall-growing, fibrous-rooted Brazilian species. The leaves are nearly circular in shape, but, as opposed to being lacerated like the others in this group, are divided up into some sixteen elliptical leaflets, only joined at the petiole. The whole plant is covered with fine hairs that are only perceptible by touch. *Luxurians* will make a plant from 2 to 3 feet in height, but requires frequent stopping if a bushy plant is required. The

136

stems and leaf stalks are reddish and there is a patch of pink where the leaflets join. The leaves are a glossy medium-green. Apart from the number of leaflets, the leaves suggest a horse chestnut leaf in appearance. An individual leaflet is up to 6 inches long but only ¾ inch across; the full leaf is some 7 inches in diameter. *Luxurians* likes warm conditions, a moist atmosphere and shade, and should be regarded as rather more difficult than any of the *haageana* or *maculata* groups, but no more difficult than the *rex*.

We are left with a few species and hybrids that do not fit very satisfactorily into any group. Among these is one of the most suitable houseplant begonias. This is

34. Begonia × 'Abel Carrière'

This handsome hybrid was made by crossing a silver-leaved *rex* begonia with the very hardy *B. evansiana*. The plant is fibrous-rooted and throws up a number of stems. The leaves are nearly heart-shaped, glossy in appearance, though slightly hairy to the touch, and silver in colour, apart from thin dark green zones along the veins. The underside of the leaf is purple. The leaf is 4 inches long and 3 inches across. To obtain a bushy specimen stopping should be applied at an early stage, and the resultant sideshoots should themselves be stopped. The small cymes of red flowers are produced from the leaf axils. Apart from seeing that sunlight does not scorch the leaves, this has proved easy of room cultivation.

35. Begonia mazae

This would appear to be a genuine species, though it seems remarkably close to the *heracleifolia-hydrocotilifolia* cross. It is a small plant, some 6 inches high with a creeping rhizome. The leaves are nearly circular, but slightly wider than long and the edge of the leaf is not quite regular. The leaf is some 2 inches long and 3 inches across, and is of a dark metallic green, that gives a shot-silk or iridescent effect. The underside of the leaves is maroon. The stems and petioles are pale green. This attractive plant is not very easy in the early stages, but once a good root system has been established it is easier to keep in good condition. It likes warm conditions, but is not exigent in its requirements and can tolerate bright light.

36. Begonia × margaritae

The pearly begonia. This is a cross between *B. echinosepala* and *B. incarnata metallica*. In habit and appearance it suggests *B. maculata*. The leaves are roughly heart-shaped with a sharp point at the end, some 6 inches long and 4 inches across. The smooth leaf is dark green with a purple sheen and is covered with small purple dots. The underside of the leaf is crimson-maroon. This is an attractive plant that will respond to the same treatment as *maculata*. It is advantageous to stop it from time to time to encourage the growth of sideshoots. The pale pink flowers in corymbs are quite large and handsome.

37. Begonia phyllomaniaca

A begonia with maniac leaves sounds most alarming, but the plant is not so terrifying as that. It is a tall plant with large leaves of the typical begonia triangle. They are over 9 inches long and 4 inches across. Pink flowers are produced in cymes from the leaf axils in the winter. It gets its name from its habit of producing small buds on the leaves and stem from which tiny leaves emerge. If these buds are removed and placed on a propagating mixture in a warm temperature, they will produce roots and so can be used for increase of stock. These curious irruptions of leaves occur most frequently in spring. They are somewhat minute and need searching for. Apart from their curious habits the large green leaves with a red edge are attractive in themselves and blend well in a group with other species.

38. Begonia × vitichotoma

This is one of an interesting group of hybrids that were raised at Riga in the first decade of this century. *Vitichotoma* is a hybrid between *B. vitifolia*, the vine-leaved begonia, and *B. dichotoma*. The plant is perhaps more curious than beautiful. It is a fibrous-rooted plant, that may grow tall, with large roundish dark green hairy leaves. Its interest lies in a number of leaf-like appendages, some ¼ to ½ inch in height, which appear at irregular intervals along the main veins of the leaves. Unlike the last species these leaf-like appendages are of no use in propagation. At some stage in its career, probably owing to illegible label-writing, the hybrid acquired the name of *vivachotoma*, and may frequently be met with under this picturesque name.

39. Begonia serratifolia

This plant was brought from New Guinea by Mr. L. Maurice Mason. As its name implies the leaf is much cut up and appears in two shapes; one long and thin, the other more rounded. It is a fibrous-rooted begonia throwing up several stems from the roots and branching naturally. The leaves are some 4 inches long, 1 inch across in the narrow form and 2 inches in the wider specimens. The ground colour of the leaves is reddish green, with red veins and rosy-purple spots, which are sometimes quite sizeable, between the veins. The stems, petioles and undersides of the leaves are red, and the flowers, which are produced in small racemes in the summer and autumn, are a pale vermilion and clash badly with the leaves and stems. The plant is hardy and easy to grow and, though it cannot appeal to all tastes, can be warmly recommended.

40. Begonia × weltoniensis (Plate 57)

This, the only tuberous begonia in our selection, is the result of a cross between two South African species: *B. dregei* and *B. sutherlandii*. As a result it is far hardier than the majority of begonias and has no objection to cool conditions. At one time it was a popular plant in cottage windows and will tolerate as much light as can be given. From the tuber arise erect branching stems to a height of some 12 inches, when pale pink flowers, an inch across in small heads, are produced from the leaf axils. The stems and petioles are red and the leaves are a yellowish green with red veins. They emerge roundish in shape, but as they expand the shape becomes more triangular and irregular. A full-sized leaf may be 4 inches long and 2 inches across, but the majority are smaller. The stems are of annual duration, dying off when flowering is complete. In its native land both parents die down to the tuber during the dry season and start into growth when the rains come. Under room or greenhouse conditions growth is continuous and new stems are starting to ascend, when the old ones have completed their cycle. This is a pretty and unusual-looking begonia. Its only fault is a proneness to mildew, but it requires drier conditions than any other begonia and this should stop the fungus from spreading.

As the number and varieties of *Begonia* suitable for house-plant work is rather confusing, we felt it might be helpful if we listed here the varieties that have so far proved the easiest and most successful for this type of work. None of the plants we have described is unsuitable, but *rajah* and *masoniana* are decidedly difficult, while the others are more or less suitable according to their different habits and consitutions. The ones we can recommend with confidence are *B. metallica, maculata, mazae, 'coro-licta'*, 'Axel Lange', 'Abel Carrière', *haageana, glaucophylla* and 'Papa de Chevalier'.

CHAPTER VIII

Piperaceae and Marantaceae

I. PIPERACEAE

The Pepper family (*Piperaceae*) consists of some seven genera, of which only two are in general cultivation. One of these is the genus *Piper*, which contains few species that are ornamental, but includes *Piper nigrum*, which is the source of pepper. The other genus is *Peperomia*, which consists of some 400 species, most of which are found in central and tropical South America; but there are species found throughout the tropics. As collectors do not appear to visit Africa much, all the houseplant *Peperomias* are American in origin.

When growing in the wild state *Peperomias* are found in very shallow soil or more frequently in the moss at the base of tree trunks or in the hollows between branches. They are not epiphytic for the most part (there are some that are true epiphytes) but they give an appearance of being so and cannot in any case absorb much nourishment from their roots. However, plants will tolerate conditions in the wild that they will not do in the artificial state of cultivation. Moreover, many true epiphytes will develop roots that function if given the opportunity. The two most commonly cultivated epiphytes are orchids and Bromeliads. Orchid growers will tell you that the composition of the compost on which the plants are placed will make a great deal of difference to their vitality and we have found that Bromeliads, particularly in their young stages, will enjoy a good leafy soil mixture.

Piperaceae and Marantaceae

Many of the cool-house Rhododendrons such as *lindleyi* are epiphytes in their native haunts, but grow as ordinary shrubs in the greenhouse.

In cultivating *Peperomias*, therefore, a good open soil mixture is necessary and at Turnford they are grown in a compost made of:

2 parts loam
1 part peat
1 part leaf mould
1 part sand.

The root system is never very extensive, and they are placed in small pots and not potted on until this is necessary for reasons of space. There is no need to worry about the plants becoming pot-bound.

In habit and leaf-shape the *Piperaceae* show many different forms, but the one constant feature is the inflorescence. This is a thin spike resembling a mouse's tail or the spadix of a small arum; occasionally this spike is branched. As it is generally whitish or yellowish in colour it is not particularly striking, but it possesses a certain architectural value and contrasts well with the curved leaves that most species possess.

Many of the *Peperomias* possess thick fleshy leaves which indicate that they are used to dry conditions, and even the thinner-leaved species such as *scandens* and *sandersii* will take far less water than most other plants. In the wild they are often seen after a dry spell looking so shrivelled that regeneration would seem impossible, yet a slight shower is enough to restore them to a turgid state. Although they should not be reduced to this condition, they require very infrequent watering and none at all in cold periods. If it is essential, when conditions do not appear to be satisfactory, be sure to use tepid water.

Species that come from a central growing point like *sandersii* and *caperata* are liable to rot if overwatered, but come to little harm if left on the dry side. It is advisable to keep a watch out for Red Spider, but if a moist atmosphere is provided the risk is lessened.

Piperaceae and Marantaceae

Propagation is generally by means of cuttings, which are taken from different parts of the plant according to the species. Seed is not easy to ripen well under greenhouse conditions, but there is always the chance of an improved variety arising from seedlings.

Peperomias do not require great heat as they are frequently found at considerable heights in the tropics, but will not relish the temperature falling below 45° and 50° is the ideal minimum.

1. Peperomia magnoliaefolia (Plate 58)

Botanists have named many of the *Peperomias* by comparing their leaves, not very happily, to those of other plants. *Magnoliaefolia* means that this plant has leaves like a magnolia, but the resemblance is far from striking. The variegated form is the only one that is offered. *P. magnoliaefolia* is a sturdy shrubby plant with compact growth and frequent sideshoots that form naturally, but can be encouraged by stopping. The leaves are a somewhat elongated oval in shape, slightly over 2 inches long and about 1¾ inches across. The new leaves have a thin grey-green streak in the centre and wide cream edges; as the leaf ages the centre portion expands and the cream fades to a lighter green. The young stem is reddish and the older stem is green with red spots. Propagation is by stem cuttings.

A cultivar known as 'Green Gold' (Plate 59) is very similar to *P. magnoliaefolia variegata*, but has slightly larger leaves and these are more brilliantly coloured. The cream portion is more yellow than in the usual form and remains coloured even after the leaf has aged.

2. Peperomia caperata (Plate 58)

Caperata presumably means resembling the caper. It is hard to believe that this belongs to the same genus as the preceding species. It throws up a mass of small heart-shaped leaves from the root: the tallest leaf is only 3 inches from the base of the plant and a fully developed leaf is about 1¼ inches long. The leaves are very corrugated and are a dark green, with purplish shades at the base of the corrugation, and a greyish green on the ridges. The petioles are pale pink. This is a fascinating miniature. It is unfortunately liable to a virus which causes distorted leaves. Propagation is by leaf-stalk cuttings and care must be taken that the plant is perfectly healthy before selecting it for propagation. The flower spikes are pure white and contrast well with the dark leaves and, uniquely among the *Peperomias*, they produce two or three-antler-like points at their tips when fully developed.

During the intervening years the virus mentioned above would seem to have been rogued out and it is only very rarely met with nowadays.

A variegated form, in which the leaves are heavily mottled with cream has now turned up, and makes a pleasing variant for those who like variegated plants.

3. Peperomia glabella

The specific epithet means 'fairly smooth', though since the leaves are entirely hairless, the qualification seems rather meaningless. *P. glabella* is a trailing plant with red stems and green leaves that are oval in shape and come to a point. The mature leaf is about 2 inches long and slightly over $1\frac{1}{2}$ inches across. It needs stopping from time to time to make a nice bushy plant. It is hardy and a quick grower. *P. glabella variegata* (Plates 60 and 61) has a great deal of cream in its leaves, and like so many variegated plants is more difficult to grow than the green form. Overwatering will quickly cause stem-rot. It is slightly more of a trailer than the type and, naturally, not so vigorous. The stems are pink rather than red. Stem cuttings are the best method of propagation.

4. Peperomia hederaefolia (Plate 60)

Hederaefolia means ivy-leaved, but anyone who can see any resemblance between the leaves of an ivy and this *Peperomia* must have sharper eyes than the present writers. The habit of the plant is similar to *P. caperata* but *hederaefolia* is larger. The leaves are heart-shaped, up to $2\frac{1}{2}$ inches long and 2 inches across, and pale grey in colour, with streaks of dark olive-green along the principal veins. This grey colour, though sombre on

50. Rhoicissus rhomboidea

51. Begonia rex, Ctenanthe oppenheimiana

52. Begonia rex, Rubus reflexus pictus

53. Begonia heracleifolia stellata, Collinia elegans,
Begonia haageana

54. Begonia heracleifolia, B. boweri

55. Begonia maculata

56. Aglaonema treubii, Begonia masoniana

59. Peperomia 'Princess Astrid', P. magnoliaefolia 'Green Gold',
P. scandens variegata

60. Peperomia glabella variegata, P. hederaefolia, P. sandersii

61. Peperomia sandersii, P. scandens variegata, P. glabella variegata

62. Calathea picturata, Maranta leuconeura Massangeana, Calathea louisae

63. Maranta leuconeura Kerchoveana, Calathea insignis, C. ornata roseo-lineata

64. Calathea ornata Sanderiana, C. mackoyana

65. Calathea zebrina

its own, is extremely effective in a mixed group. The surface of the leaf is not corrugated as in *caperata,* but slightly undulating, giving a quilted effect. Propagation is by leaf cuttings. Cut the leaf with a portion of the leaf stalk and just insert the stalk in the propagating medium; it will root fairly rapidly at a temperature of 65° which is necessary for propagating all *Peperomias.* If the stalk is inserted too far, the young leaves will be strangled as they emerge from the base of the stalk and a less satisfactory plant will take longer to produce.

5. Peperomia metallica

This gets its name from the copper colouring of the leaves and stem. It is a bushy plant with erect stems that will throw side-shoots. The leaves are about 1½ inches long when fully developed and are an oblong oval in shape, ending in a point. This is not really a very satisfactory houseplant, as it requires a warm, moist atmosphere, and is liable to rot if it does not receive one. It is propagated by stem cuttings.

6. Peperomia obtusifolia (Plate 58)

The blunt-leaved *Peperomia* is a handsome plant eventually reaching a foot in height and having many branches. The leaves are over 4 inches long and 2 inches wide, and are a dark green with a purple edge, while the stem is purplish in colour. The leaves are thick and fleshy, and the plant can tolerate dry conditions for a long time. Provided it is not watered too frequently this is one of the hardiest and easiest of the *Peperomias.* Propagation is by stem cuttings. There are variegated and albino varieties recorded, but they do not appear to be in commerce over here.

7. Peperomia sandersii (Plates 60 and 61)

There seems to be considerable doubt as to whether the most beautiful of the *Peperomias* commemorates Mr. Sanders or Mr. Saunders, but the problem no longer exists as it has been decided that the correct name is *P. argyreia,* the silvered *Peperomia.* The thick smooth leaves are nearly round but taper off to a point at the end. They are marked in alternate bands of silver and dark green. If you turn the leaf over you can see that the dark green parts show the position of the principal veins. The leaf stalks are dark red, but in a well-grown plant they are invisible unless the leaves are parted. The mature leaf is 4 inches long and 3 inches across. Apart from disliking draughts this is not a difficult plant, but it will soon rot is overwatered. It is safest to let it dry out between waterings; although the leaves are not so fleshy as *P. magnoliaefolia* or *obtusifolia* they are sufficiently so to store enough water to prevent flagging. Propagation by leaf-stalk cuttings is possible, but the simplest method is to cut the leaf in half or in four and insert the cut surface in the propagating medium. Plantlets will come from the base of each principal vein.

8. Peperomia scandens (Plates 59 and 61)

Although *scandens* means climbing, this is most effective as a trailer, when it will extend to 4 or 5 feet if allowed. The type is not available in commerce, only the variegated variety. The leaves are similar in shape to *Philodendron scandens*, though only a little over 2 inches in length and 1¾ inches across, and they are slightly asymmetric as they mature. The young leaves are pale green with a cream border, but as they mature, the green spreads over to the left side of the leaf and the amount of cream is diminished. The main stems are pale green, but the petioles are flushed with pink This. is rather a difficult plant in the early stages, and it is not easy to avoid some leaf drop; once the plant has become fairly sizeable it is much easier to keep in good condition. It is propagated by stem cuttings.

9. Peperomia tithymaloides variegata

This is a rather floppy plant, which would probably do well in a hanging container. The stems are thick and fleshy and have a pinkish tinge, while the leaves are oval or rounded, often pure ivory when they first unfurl, later becoming green in the centre and finally becoming almost entirely green. They are about 2 inches long and an inch across. The plant is fairly close to *P.*

magnoliaefolia, but it lacks the erect habit of this plant and the leaves are somewhat smaller. It responds to similar treatment.

10. Peperomia 'Princess Astrid' (Plate 59)

As there are some 400 different *Peperomias*, it is not easy to say of which species this is a cultivar. It is a small bushy plant with branching stems covered with small leaves that do not exceed 1½ inches in length and 1 inch in breadth. The leaves and stem are covered with fine hairs. The leaves are a middle green with a pale grey zone down the midrib. It is scarcely interesting enough to grow as a specimen but makes its effect in mixed groups. It is increased by stem cuttings.

11. Peperomia verschaffeltii

Named in honour of Alexandre Verschaffelt who had a famous nursery at Ghent in the mid-nineteenth century, this is a very low-growing plant with leaves that are similar in coloration to those of *P. sandersii*. However the leaves are an oblong-oval not a rugby-football shape and are not more than 2½ inches long and 1½ inches across. The leaf stalks are green, not red as in *P. sandersii*. The plant is no easier to grow than *P. sandersii*, but has a subtle charm which makes it a plant of some distinction.

Genus PIPER

The pepper plants are mostly climbers. Only one species is in cultivation at the moment and that is a recent introduction. It is not unlikely that others will be introduced later.

1. Piper ornatum (Plate 72)

The ornate pepper is a native of the Celebes, off S.E. Asia and enjoys a warm moist climate. It is a climbing plant with heart-shaped bronzy green leaves, with the main veins picked out in pale pink spots. The plant may be being offered under an incorrect name as the description accords better with *P. porphyrophyllum* (with leaves like porphyry). *P. ornatum* is described as having rounded leaves with a bright green ground colour. The plant is not easy of cultivation, and is liable to drop its leaves in winter if it gets cold even for quite a short period. If it gets cold for a long period it soon dies: 60° should be regarded as the ideal minimum temperature. It will survive at 10° lower, but only at the cost of some leaf fall. As it is a climber it will tolerate shade as well as light, but the leaves will be a better colour if they receive light, and the combination of bronze and pink suggests that this can scarcely be too strong. On the other hand the leaves will be larger under shaded conditions. Although we have said that it is not easy of cultivation, this is not strictly true: given the higher temperatures that it requires it will grow without further trouble. It produces aerial roots at the leaf nodes, and these should be given water in some way as it does not produce a large terrestrial root system. It can be treated as a climbing *Philodendron* and trained on bark or a mossy cylinder with advantage. It will grow quite happily without such aids, but in this case should be watered with care.

II. MARANTACEAE

The *Marantaceae* are a family of monocotyledons related to the Ginger family, and also to the Canna family, though this relationship is not at all apparent to the eye. The family is now divided into some twenty-six genera and 280 species, but the difference between them generally depends on small botanical differences. *Maranta arundinacea* is the source of arrowroot, which was at one time regarded as excellent for invalids, but the majority of the family have no economic importance, though possessing some of the most ornamental leaves of all plants. It is a sobering thought that one of the most lovely, *Calathea roseo-picta*, with shiny green leaves, a deep pink zone around the margin of the leaf and a pink band along the midrib, though introduced in 1866 seems to have entirely vanished from cultivation, and never to have been re-collected.[1] Anyone who is travelling up the Amazon should look out for this plant and re-introduce it. It would certainly help to pay part of the travelling expenses. Although, as

[1] Since the above was written we have received some plants that are ostensibly *C. roseo-picta*, but, if correct, this must be a very variable species, as the plants received were far less attractive than those depicted in contemporary illustrations. It is obviously essential to get the right form as well as the right species.

we shall see, they are not the easiest of houseplants, they are certainly among the most beautiful, and are well worth the extra trouble necessary to keep them in good health. They are found throughout the tropics, but the vast majority of the family are natives of South America, particularly Brazil. They require a warm moist atmosphere which should not be allowed to drop below 50°, although *Ctenanthe lubbersiana* will tolerate considerably lower temperatures without apparent damage and so, to a lesser extent, will the forms of *Maranta leuconeura*. The moister the atmosphere is the more they will flourish, and it is beneficial to moisten the material around the pots with warm water in the winter. If the pots are not surrounded by absorbent material, they can be stood in a bowl and some hot water can be poured therein; but great care must be taken not to damage the plants under these circumstances. The water can be well heated, but boiling water would probably be too hot and the steam might damage the leaves, while if any touched the soil it would kill the roots.

All the *Marantaceae* appear to be shade lovers and too bright sunlight will cause the leaves to curl up and they will lose their coloration. They should be kept on the damp side, as prolonged drought will cause them to curl and brown at the tips. Owing to this need they require an open compost such as:

3 parts light loam
3 parts peat
3 parts leaf mould
1 part sand.

This is sufficiently open to prevent water from clogging the soil and causing root-rot. Propagation, which is best undertaken in April or May, is principally by division, but cuttings can be taken of some varieties. All *Marantas* have a creeping rhizome or underground stem. Most of the plants have their leaves flat by day, but erect at night, which has given them the name of Prayer Plants. The lower leaves will die off after a time, but more are constantly produced during the growing season, from April to October.

149

Genus CALATHEA

The derivation is from the Greek word for a basket, perhaps in view of the markings on some of the leaves, or possibly the Brazilians used to make baskets from them. The genus contains some of the most brilliantly marked leaves among all plants. Most of the species come from Brazil.

1. Calathea backemiana

This charming plant is said to have tuberous roots and, like the majority of *Calatheas*, comes from Brazil. The leaves are long in comparison to their width. In a normal plant the length is $5\frac{1}{2}$ inches and the width $1\frac{1}{2}$ inches, though with large plants the dimensions are increased. The basic colour of the leaf is a silver-grey, but it is diversified by oval emerald-green blotches that stem from the midrib on both sides and give the impression of an archaic painting of a tree.

2. Calathea crocata

Crocatus means the colour of saffron and refers here, although not with much accuracy, to the colour of the inflorescence. This is, indeed, probably the only *Calathea* which is grown as much for its flowers as for its leaves. These latter are oblong-oval in shape and borne on the end of a broad keeled pale purple stalk, which is not more than 4 inches long. The blades are about 4 inches long and 2 inches across and are maroon-purple on the underside, while the upper surface consists of alternate bands of dark and light green; the darker portion along the lateral veins, the lighter portions in the interstices. The plant produces a number of separate tufts. During the summer it will send up flower spikes on a bare stem about 9 inches tall at the end of which the flowers are grouped in a dense head. The flowers themselves are orange, but they emerge from pink bracts and make a surprisingly showy display. To make up for this display one must resign oneself to the fact that many of the older leaves are going to get discoloured and ragged during the winter months and will eventually have to be removed. They are soon replaced by the new foliage. The plant is native to Brazil and should have a temperature of 55° at least during the winter, while 60° is to be preferred. The plants naturally inhabit rain forests, so that they require a moist atmosphere, particularly during their growing season. In rooms this can only be obtained by plunging the pots in containers with some sodden material, which will throw up the water vapour, and spraying the leaves during hot weather.

3. Calathea kegeliana

This is very similar to *backemiana*, of which it may prove to be only a variety. The coloration and markings of the leaf are identical but the plant is very much larger, with the leaf reaching a length of 8 inches and a width of 4 inches.

4. Calathea insignis (Plate 63)

Insignis means striking, an epithet that could be applied to most of the genus, though this particular species does not seem in any way outstanding. The leaf is some $5\frac{1}{2}$ inches long and $1\frac{1}{2}$ inches across, and is of a medium light green in colour. This is diversified by dark green blotches springing from the midrib. The underside of the leaf is a dark wine-purple.

5. Calathea lindeniana

This species is named in honour of J. J. Linden, a very famous Belgian horticulturist of the last century. The leaf is an oblong-oval some 6 inches long and 3 inches across. The ground colour is dark green, and this is diversified with an emerald-green zone around the centre of the leaf and a thinner one outlining the edge of the leaf, but about $\frac{3}{4}$ of an inch from the margin. The underside of the leaf is maroon, apart from the light green zones which are green on the underside.

6. Calathea picturata (Plate 62)

This is very similar to *lindeniana* but the leaf is more elliptical in outline and somewhat larger, measuring 7 inches long and $3\frac{3}{4}$ inches across. The zones are not emerald-green but silvery, and the underside is entirely maroon. The appearance is thus rather more striking than *lindeniana*, but the basic leaf pattern is the same.

7. Calathea louisae (Plate 62)

This species is named in honour of Queen Louise of Belgium. This has the usual oblong lance-shaped leaf, which reaches a length of 7 inches and a width of only 2¾ inches. The ground colour is a medium green and there are irregular variegated zones centre on the midrib. The underside of the leaf is a greenish purple with a marked green margin.

8. Calathea mackoyana (Plate 64)

This is also known as *Maranta mackoyana*, the difference between *Calathea* and *Maranta* being that the ovaries of *Calathea* contain three cells and those of *Maranta* only one. *Calathea mackoyana,* which is known in the United States as the Peacock Plant, is one of the most striking of all ornamental-leaved plants. It is said to reach a height of 4 feet when fully grown, but when purchased will probably not be more than 8 inches tall. At this stage a mature leaf will be about 6 inches long and 4 inches wide and an oblong oval in shape. This leaf is on a stalk some 4 inches long rising direct from the rhizome. The upper side of the leaf has a middle-green edging and a silvery-green ground colour on which are markings in dark green, along the principal veins, so arranged as to give the outline of a rather archaic tree. On the underside of the leaf the dark green portions are a reddish purple, while seen against the light, the silvery-green portion appears transparent and the dark green portion acquires a rosy glow from the underside. It is natural with so ornamental a leaf to seek to use it in flower arrangements, but it will wilt immediately unless it is plunged for a few minutes in boiling water, with a little sugar added, immediately after cutting.

9. Calathea ornata (Plates 63 and 64)

Ornata means showy and is an apt name for this plant. It is described as growing from 18 inches to 8 feet in height, but the first figure is the most that it will attain as a houseplant. The leaves are about 7 inches long and 5 inches across, rather more elongated than *mackoyana*. This is a variable plant, but the Turnford form has dark green leaves with pale pink lines between the principal veins, which fade to cream as the leaf ages. The underside of the leaves is dark purple. As the plant increases in size so do the dimensions of the leaves, and a really large specimen may have leaves as large as 2 feet in length.

10. Calathea veitchiana

Named after the famous nurseryman James Veitch, this *Calathea* has a longer leaf stalk than the majority. The leaf is also more rounded than most *Calatheas* and is $5\frac{1}{2}$ inches long and $3\frac{1}{2}$ inches across. The leaf is a blend of four shades of green. Around the midrib is an irregular zone of light green, this is followed by a zone of very dark green, which is edged with a thin band of emerald-green and finally the leaf margin shows a medium-green band about $\frac{1}{2}$ inch across. The underside of the leaf is olive-green, except where the upper side is very dark green; this is maroon on the underside. The plant is a native of Venezuela.

11. Calathea zebrina (Plate 65)

Zebrina means that the leaves are striped like a Zebra. In this case the ground colour of the leaves is a dark emerald-green and the stripes are an even darker green on the surface; on the underside the dark green shows as a dark purple and the light green as a greenish purple. The plant has a graceful palm-like habit. When fully grown the plant will reach about $1\frac{1}{2}$ feet in height and will carry leaves some 12 inches long, but about half these dimensions are more usual. *C. pulcherrima* is very similar to *C. zebrina* but the underside of the leaf is the same colour as the top.

Genus CTENANTHE

The derivation is from two Greek words meaning 'comb' and

153

'flower' as the inflorescences are supposed to resemble a comb. As a general rule *Ctenanthes* are sold under the name *Calathea*, since their correct name is difficult to pronounce and therefore commercially bad. They can be distinguished from *Calatheas* by their more tufted habit, suggesting a small banana tree, and by their narrower leaves.

1. Ctenanthe lubbersiana (Plates 16 and 66)

Named after the same C. Lubbers of *Begonia lubbersii* (see p. 129). This is one of the hardiest and most vigorous of the *Marantaceae* and seems tolerant of far lower temperatures. The leaves are not dissimilar to those of a *Calathea* in shape and attain some 7 inches in length and 3 inches across. They are either light green mottled with dark green or light green mottled with cream, depending on the amount of light the plant receives and also on the age of the plant; the cream appears more frequently as the plant ages. To start with, the plant will throw several tufts from the rhizome, but as it increases in size it will throw up a bamboo-like stem, at the end of which a further tuft of leaves will appear and, eventually, the inconspicuous white flowers. Mature specimens are said to attain a height of 18 inches, with leaves up to 13 inches long, but though the first statement appears reasonable, the second seems exaggerated.

2. Ctenanthe oppenheimiana (Plate 51)

We have been unable to find out which Oppenheim gave his name to this plant. This plant is capable of reaching a height of 3 feet, with leaves 15 inches long. As purchased, however, it is about 6 inches high, with mature leaves 5 inches long and 2 inches across. The leaf stalk is long and the leaves turn at a right angle and are parallel to the ground. The upper side of the leaves are marked with alternate bands of dark green and silver-green and the underside is a lurid purple.

3. Ctenanthe oppenheimiana var. tricolor

The leaves are much narrower than in the type and the bands are less clearly marked. In addition parts of the upper side of the leaf are variegated with irregular cream blotches, which show a rosy red on the underside. All the family, as we have seen, dislike strong light, but *C. oppenheimiana tricolor* if exposed to bright sunlight will curl its leaves up, and they will remain curled for some days even if removed from the light. Both the *oppenheimiana* have an attractive fan-shaped habit of growth.

Genus MARANTA

The genus is named in honour of a sixteenth-century botanist, Bartolomeo Maranti. As far as houseplants are concerned the leaves are smaller and more rounded than the other genera of the family. They tend to lie flat, whereas *Calathea* and *Ctenanthe* grow upright; the leaf surface is less shiny and the plant is generally smaller.

1. Maranta leuconeura

Leuconeura comes from two Greek words and indicates that the leaves have white veins. This is a variable species and three varieties are generally sold as houseplants.

(*a*) Var. *Kerchoveana*. Who M. Kerchov was we do not know. This is an attractive low growing plant with oblong-oval leaves some 5 inches long and $3\frac{1}{2}$ inches in width. The leaves emerge emerald-green with red blotches between the principal veins, but as they age they darken to a darker green with maroon blotches. (Plate 63)

(*b*) Var. *Massangeana*. M. de Massange was an enthusiastic orchid grower who flourished in the 1870s. This plant is more spreading than *Kerchoveana*, and the leaves are marked differently and are less pointed at the end. The principal veins are a prominent white in colour, giving the leaf a herring-bone pattern; in addition there is a zone of silver along the midrib. The maroon between the veins is not so marked as in *Kerchoveana* and fades to a dark green. The underside of the leaf is a rosy purple, but, unlike the tall-growing *Calatheas*, it is not easy to see the underside of the leaves. They are not so large as in the other variety, being some 4 inches long and $2\frac{1}{2}$ inches across. (Plate 62)

(c) Var. *Erythrophylla*. This plant has only been introduced comparatively recently and is sometimes sold under the name *'Tricolor'*. *Erythrophylla* comes from two Greek words meaning 'red leaves', but it is not the leaves that are red but the principal veins. In fact the plant looks much like the var. *Massangeana* with red in place of white veins. There are the same pale blotches along the midrib between the veins, but these are creamy-green rather than silver, while the main ground colour is a dark olive green. The plant is much larger than the other two varieties described above, with leaves that may be more than 6 inches long, although the width is still about 3 inches. They are thus less rounded in appearance than those of the others. It also appears to be tolerant of rather lower temperatures, although ideally they should not drop below 55° for any length of time.

All these *Marantas* are vigorous growers and can take plenty of feeding during the growing period. Sometimes the roots grow so vigorously that they will push the plant out of the pot. If this happens it is necessary to pot the plant on, but this should not be done after the end of May or before growth is seen.

Genus STROMANTHE

The derivation is from two Greek words meaning 'bed' and 'flower', though the idea that the inflorescence is bed-shaped is not one that would present itself to most observers.

1. Stromanthe sanguinea

The epithet 'sanguine' presumably refers to the colour of the underside of the leaf, though maroon is a more accurate description. This is a rhizomatous plant with very long and narrow lance-shaped leaves. The blade is 13 inches long and 4½ inches across, of a dark shining green. Some specimens are described as having a white midrib. The underside of the leaf is a glowing maroon. Like so many of this family it is a native of Brazil. It needs treatment similar to the *Calatheas*, but will tolerate more light than the majority of this family.

CHAPTER IX

Bromeliaceae

———————⊱※⊰———————

The Bromeliads are a family of monocotyledons subsumed in some fifty-one genera and over 1,000 species, confined to the American continent and the Caribbean islands. The majority are found within the tropics, but the well-known 'Spanish Moss' of the Florida Everglades is found elsewhere in the Southern United States and some species of *Puya* are found in the cooler parts of Chile.

With the exception of the pineapple, *Ananas comosus*, the family is of purely decorative interest, and it is only very recently that they have been recognized as being particularly suitable for houseplant use. Previously they had been regarded as rather difficult of cultivation and needing considerable heat, and it is only in the last few years that they have been recognized as being surprisingly hardy and capable of surviving low temperatures without injury. As many of the species are extremely spectacular, both in leaf and in flower, they form a most welcome addition to the list of the more easily grown houseplants. They are even said to withstand frost, though this should probably not be put to the proof, as a certain amount of leaf damage would certainly ensue.

The majority of Bromeliads cultivated as houseplants are epiphytes in their native state and grow along the branches of trees, or occasionally on rocks. One species, *Tillandsia recurvata*, of no decorative interest, even grows on telegraph wires. The terrestrial species with a normal root system include many decorative species, but they are mostly so large that their

157

cultivation is impracticable; rosettes of leaves 6 feet across are not unusual. However, one genus, *Billbergia*, is an easily-grown terrestrial Bromeliad. The epiphytic character of the majority of Bromeliads appears to be the result of necessity, as occasionally one sees plants that have succeeded in growing in soil or leaf mould, and these are usually larger than the tree-borne plants and have a mere extensive root system. It follows therefore that although the roots' main function is as an anchor for the plant, they are also capable of taking up a certain amount of nourishment and so the selection of the potting compost is of some importance. Young plants appear to do best in a mixture such as

one-third pine needles (*Pinus sylvestris*)
one-third leaf mould (oak or birch is preferable to beech)
one-third peat.

Older plants will do best in a mixture of equal parts of peat, sand and Osmunda fibre, while *Aechmea*, *Billbergia* and *Nidularium* will thrive in a mixture of this with well-rotted leaf mould and pulverized cow dung.

The typical form of most Bromeliads is a rosette of leaves with an empty cup-like space in the centre. This is usually referred to as the 'vase' and should be kept full of water, preferably rain water. During the growing season a very mild liquid fertilizer can be added once a month, but this must be done with discretion. In the wild, water will be found in these vases even in the driest season, with the result that many of the larger species have a special fauna of frogs and toads, who probably add the equivalent of liquid fertilizer. This water is evidently collected as much from dew as from rain, and so the presence of Bromeliads will suggest either a permanently moist atmosphere, or alternately, and perhaps more frequently, an atmosphere with a marked difference between the day and night temperature, which will encourage the precipitation of dew.

In their early stages high temperatures are necessary for Bromeliads, 80° to 85° for seed germination and 70° to 80° to encourage offshoots to root. Once a Bromeliad has flowered the central rosette dies, leaving a number of offshoots, which will grow best if left attached to the original plant as long as possible. If they are removed at an earlier stage, they will take a longer time to get away; but against this disadvantage, the original rosette will probably produce further offsets. These offsets should be potted in a mixture containing one-third each of leaf mould, sphagnum moss and peat; care must be taken that the vase is kept full of water. A temperature of between 70° and 80°, with bottom heat, is recommended and in summer the plants should be shaded. Sphagnum moss can be replaced with the needles of *Pinus sylvestris* if these are more easily obtainable, and oak or birch leaf mould is to be preferred to that of beech, which appears too calcareous. Once established the plants can be moved to a more airy and better lighted situation. Young growing plants appear to do best under clear glass from October to March, and require medium shading during the late spring and summer. If possible, the best time for taking offshoots is in late spring and these are potted on in August. Bromeliads should always be placed in the smallest possible pot and should be potted on only when absolutely necessary. This will be caused by the size of the rosette, rather than root action, and the plant should be moved to a size of pot that prevents lack of balance.

For the growing of Bromeliads on a large scale it is necessary to propagate from seed. This is a slow business, as it may take from three to four years to produce a flowering-size plant. As the seed loses viability after six months, much better results are obtained by using one's own seed, rather than buying it from abroad. This will entail pollinating the flowers with a fine paint brush. Many Bromeliads appear to be self-sterile under greenhouse conditions, and it is as well to have more than one plant of the same species in flower at the same time, so that cross-pollination can take place. Why this should be necessary is obscure; cross-pollination can certainly not always take place under natural conditions, but appears essential in the glasshouse. Care must be taken that while the seed is ripening (which may take from two to six months) the temperature does not fall too low. When the seed is ripe it should be sown as soon as possible.

Bromeliaceae

The seeds of *Tillandsia* and *Vriesia* are naturally wind borne and are light and feathery, like dandelion seeds. *Aechmea* and *Bilbergia* produce a berry-like seed capsule, and the seeds must be washed clear of the pulp before sowing. Under natural conditions these seeds are presumably distributed by birds.

Cryptanthus provides an exception to most of the other Bromeliads. The centre cluster of flowers are imperfect, having stamens but no stigmas or ovaries, while bi-sexual flowers appear later in the leaf axils. As by this time the main cluster of male flowers has usually faded, it is simplest to self-pollinate these late perfect flowers: *Cryptanthus* does not object to self-pollination. Interspecific hybrids are easy to obtain in most genera; there are also some so-called intergeneric hybrids, but this may be due to the fact that plants have been placed in the wrong genera. Plants glide from genus to genus in the most baffling way, and the taxonomy of the family is exceptionally confused, even for specialists in the field, which we make no claim to be.

A number of soil mixtures are recommended for seed sowing, the essential being a fairly acid reaction, a pH of 4 to 4·5 being the ideal. The sowing medium should be sterilized. The following mixtures have all shown satisfactory results:

    i. Leaf mould with a top layer of sharp sand
    ii. Chopped sphagnum and sand
    iii. Peat covered with a layer of Osmunda fibre
    iv. Well-rotted pine needles
    v. Very light soil firmed with a very light sift of sand.

In all cases the seed is placed on the surface of the soil mixture and watered in with a solution of some fungicide to combat any *fusarium*. The pans are then covered with a pane of glass or a sheet of polythene, and placed under the bench in a temperature of 80° to 85°. Germination should take place within three weeks and the seedlings should gradually be inured to more light. The seedlings will stay in the seed pans for from four to six months (*Vriesias* are very slow growers and will require the longer period) and will then require pricking out. This will be repeated several times during the first year, but once the plants are large enough to be placed in thumb pots the tempo can slow down and one repotting a year is usually sufficient. Bromeliads appear to do best in the smallest possible pot and potting on is usually a question of balance, rather than root growth. Although so many of the family are naturally epiphytic, Dr. J. Sieber, in a series of interesting experiments, showed that feeding through the roots gave more satisfactory results than feeding through the leaves; though a combination of the two was even more satisfactory. He further elucidated the interesting facts that, under greenhouse cultivation, phosphorus and potash were absorbed to a greater extent through the roots and nitrogen to a greater extent through the leaves. This phenomenon is more marked in the early stages of the plant's life and in general the older plants respond best to leaf feeding. How these results can be reconciled with the plant's habits in the wild state it is not easy to see. As far as the houseplant grower is concerned an occasional very light addition of a balanced fertilizer to the water in the plant's vase is all that is necessary, but to the nurseryman a little root-feeding is evidently helpful in the early stages.

In the home Bromeliads can be given as much light as possible, but in the greenhouse some shading will be necessary, though the amount varies from one species to another. The leaf colouring will generally give one some idea as to the amount of shade required. Most of the dark green and mottled varieties, such as *Vriesia fenestralis* and *hieroglyphica*, need shading from early spring until the end of September. The red and purple leaved species, such as *Aechmea fulgens* and *Nidularium innocentii*, can do with less shading, and it need not be applied until the end of May. Many of the terrestrial varieties, such as the *Billbergias*, can dispense with shading altogether, except on the brightest and hottest days when light shading is beneficial. Plenty of fresh air would seem to be an essential and many of the *Tillandsias* will only do well if placed in a hanging basket filled with Osmunda fibre or encouraged to root on a piece of cork bark which can be suspended from the roof. Thrips are sometimes a nuisance with young seedlings and an occasional nicotine spray will keep

L   161

Bromeliaceae

these under control. Mature plants may be infested with scale and some application such as Volck should be given.

Genus AECHMEA

The name is derived from the Greek word for a point; the calices have very rigid points.

1. Aechmea chantinii

This makes a medium-sized rosette of leaves which are held fairly upright and are banded alternatively green and white. They are about 10 inches long and 1½ inches across and are very finely toothed on the margins. The flowers are borne on the end of a foot high scape in a dense egg-shaped panicle. The top of the flower scape has bright red leaves, while the inflorescence itself is reddish-yellow; both the flowers and the sepals being the same colour, a comparatively unusual phenomenon among Bromeliads. The plant is native to Brazil.

2. Aechmea fasciata (Colour Plate II. Plate 69)

This is, apparently, the correct name for the plant sold as *A. rhodocyanea*, the rosy-blue *Aechmea*, which is a much more descriptive name. This makes a large rosette of grey-green leaves with horizontal grey bands, which vary in size from one plant to another. A well-grown specimen may be as much as 2 feet across and the leaves will rise for about 12 inches. The individual leaves are some 18 inches long and 3 to 4 inches across. The showy flower-scape is rosy pink and opens out into numerous pink spiny bracts from which the lavender-blue flowers emerge. The scape is borne on an 18-inch stem and the stem and bracts will keep their colour for six months. The plant is hardy, although native around Rio de Janeiro, and needs all the light that can be given. During the winter it is advisable to fill the vase with warm water. *A. fasciata* is prolific in throwing sideshoots and under room conditions these can be left in the pot, after the central rosette has withered. The plant is generally offered for sale when the flower-scape is about half developed.

162

II. Neoregelia carolinae tricolor, Aechmea fasciata,
Cryptanthus tricolor

Bromeliaceae

3. Aechmea fulgens (Plates 68 and 70)

The specific epithet, which means 'blazing', refers to the brilliant scarlet of the flower-scape. The type, a native of French Guiana, has dark green leaves; but the variety *discolor*, which is found in Brazil, has the underside of the leaves a dark maroon-purple. The upper side is olive-green in colour, and as the leaves age they become covered with a greyish indumentum, which almost suggests mildew. The rosette is nearly as large as that of *A. fasciata*, but the leaves are narrower and the plant has a more slender appearance. The actual flowers are purplish blue and last only a couple of days, but the sepals, which enclose them, are a bright scarlet and berry-like in appearance: the flower stem is similarly coloured and the inflorescence will retain its brilliant coloration for six to seven weeks. The edges of the leaves are minutely prickly, but are incapable of causing any injury. *A. fulgens* is slightly less hardy than *A. fasciata*, but cannot be reckoned a difficult plant.

These two *Aechmeas* are those most generally offered, but it can only be a matter of time before *A. macracantha* with wine-red leaves in a large rosette, from the comparative coolness of Mexico, and *A. mariae-reginae*, with a 2-foot flower-scape ornamented with 4-inch long rosy-pink boat-shaped bracts are introduced. The latter plant is found in Costa Rica and should not prove difficult. There are other very handsome members of the genus, but many of them are rather large.

Genus ANANAS

This is the genus containing the pineapple and is terrestrial not epiphytic and liable to make a very large plant, which requires a rich soil mixture and plenty of root room. Although it is possible to root the tuft at the top of a pineapple, you are not likely to get pineapples forming in your room, as considerable heat is needed for this.

1. Ananas bracteatus striatus

A form of the pineapple with bright green leaves which have

wide cream margins, tinged red towards the tips and suffused with red while still not fully developed. This is a very decorative plant, which withstands room conditions quite well, if not exposed to draughts. It does, however, require a winter temperature of 60° and will eventually require a 9-inch pot, which makes it rather bulky. The plants produce suckers, when well established and these can be used for propagation. Being a terrestrial plant it requires moisture during the growing season, while there is no necessity to put water in the vase.

Genus BILLBERGIA

The genus is named in honour of a Swedish botanist, J. G. Billberg.

1. Billbergia nutans (Plate 67)

Nutans means 'nodding' and refers to the shape of the flower spikes, which are like those of a bluebell. *Billbergias* are terrestrial and can use more soil than most other Bromeliads. *B. nutans* is extremely hardy and throws sideshoots with such profusion that it can make a large clump of rosettes and will need potting-on fairly frequently, say once every two years. The greyish leaves are long and narrow and end in a point. The inflorescence is chiefly conspicuous by reason of the pink bracts that surround the flowers. These are greenish in colour and not very showy. The plant is one of the least decorative of all Bromeliads, but it is so easy to grow, that it will always be popular.

2. Billbergia × windii (Plate 67)

This is a hybrid made by crossing the hardy *B. nutans* with the more decorative, but tenderer, *B. decora*. This makes a handsome plant with medium-green leaves, not so erect as in *B. nutans* and some 1 to 2 inches across. The plant grows some 12 to 18 inches high and is about 12 inches across. The flower-scape is some 8 inches long before the light red bracts, which prolong it for a further 6 to 8 inches, appear. The flowers are pale green, tipped with blue, and have prominent yellow stamens and are not long lasting. The inflorescence as a whole does not usually survive for more than a fortnight. Although less vigorous than *B. nutans* and very slightly less hardy, this plant can be relied upon to flower regularly and is considerably more decorative both in leaf and in flower.

Genus CARAGUATA

Officially this genus has ceased to exist, most of its species now being found under *Guzmania*. *C. peacockii* does not appear to fit in *Guzmania* very satisfactorily and the name is here retained for convenience.

1. Caraguata peacockii (Plate 75)

This plant, in the wild state, is either epiphytic or terrestrial, though it is more usually found growing on the boughs of trees. It is a fairly compact plant with a rosette only a little over a foot in diameter, composed of strap-shaped leaves, some $1\frac{1}{2}$ inches wide, of a pale claret colour. The plant is often found high in the mountains and will tolerate quite low temperatures with ease; although young plants are liable to damp off if kept too cold. The inflorescence, borne on a scape some 9 to 11 inches high, consists of a funnel-shaped cluster of wine-red bracts, 2 inches long and 4 inches across, from which the pale yellow flowers barely emerge. The bracts will retain their colour for six to eight weeks but when the plant starts flowering the leaves tend to lose colour; this happens with many of the Bromeliads. *C. peacockii* likes plenty of air around it and in the room will tolerate as much light as can be given. In the glasshouse it needs light shading in the summer to prevent scorching.

Genus CRYPTANTHUS

The derivation is from two Greek words meaning 'hidden flowers', as, like most of the family, the flowers are concealed in the bracts. These 'Earth Stars', as they are popularly called, are terrestrial in habit, although the root system is not very large. They tend to grow on rocks and do not have the typical 'vase' of most of the family. As a result watering is more difficult, though a simple rule of thumb method is to keep the compost moist in summer and dry in winter. The flowers appear in the centre of the rosette and in the leaf axils, but are not very conspicuous. The leaves on the other hand are brilliantly coloured. All *Cryptanthus* are very hardy and easy to keep, and appreciate good light.

Most *Cryptanthus* are small-growing, stemless plants; though *C. tricolor* and *fosterianus* are larger than the majority. They are being imported and propagated in ever-increasing numbers and the list we give will probably be considerably augmented in the near future. At the moment the following are those in commercial supply.

1. Cryptanthus acaulis (Plate 75)

The specific epithet means 'stemless' and could apply to the whole genus. The type plant has a compact rosette of broad rather fleshy leaves of soft green. The variety *rubra* has brownish red leaves.

2. Cryptanthus bivittatus (Plate 72)

Bivittatus means 'having two stripes' and refers to the marking of the leaves. The variety usually offered is *roseo-pictus* (Plate 71), painted with pink. The plant makes a flattish rosette about 6 to 8 inches across and looks like some exotic starfish. The leaf-colour varies with the intensity of light: if kept in bright light the leaf is mainly pink with cream stripes, while in the shade the leaves are light and dark green. It is possible to get the colours to change in about ten days, by altering the intensity of light. A larger version of the plant has the varietal name *major* (Plate 71).

3. Cryptanthus beuckeri (Plate 74)

Beucker's *Cryptanthus* has leaves differing in shape from the majority of the genus. Most of the plants have elongated leaves coming to a point at the end, but otherwise of the same width for the whole of their length; *C. beuckeri* has a leaf shaped rather like a teaspoon, with a thin stem-like portion springing from the rosette, which suddenly opens out into a flat oval. The leaf is beautifully mottled green and cream.

4. Cryptanthus fosterianus (Plate 73)

Foster's *Cryptanthus* is the largest and most handsome of the genus and its habit of growth is more upright than the majority of Earth Stars. The colouring of the leaves is best compared to the tail feathers of a pheasant, with red and grey predominating.

5. Cryptanthus lacerdae (Plate 70)

This is one of the smaller members of the genus. The leaves are banded alternately dark green and silver-grey. The plant is very compact.

6. Cryptanthus osyanthus

This is distinguished by its brownish red unstriped leaves. It requires a very well-lit situation.

7. Cryptanthus tricolor (Colour Plate II)

This should correctly be known as *C. bromelioides* var. *tricolor*. It is larger than the majority, though smaller than *C. fosterianus*, and is very vigorous, making numerous sideshoots. The inch-wide leaves attain some 10 inches in length and are cream in colour, with a few narrow dark green stripes running lengthwise; the whole suffused with a pinkish glow, which is most marked at the centre of the rosette.

8. Cryptanthus unicolor (Plate 76)

This charming little plant has pale pink leaves, which rise in the centre, with a fountain-like effect and the leaf-tips curl over the edge of the pot.

9. Cryptanthus zonatus

The zoned *Cryptanthus* is similar in shape to *bivittatus*, though the leaves are somewhat broader. There are two varieties: *argyraeus* (Plate 73) is characterized by irregular bands of green and golden brown (why it is called *argyraeus*, silvered, is obscure), while *zebrinus* (Plate 76) has the colours grey and maroon, like a smaller and less brilliant *fosterianus*.

The hybridist has been working on *Cryptanthus* and a number of attractive plants have been bred, while a number of sports from the genuine species with more attractive leaves have also been noted. Among these is an American hybrid called 'It', which is like a flatter, pinker and rather larger *C. tricolor* and may possibly be that species hybridized with *C. bivittatus*. *Feuerzauber* (Flower Magic) raised in Germany has the markings of *C. fosterianus*, but as the leaves age they become suffused with deep red; possibly the plant is a hybrid between *C. fosterianus* and *C. tricolor*. The trouble with these hybrids and with the various sports is that they can only be propagated asexually, by rooting offshoots, which means that increase is very slow. There is no guarantee that plants from seed would show the same characters, so that at the moment they are very scarce and expensive. There is at least one nursery in Europe which is specializing in these sports and hybrids and we may expect them to come into commerce in the course of a few years. In 1959 we prophesied that more *Cryptanthus* would soon be introduced. It now looks as though that prophecy will eventually justify itself.

Genus GUZMANIA

Named in honour of a Spanish botanist, A. Guzman.

1. Guzmania zahnii

There are three Zahns who are honoured in botanic nomenclature. This one was Gottlieb Zahn, a plant collector in Central America where he was drowned in 1870 when on a mission for Robert Veitch. This is a most brilliant plant, found in Costa Rica, with leaves some 20 inches long, with a yellow ground colour, striped with crimson and with the upper part of the leaf bright crimson. The flower spike consists of a large panicle 9 inches long and 4 inches across with a large number of yellow flowers that are short-lived, but so numerous that the spike is conspicuous for some six weeks. This species is a little more delicate than those we have described so far, but will thrive in a temperature of 50° or over.

2. Guzmania sanguinea

As the name implies this species has blood-red leaves. It is similar in size to the last-mentioned species with leaves up to 20 inches long and a rosette of some 2 feet in diameter. The flower spike is borne on a tall stem over 12 inches high, ornamented with red bracts and the 6-inch flower spike is equally showy. The yellow flowers are fugacious, but numerous.

Guzmanias are epiphytes with the typical Bromeliad 'vase'.

Genus NEOREGELIA

This genus is named in honour of the Russian botanist, E. A. von Regel. The genus was originally named *Regelia* and subsequently *Aregelia* and the plants listed below may be found under either of these generic names. In appearance the plants are like many of the other Bromeliads, but the flowers do not appear on a spike, but just emerge above the water in the 'vase' and look like miniature water-lilies. As a result the species grown are selected for their brilliant leaf colour.

1. Neoregelia carolinae tricolor (Colour Plate II. Plate 3 and 69)

The leaves are somewhat narrow and of a medium green with the centre variegated with cream and pink, though the pink vanishes as the leaf ages. The leaf may be as much as 15 inches long, but is only 1 inch across. A mature plant is about 18 to 24 inches in diameter, but may be more. Like most of the species in this genus, the last leaves to appear before the flowers are short and very brilliantly coloured; in this species they are bright red. The flowers are a light blue, about half an inch across and appear first from the outside of the flower cluster. *Neoregelias* like a somewhat warmer temperature and rather more shade than most of the other Bromeliads.

2. Neoregelia marechatii (Plate 3)

Presumably named in honour of a M. Marechat but we can

find no trace of him. The leaves are wider than in the preceding species and slightly prickly on the sides. They are a medium-green, flushed with wine-red as they emerge, but this gets lost as the leaf elongates and ages. The rosette is a little less in diameter than the former species, although the leaves tend to be slightly longer. This results in a somewhat taller plant with a deeper 'vase'. The flowers are again surrounded with bright crimson leaves.

3. Neoregelia meyendorfii

Meyendorff's *Neoregelia* is characterized by pink rather than crimson leaves around the flowers. The other leaves are a some-what light green and the whole plant is slightly smaller in all its parts than the other species in cultivation.

4. Neoregelia spectabilis (Plate 74)

Spectabilis may be translated 'showy' and this is easily the most ornate member of the genus. The rather narrow leaves are characterized by a crimson tip, while the main portion of the leaf is green on the upper side, sometimes with red flecks, and ash-grey and banded on the underside. To make up for the brilliance of the leaves, the ones that immediately precede the appearance of the flowers are a dull purple and considerably less brilliant than in the other species. However, the general appearance of the plant is so conspicuous that it is easily the favourite of the genus.

Genus NIDULARIUM

The name means a little bird's nest. This genus is very similar to the last, from which it may be distinguished by the petals being erect instead of spreading and by the fact that the inflorescence is branched; although dissection is necessary to establish this point.

1. Nidularium innocentii

Presumably named in honour of a Pope Innocent. This is one of the plants mentioned by Huysmans in *A Rebours*, where he describes it as having leaves the colour of wine-must. This makes a sizeable rosette of leaves about 15 inches long and 1½ inches in width, very slightly serrated at the edge. These leaves are dark green, flecked with purple on the top side and a very dark claret colour on the underside. As the flowers emerge, the centre of the rosette turns bright crimson. The flowers themselves, which barely emerge from the water in the vase, are a greenish white and of little interest. This plant is quite hardy and easy to keep, though it would be unwise to let the temperature fall below 50°. *N. innocentii* would seem to be the only member of the genus in cultivation at the moment, but it can only be a matter of time before *N. rutilans*, with spotted leaves and scarlet flowers, is re-introduced.

Genus TILLANDSIA

Named in honour of a Swedish botanist, Elias Tillands.

This is a large genus containing nearly 400 species and its interest lies mainly in the flowers. These are generally borne on a tall scape, which may or may not be coloured, and emerge from bracts which are generally brightly coloured and overlap each other, so that the inflorescence has the appearance of a lobster claw. In general the leaves are not very showy and this helps to distinguish the genus from the rather similar *Vriesia*.

1. Tillandsia cyanea (Plate 71)

The specific epithet means blue. The plant makes a rosette some 21 inches across of narrow medium-green leaves. The flower-scape is ornamented with pink bracts from which the large blue flowers emerge. The flower stem is some 5 inches high and the inflorescence some 4 inches long and as much across. The bracts keep their colour for eight weeks. The flowers, which start from the bottom of the sheath, last from three to five days and there is a continual succession. Although not exigent in regard to heat, *Tillandsias* require an airy position and bright light. These conditions are not always easy to provide in the home. Without them there is no great difficulty in keeping the plant alive, but flowering may be long delayed.

171

Bromeliaceae

2. Tillandsia lindeniana (Plate 69)

This species is named in honour of the famous Belgian gardener, J. J. Linden and is sometimes known as *T. lindeni*. This is a native of Peru, and one of the few *Tillandsias* with ornamental leaves as well as large showy flowers. The rosette is wider and the leaves slightly broader than *T. cyanea*. The leaves are green, flushed with purple and are numerous. The bracts are borne on a stem some 5 inches high, and extend this for a further 7 to 8 inches. The inflorescence is about 1½ inches across. The bracts are a coral-pink in colour and keep their colour for six weeks. The large violet-blue flowers are short-lived, but there are many to emerge and flowering will continue for some time. This is a most handsome plant.

Genus VRIESIA

Named in honour of a Dutch botanist, W. H. de Vriese, this is very similar to *Tillandsia*, though, as far as houseplants are concerned, they can be distinguished by the broader leaves with more ornamental markings and the smaller flowers. Although great heat was formerly regarded as necessary, they have now proved themselves to be extremely hardy: the most difficult being *V. fenestralis*.

1. Vriesia carinata (Plate 73)

'*Carinata*' means 'keeled' and refers to the shape of the bracts. This is a small plant with a rosette some 6 inches across and with leaves about the same length, ½ to ¾ inch across, of a medium green. The bracts are borne on a stem 4 inches high and are red and yellow and will remain conspicuous for at least eight weeks. The inflorescence is 3 inches long and 2 inches across. The yellow flowers last for one day only.

2. Vriesia hieroglyphica (Plate 76)

This is a large plant with broad strap-shaped leaves of a dark green, irregularly banded with black. The plant may be as much as 2 feet across and the leaves are 3 inches across and 18 inches long. The plant is about 16 inches high. The interest in the plant is in the leaves, the inflorescence has yellowish bracts from which yellow flowers emerge.

3. Vriesia fenestralis (Plate 77)

Fenestralis means like a window. This is about the same size as the last species and has light green leaves, beautifully reticulated with darker green lines. The inflorescence is dull, being composed of green bracts, spotted with brown from which long, greenish-yellow flowers emerge. This is more tender than the other *Vriesias*, but is not unduly difficult and has remarkably beautiful leaves to which no description can do justice.

4. Vriesia saundersii (Plates 57 and 70)

Also known as *Encholirion saundersii*. The leaves are $1\frac{3}{4}$ inches wide, 8 to 10 inches in length and recurved. The upper sides are mid-grey in colour except at the base near the centre of the rosette where they are pale sea-green flecked with small irregular red blotches. The undersides are pale green but thickly covered with red-blotch markings. The flower-scape is 18 to 20 inches in height, with 5 branches at the top each bearing several yellow cigar-shaped bracts about 1 inch in length; from these, yellow tubular flowers emerge some 2 inches in length. The flower is not attractive and the main attraction of this plant would seem to be its unusual leaf-colouring.

5. Vriesia splendens (Plates 74 and 77)

The showiest species in the genus and one of the easiest to grow, *V. splendens* makes a large rosette of broad strap-shaped leaves of a dark green with claret-coloured transverse bands. The rosette is some 19 inches across and about a foot high and the leaves are some 3 inches wide and about a foot long. As the flower-scape emerges the leaves lose their colouring. The flower stem is some 8 inches long and the inflorescence may be as much as 15 inches long and is about $1\frac{1}{2}$ inches across. The bracts are bright red and retain their colour for at least eight weeks. The ephemeral flowers are yellow in colour.

Bromeliaceae

As the various genera are hard to distinguish, the following key may be helpful. It should be emphasized that it refers only to houseplant Bromeliads and is of no value botanically.

1. Leaves grey-green, sedge-like, no 'vase' *Billbergia*
2. Rosette flat resembling starfish, no 'vase' *Cryptanthus*
3. Flowers not emerging from 'vase' *Nidularium, Neoregelia*

    (*a*) Flowers blue, petals spreading *Neoregelia*
    (*b*) Flowers white, petals erect *Nidularium*

4. Leaves narrow, inflorescence of sheathed bracts, flowers large and blue *Tillandsia*
5. Leaves broad, inflorescence of sheathed bracts. Flowers tubular, generally yellow *Vriesia*
6. Leaves broad, inflorescence berry-like *Aechmea fulgens*
7. Leaves broad, inflorescence branched and spiny *Aechmea fasciata*

8. Flowers in clusters, yellow bracts on stem below inflorescence *Guzmania*
9. Inflorescence wider than length. Flowers small *Caraguata*

CHAPTER X

Palms and Ferns

I. PALMS

Everyone knows what a palm is, but it is by no means easy to describe botanically. They can scarcely be described as trees, yet they are usually woody. Usually each palm has a single unbranched stem, which can be so short as to be barely detectable or over 100 feet high. There are a few exceptions to this. Plants of the genus *Hyphaene* do produce branches, while *Calamus* and *Desmoncus* are twining plants. The plants are monocotyledons, but rather unusually for this group they have compound leaves. Without researching the matter the only other monocotyledon with compound leaves we can think of on the spur of the moment is the *Araceae* and, like these, the young seedling leaves of palms are usually undivided. Palm leaves are generally either palmate, with a number of leaflets radiating from the top of the stem, or pinnate, with the leaflets emerging from the stem along its upper length, the stem, indeed, serving as a midrib. Palms generally inhabit hot regions, although a few have proved sufficiently sturdy to survive outside in Great Britain. Generally they are very slow growing, although the dwarf palms sold under the names of *Cocos weddeliana* and *Neanthe bella* (neither, apparently, correct botanically) will make respectable plants some three years from seed sowing. Some species, when sufficiently established, will throw up suckers from the roots and these can be detached and potted up separately, but with the majority seed is the only satisfactory method of propagation.

175

Palms and Ferns

Most palms in the wild grow in full sunlight, but in cultivation they seem remarkably tolerant of quite shady conditions. Indeed *Howea* will tolerate dark shade for quite long periods without discomfort. In theory palms grow all the year round, but in practice they will make little growth during the dark days of winter, even if kept at a high temperature. Their soil should not be excessively rich. JIP 2 will be quite sufficient even for large specimens and so will the Ivy compost. Most Victorian gardening books recommend a compost of two parts loam to one part sharp sand (they, indeed, specified silver sand) and since those were the great days of palm culture, this might well prove the best mixture where good loam is obtainable. Palms require ample water during spring and summer and should be kept moist during autumn and winter. They seem to do best with their roots somewhat restricted and, once the required size has been attained, they are only potted on about every three years. When this is done care must be taken not to damage the roots as palms are very sensitive to any root damage and some may even die if this is excessive. As a general rule palms do not flower as small plants, but *Neanthe bella* may produce a rather dreary little spike of greenish flowers, which has no decorative value at all. It would seem that almost all the houseplant palms are sold under incorrect names. We give here the correct names, or to be more accurate, the names that are given as correct at present and will note the more popular names at the same time.

Genus CHAMAEROPS

There is only the one species in this genus, which is not outstandingly ornamental, but is interesting as being the only palm that is native to Europe. It is basically North African, but gets across the Mediterranean in Spain, Sicily and parts of Southern Italy.

1. Chamaerops humilis

Normally a dwarf tufted plant, but apparently it can produce a trunk over 6 foot high on rare occasions. The leaves are fan-shaped and split nearly to the top of the leaf-stalk into a large number of narrow segments. The leaves may be 18 inches long

66. Ctenanthe lubbersiana

67. Billbergia nutans, B. × windii

68. Philodendron bipinnatifidum, Aechmea fulgens discolor

69. Aechmea fasciata, Neoregelia carolinae tricolor,
Tillandsia lindeniana

70. Vriesia saundersii, Aechmea fulgens, Cryptanthus lacerdae

71. Tillandsia cyanea, Cryptanthus bivittatus roseo-pictus, C. b. major

72. Piper ornatum, Hedera helix 'Lutzii', Cryptanthus bivittatus

73. Cryptanthus fosterianus, Vriesia carinata, Cryptanthus zonatus argyraeus

74. Vriesia splendens, Neoregelia spectabilis, Cryptanthus beuckeri

75. Caraguata peacockii, Cryptanthus acaulis

76. Vriesia hieroglyphica, Cryptanthus unicolor, C. zonatus zebrinus

77. Vriesia fenestralis, V. splendens

78. Howea forsteriana

79. Syagrus weddelianus

80. Asplenium nidus

81. Adiantum tenerum

82. Nephrolepis exaltata 'Whitmannii'

and a foot across and are borne on the end of rather spiny stems, usually about 9–12 inches long, but reaching as much as 4 feet in very vigorous plants. The leaves are grey-green in colour and the emerging leaves are covered with a grey wool. Forms have been recorded with silvery leaves and also with rather smaller more delicate leaves and these were given the names *argentea* and *elegans*. The plant needs full light, but is tolerant of low temperatures, surviving outside in sheltered parts of southern England, so that a winter minimum of 45° is more than adequate. In the wild they must be moist in winter and spring and rather dry in the summer, but it is not advisable to let them dry out too much in pots, even in the summer. Plants in the wild produce suckers freely and these can be detached and potted up separately.

Genus COCOS. See *Syagrus*

Genus COLLINIA

This is, apparently, the correct name for the plant which is well known under the names *Neanthe bella* and *Chamaedorea elegans*, but which looks very strange to most of us under its correct name of

1. Collinia elegans (Plate 53)

This is always a small palm, although really mature wild plants can reach a height of 4 feet with leaves over 2 feet long. It makes, however, a very elegant little plant only two years from seed, when it will have leaves up to 8 inches long, which are feathery in appearance, as a number of small leaflets radiate from the central stem. These individual leaflets are up to 4 inches long and an inch across and are elliptic in shape. As the plant ages its leaves become longer and the leaflets also become larger and coarser, so the plant loses some of its original elegance. It will bear a rather unexciting green inflorescence at an early age, but if fruit is set, this is quite decorative. The plant can be kept rather drier than most palms during the winter months, but this should not be carried to excess as prolonged dryness will have a

M   177

bad effect. The plant seems to tolerate a dry atmosphere with equanimity, and will also survive in light shade, although they are not happy if it is too dark. A winter temperature of 50° is advisable and the plant should only rarely be fed during the summer.

Genus HOWEA

So called as the plants are found only on the Lord Howe Islands in the Pacific. The capital of these islands is a town called Kentia and these palms are often sold as Kentias. These are the palms of the Palm Court and are very tolerant of quite dark conditions, although they are happier if this is not overdone. There are theoretically two species, but they are so similar, one would have thought that they could be reduced to two varieties of a single species.

1. Howea belmoreana

It is only seedling plants of *Howeas* that are grown. In the wild they attain a height of 35 feet and by then the leaves may be 8 feet long. In commerce they are usually from 30 inches to 4 feet in height with a head of pinnate leaves that will attain a length of 2 feet in large specimens and a width of about a foot, while the leaf-segments themselves may be a foot in length. These segments are held more or less horizontally. This constitutes the main distinction between this species and

2. Howea forsteriana (Plate 78)

which is characterized by drooping segments. There are also on an average less segments per leaf and the leaves are rather less densely crowded on the plant. The graceful drooping pinnae make this the more attractive of the two. Both species need similar conditions. A winter temperature of 55° is desirable and the plants must be kept moist at all seasons, although naturally more water is required during the period when the new leaves are appearing. The plants appear to resent strong sunlight, although why this should be so is not very clear. One would have thought that there was plenty of sunshine in the Pacific.

3. Howea canterburyana

Although this plant is invariably sold under the above name (or as *Kentia canterburyana*) it belongs, in reality to a different genus and should correctly be known as *Hedyscepe canterburyana*. It differs from *Howea* in the shape of the inflorescence and the dry, not fleshy, fruits, and also in the fact that the leaves are truly pinnate, while those of *Howea* proper would more accurately be described as pinnatisect; the leaflets are not quite separate. The treatment is the same as for the other two species.

Genus LIVISTONA

One species of this was very popular in Victorian days, before the introduction of the *Howeas*. It was then known as *Latania borbonica*. It is probably not easily obtained nowadays, but since Victoriana are making a comeback, it seems as well to describe it.

1. Livistona chinensis

Mature plants of this would prove rather unmanageable with a trunk up to 6 feet high and leaves up to 5 feet across, but young plants were highly thought of for room decoration in the 1860s. The leaves are kidney-shaped in outline, but cut up into numerous hanging segments, while these segments themselves are deeply forked with threads adhering between the forks. The stems are from 1 to 2 feet long, depending on the age of the plant and young specimens will have the leaves about 18 inches or 2 feet across; very young plants will be more manageable in size, but the leaves will not be so segmented. Plants survived outside for many years in Cornwall, so that a winter temperature of 45° will prove more than adequate, while the plants should be kept moist at all seasons. Shady conditions are tolerated with ease and also well-lit situations. The plant seems rather greedier than most palms and requires feeding during the summer months.

179

Palms and Ferns

Genus PHOENIX

The best-known member of this genus (which is not large, but the number of species depends on what authority you accept. Probably about twelve is the best estimate) is the Date Palm, *P. dactylifera*, and, indeed, you can acquire a quick do-it-yourself houseplant by sowing date stones. It will be about three years before you have anything worth looking at, but it will then keep going for some time, before it becomes too large for comfort. There are a number of dwarf species, but only one is usually available. The others need the same treatment. To revert to our date stones for a moment; 45° is an adequate winter temperature, far less than is required for the true dwarf species.

1. Phoenix canariensis

This palm, which is closely allied to the Date Palm, is often used in large arrangements, but is too bulky for most homes. Eventually it makes a tall palm with very slender leaves, composed of numerous leaflets, which may be up to 10 inches long and which are held at first erect, although they may droop slightly subsequently. When full-grown the palms may carry leaves 20 feet long and even small specimens may have leaves up to 6 feet long. As its name implies the plant is native to the Canary Islands, where it may be exposed to quite low temperatures occasionally and so it will come to no harm with a winter temperature of 45°, although 50° is to be preferred. The palm is often planted for ornament in Mediterranean countries, where they are occasionally exposed to severe frosts. These kill off all the existing leaves, but the plants appear to regenerate and soon replace the damaged foliage. Young plants would probably suffer more severely, but if kept free from frost the plants will survive, even though they may not thrive in too low a temperature.

2. Phoenix roebelinii

A suckering plant with a rather swollen stem about 2 foot high at the most, but often less. The pinnate leaves are about a foot long, while the pinnae are rather narrow but up to 7 inches long. They are clustered along the stem rather irregularly and, unlike the majority of Phoenix leaves are soft and not spiny. This is sometimes described as a variety of the widespread *P. humilis*, with a shorter trunk and rather rigid grey-green leaves and this is quite close to *P. acaulis*, which has practically no trunk (although what it has is very spiny) but which can produce much larger leaves than *P. robelinii*. All these plants are native to India, but both *P. robelinii* and *P. humilis* are also found much further east. None are difficult to keep in good condition, provided that a fairly high winter temperature can be provided, preferably 60° or slightly higher. The plants should be kept to a single stem, any suckers that appear should be either rubbed out or detached and potted up. Since the plants are unisexual, there is no chance of obtaining fruit from them, although that of *P. acaulis* is rather striking.

Genus REINHARDTIA

A small genus of very dwarf, delicate palms from Central America. They are not in general cultivation at the present time, but they can probably be expected in the not too distant future. They have also been known as *Geonoma* and *Malortiea*.

1. Reinhardtia gracilis

This has pinnate leaves borne on slender stalks which radiate from a rather slender trunk, that can eventually reach a height of 2 feet or more, but not for a long time and it is usually seen as a stemless plant with the leaves borne on stalks about 9 inches long, while the leaves themselves are up to a foot long. The plant needs ample water and high temperatures, but used to be recommended for cultivation in Wardian Cases, which suggests that they might prove successful in closed glass containers.

Genus RHAPIS

The name comes from the Greek word for a needle. A number of dwarf Chinese and Japanese palms are included in this genus, but only one has proved popular.

1. Rhapis excelsa

This was known in the great days of palm growing as *R. flabelliformis*, and is a dwarf palm, eventually producing a thin trunk up to 18 inches high, which is sheathed in the base of the leaf stalks. The fan-shaped leaves are deeply divided, less so in seedling plants or those only a few years old. The plant forms tufts, rather like *Chamaerops* and needs very similar treatment. At one time a form with variegated leaves was available, but may well be lost now. It was brought back from Japan in 1861 by the great Robert Fortune, who greatly enhanced the appreciation of variegated plants by his Japanese collections. The green plant is found in both Japan and in China. The leaves are usually about 9 inches across and long.

Genus SYAGRUS

This is one of the genera resulting in the breaking up of the genus *Cocos*, which is now restricted to the Coconut Palm alone.

1. Syagrus weddelianus (Plate 79)

Named in honour of Dr. H. A. Weddell, who botanized in Peru in the mid-nineteenth century, this plant is always sold in this country as *Cocos weddelianus*, while in the U.S.A. apparently it is known as *Microcoelum mortianum*. This is arguably the most elegant of the smaller palms, with its slender arched stems, bearing fine feathery leaflets. This is always offered as a small seedling plant with leaves about 6 inches long, but if it can be preserved (and this is not easy for long) it will get leaves over a foot long and start to form a slender trunk. It does require rather warm conditions with a winter temperature of 65° if it is to do well, although it will survive at 60° and higher temperatures during the summer. As the plant ages the leaves and leaflets get larger, but they never look coarse. The leaves are dark green above and a glaucous grey below. Not the easiest of plants to keep for long, but well worth the trouble.

II. FERNS

Although the majority of houseplants are grown for the sake of their leaves rather than their flowers, they do, at least, produce flowers, even though they may not be particularly showy or often seen in cultivation. Ferns on the other hand produce no flowers at all, nor do they grow from seeds, like the majority of plants. They belong to a different branch of the vegetable kingdom from the flowering plants and are, indeed, very much older; fossil ferns having been found in old deposits, probably long before flowering plants had evolved. Although the culture of ferns does not differ in any marked way from that of other plants, it is necessary to learn a small vocabulary to recognize the various parts and perhaps it would be as well to get that out of the way first, before we discuss them further. The majority of ferns send up their leaves from a central growing point, but some have a long creeping rhizome, or underground stem, from which leaves are only produced at intervals. These latter are not liable to worry the houseplant grower much, unless he grows *Davallia bullata*. The stem which carries the fronds is known as a *stipe*. Some ferns have simple leaves, but the majority are made up of numerous leaflets and they are designated as follows. The fronds that emerge direct from the stipe are known as *pinnae*, while fronds that emerge from the pinnae are referred to as *pinnules*. These latter are normally rather minute, but in the case of some of the Maidenhair ferns (*Adiantum* spp.) they may be quite sizeable. Some ferns bear distinct fronds, some of which are sterile, while others are fertile and in some species these may be of different shapes. However in the majority of ferns all the leaves are fertile. If you look at the underside of one of these fern leaves you will see a number of small round dark dots near the edge of the leaf. These are known as *sori*. Each sorus, if examined with a powerful lens will be seen to consist of a number of minute sacs, which are known as *sporangia* and these contain a number of very fine dust-like *spores*. These are so fine that they can be transported in air currents quite literally

183

around the world. There is no temperate climate and there are not many tropical ones, where Bracken is not found. The Maidenhair fern, *Adiantum capillus-veneris* is not only a rare British plant, but turns up in places as far apart as South Africa, Polynesia, Ceylon, the U.S.A. and the banks of the Amazon. We probably breathe in fern spores in almost every breath we take. When the spore settles on a suitable spot it starts to grow and forms a flat green plate known as a prothallus, which is only one cell thick and rarely more than $\frac{1}{4}$ inch across. On the underside of this the sexual organs are developed and fertilization is effected by the male *antherozoid* swimming over to the female organ, the *oosphere*. Once this has taken place, and it can only be done under moist conditions, the true fern plant will start to appear. Although it would seem very improbable, on occasions where different spores have landed in close proximity, hybrids have occurred. Possibly with electron microscopes it might now be possible to produce these artificially, but we do not think that it has yet been done. Raising ferns from spores is not unduly difficult, but it is usually left to specialists, as the technique is somewhat different from raising flowering plants from seed.

So much for this rather tedious aspect of ferns. Let us now turn to their cultivation. Many are very suitable for room work as they may generally be expected to tolerate shady conditions, although by no means all ferns are shade lovers. They require ample moisture during the growing season and are generally intolerant of drought at all times, although there are a few exceptions which need not worry the houseplant grower, who should keep his ferns rather drier in the dark months, but never let them dry out completely at any time. Ferns also require perfect drainage, with the exception of some marsh dwellers, which, once more, will not be met by the houseplant grower. The classical compost for most ferns is composed of equal parts of peat, leaf mould and good loam with a quarter part each of sharp sand and granulated charcoal. For epiphytic species, which for us means *Asplenium nidus* and *Platycerium bifurcatum*, the great fern growers of the last century used a mixture of equal parts of peat and sharp sand. They will all succeed fairly well in loamless mixtures. Ferns should never be overpotted, but equally they do not do well if they become too pot-bound and are usually potted on yearly, at the end of March and sometimes again at the end of June if they are growing vigorously and a large specimen is wanted. Ferns are very sensitive to any damage to their roots and care must, therefore, be taken to see that they are not harmed when repotting is taking place.

It is perhaps rather interesting to note that the first large scale introduction of tropical ferns into this country was due to Captain Bligh. After his first attempt to bring Breadfruit plants from Tahiti to the West Indies was foiled by the famous mutiny on *Bounty*, he made a second and successful attempt on *Providence* and brought back a large collection of plants from the West Indies for the Royal Gardens at Kew, including thirty-seven species of ferns. The naming of ferns is even more capricious than in most other branches of plant life and our names are those under which the plants are liable to be offered. They are only just starting to make a comeback after their great popularity in the last century and, although the number of species suitable for houseplants is very large, the amount that are obtainable is by no means commensurate. The Ferns have been arranged by botanists into a small number of families, but all the ones with which we shall be concerned are placed in the *Polypodiaceae*.

The earliest writers included the *Selaginellas* among the ferns, but they seem to occupy an intermediate position between the ferns and the mosses and, although very ornamental, tend to need too moist an atmosphere to prove very satisfactory as houseplants, although they are, apparently, grown on the Continent, so possibly some species might be worth considering. They are grown in shallow pans in a mixture of peat, sand and chopped sphagnum moss, although any open mixture appears satisfactory. The majority need shady conditions and a constant temperature of 55°–65° throughout the year, with as little variation as possible.

As can be seen with *Philodendrons*, with their leaves varying in shape from the jagged leaves of *P. bipinatifidum* to the heart-shaped leaves of *P. scandens*, leaf shape is by no means a constant in many genera and the shape of the fronds is not a guide to the genus of a fern. Even the Maidenhair ferns, although easily distinguished and all belonging to the genus *Adiantum* do not necessarily characterize this genus. There are other *Adiantums,* which do not look remotely like a Maidenhair and the assignation of a fern to its proper genus is a matter for a specialist, armed with lens and microscope. Unless you move in pteridological circles, which neither of us do, it is not possible to always be sure even of the correct genus of a fern, let alone its specific identity and we are sticking here to the names in the *R.H.S. Dictionary of Gardening* and hoping for the best.

Genus ADIANTUM

Adiantos is the Greek for dry, and if you immerse a frond of *Adiantum* in water, you will see that it does not get wet, but is protected by a silvery layer of air bubbles. Here are found the graceful Maidenhair ferns, with their characteristic thin black stipes and stalked pinnules, which are usually more or less rectangular.

1. Adiantum cuneatum

Cuneatum means that the pinnules are wedge-shaped. This is a very variable fern, but the stipes are usually from 6 to 9 inches long, while the fronds may be as much as twice this length and are three or four pinnate. A particularly graceful form has been named *A. gracillimum.* This does not need great heat, although it is a native of Brazil, and a minimum of 50° in winter is quite sufficient. Like almost all ferns, it must never be allowed to dry out completely and it likes shaded conditions, but these should not be too dark.

2. Adiantum tenerum (Plate 81)

This is, probably in the form known as *farleyense,* the most splendid as well as the best-known Maidenhair. A form slightly less splendid than *farleyense,* but easier for room conditions, is now known as var. *Ghiesbreghtii,* but used to be known as *A. scutum. Scutum* is the Latin for a shield and the pinnules are

186

shield-shaped. This has stipes up to a foot high and fronds that may be twice as long, which are a bright green in colour. The var. *gloriosum*, sometimes called *scutum roseum* has the young fronds a delicate salmon pink in colour. This plant should have a winter temperature of 60° although 55° is quite possible, and given a well-lit situation, which will not receive direct sunshine. It will take plenty of water during summer, but must be watered fairly sparingly in the winter, although it can never be allowed to dry out completely.

All these *Adiantums* are evergreen, but eventually the fronds will die and must then be tracked down to their base and cut out. They enjoy feeding, but should only be potted on when they have filled their pot completely. They resent water on the fronds and should not be syringed. Species that might well be re-introduced are *A. fulvum*, a strong growing plant from New Zealand, with delicate pink young fronds, which would tolerate cool conditions and *A. rubellum* and *A. tinctum*, both from Peru and both with bright crimson young fronds. These would need a winter temperature of 60°.

Genus ASPLENIUM

In medieval days an extract from the fronds of this fern were thought to be a good medicine for diseases of the spleen, but when Linnaeus came to name the genus, this had been disproved, so Linnaeus called it from the Greek *a*, meaning not, and *splen*, the spleen; not for the spleen. This is a wildly confusing genus of about 700 species, all with somewhat thick fronds of very varying shapes. All *Aspleniums* must have extremely well-drained soil. A distinguishing feature of the genus is the position of the sori, which are usually near the midrib and never on the margin of the leaves, as in so many other ferns.

1. Asplenium bulbiferum

A tufted plant with all the fronds arising from a central growing point. The stipes are up to a foot long, usually less, while the fronds, which arch over at the ends, are up to 2 feet long and half as broad. Usually the fronds are considerably smaller. They are two or three pinnate and light green in colour. When the plants are mature they produce small bulbils on the upper surface of the leaves and these will soon start to produce fronds. If these are removed, when they have two or three little fronds and pressed on to a box of a peat, sand and loam mixture, they will soon root and can be potted up when sufficiently large, so that it is easy to increase your stock. The plant will survive with a winter temperature as low as 45°, although 50° is much to be preferred and will tolerate some direct sunlight, although this is not at all essential. They will even survive for some time in quite dark shade, although they will not enjoy it. This is an ideal plant for children, as they can grow on the babies and one of us dates his love of plants from the appearance of one of these in the schoolroom.

2. Asplenium nidus (Plate 80)

The Bird's Nest Fern is a plant with a large distribution in the tropics, while var. *australasicum* gets as far south as New South Wales and is the hardiest form. It has simple fronds, lanceolate in shape and, in really mature plants, they can reach a length of 4 feet and a width of 8 inches. The hardiest variety can be distinguished by its black midrib and this will survive with a winter temperature of 50°. Plants with green midribs should have a winter temperature of 60°. They are small plants when purchased and require to be potted on from time to time, although, since they are epiphytic in the wild, they do not make much in the way of roots, so that it is a question of balance rather than soil which will guide you as to when to pot on. Being epiphytic they need a very moist atmosphere in the spring and summer and so the pot is best placed in a larger container, with peat or some other water-retaining substance and this must be always kept very damp, while the compost for the fern should always be moist but never more. In Victorian Days, the var. *australasicum* was put out of doors during the summer as a feature in the subtropical bedding that was favoured in those days. It might, therefore, advantageous to stand our plants outside in shady situations be during the period mid-June to mid-August. Perfect drainage is essential for this fern, so that the loamless composts are very suitable when you are potting the plants on. Owing to their small root system they respond better to foliar feeds than to the more normal type. Owing to its entire fronds, so different from any other *Asplenium*, it was at one time placed in a genus of its own, *Thamnopteris*.

The *R.H.S. Dictionary* states that 'two species that may be regarded as indispensable to any good collection of ferns are *A. flabellifolium* and *A. flaccidum*', but at the moment they must, perforce, be dispensed with, as they are not generally obtainable.

Genus CYRTOMIUM

Named from *cyrtos*, the Greek for an arch, although their foliage is not, in reality, particularly arched, but somewhat rigid.

1. Cyrtomium falcatum

Sometimes known as the Holly Fern, although it shares this name with some others, this makes a tufted plant, with rather short stipes, usually only about 6 inches long and massive fronds, up to 18 inches long. These are simply pinnate and the pinnules are sickle-shaped (falcate), about 3 or 4 inches long and up to $1\frac{1}{2}$ inches across. They are very thick and leathery, somewhat glossy and rather dark green for a fern. It is a rapid grower and will thrive in quite dark situations and, what is even more uncommon among houseplants, has no objection to draughts. The recommended compost for this fern is equal parts of loam, peat and sharp sand. During the winter it should be kept on the dry side, but when the new fronds start to elongate it should have plenty of water throughout its growing season and also enjoys its leaves being sprayed in hot weather. It likes cool conditions and, indeed, will grow out of doors in many places. 45° is a perfectly acceptable winter minimum. In the wild the plant has a wide distribution from India to Hawaii, with the hardiest forms originating in Japan and China. This fern must have shady conditions.

189

Genus DAVALLIA

Named in honour of a Swiss botanist, E. Davall. The species grown as houseplants are, rather unusually, deciduous, and their creeping rhizome, which has been thought to resemble a hare's foot, is very attractive in itself as it is cylindrical in shape and covered with bristles or scales. This rhizome grows on the top of the soil and once it has filled its container it will grow over the side and tend to encircle it. Owing to its creeping habit and shallow rooting, ordinary flower pots are not the most suitable containers for these ferns. The most suitable, if they are obtainable, are orchid rafts, which are composed of wooden slats with large interstices, which allow the rhizome to emerge from the sides as well as the surface. Failing these, pans are probably the most suitable, although hanging baskets are also employed. Hanging baskets are a nuisance to water, although they look attractive otherwise. A light compost is required for these ferns and one recommended is composed of three parts peat, one part leaf mould and one part sharp sand. The plants require ample water in the growing season and to be kept just moist during the autumn and winter.

1. Davallia bullata

Sometimes known as the Squirrel's Foot fern, this produces a stout rhizome, which contorts itself around the surface of the pot, often forking as it goes. The stipes are up to 4 inches long and the fronds up to 8 inches, forming a triangular shape and they are four-pinnate, giving a very feathery impression and a good bright green in colour. The plant requires to be kept cool in the winter, not higher than 50°, and also to be kept shaded. *D. mariesii* with a rather more slender rhizome is hardy outside.

2. Davallia canariensis

The Hare's Foot fern is larger in all its parts than *D. bullata* and the thick rhizome is covered with hairy scales, so that it does look very like a hare's foot. The fronds can reach a length of 15 inches, but are similar in shape to those of *D. bullata*, but a rather darker green. The scales on the rhizome of *D. bullata* are a reddish brown, while those on *D. canariensis* are light brown. *D. canariensis* tends to keep its fronds over the winter and can therefore tolerate a little more water during this period. It will be quite happy with a winter temperature as low as 45°.

Genus NEPHROLEPIS

From the Greek words *nephros*, kidney and *lepis* a scale, as the sori are kidney-shaped.

1. Nephrolepis cordifolia var. compacta

The various forms of *N. cordata* are liable to bear tubers on their roots when well established and these will produce separate plants the following season, so that propagation is not difficult. If placed in a hanging basket, they are liable to colonize the outside, so that the basket itself is well-nigh invisible. The var. *compacta* has arching fronds, about 18 inches long, which are simply pinnate; the pinnules are about an inch long, so that the breadth of the frond is 2 inches. The fronds are somewhat leathery and are toothed at the margins. If *Nephrolepis* are allowed to dry out for any length of time, they drop all their pinnules, but soon recover to make fresh fronds, although it is naturally better that they should not dry out. *N. cordifolia* requires a winter temperature of 50° and has no objection to quite bright light, although it will also tolerate shady conditions.

2. Nephrolepis exaltata (Plate 82)

This is often claimed to be the best fern for growing in rooms. It makes a rosette of rather stiff fronds, generally simply pinnate, but bipinnate in the form known as 'Whitmannii', the fronds may be as much as 30 inches long and 6 inches across at their base; the stipes are from 4 to 6 inches long. The plant is a little sensitive to draughts, but otherwise seems to be trouble free. It requires a winter temperature not lower than 50° and ample water during the growing season, while it is kept moist at all times. It is said that if the end of the frond is pegged down, it will root, but since fresh plants are produced fairly freely from the wiry rhizome, it is probably not worth experimenting. Wire baskets, lined with moss, are probably better than pots for *Nephrolepis*, as the young plants can emerge from all round, but they do pose questions of watering and are probably best avoided in normal rooms, however excellent they may be in the conservatory.

Genus PLATYCERIUM

From the Greek *platys* broad and *keras*, horn, in reference to the very characteristic shape of the fertile fronds. This is a genus of epiphytal ferns that are immediately recognizable. They produce two types of fronds: the sterile ones are circular and clasp the tree branch or whatever is acting as host for the plant, while the fertile fronds are shaped like antlers and are held erect. The majority of species need high temperatures but, like *Asplenium nidus*, there is an outlier in New South Wales, which will tolerate quite low temperatures.

1. Platycerium bifurcatum

Sometimes met with as *P. alcicorne*, the Elk's Horn fern. Both the sterile and fertile fronds are covered with down when young and a sort of waxy secretion when mature, which seems to keep the fronds free from dust and the fronds should, therefore, neither be sprayed nor sponged. The sterile fronds are circular and die off each year, to be replaced by further circles; the plant seems to derive some nourishment from the old fronds and they should be left on the plant, even after they have apparently died. The plants like a moist atmosphere, but not too much water around their roots and can be left until they flag and then watered thoroughly. In the greenhouse they are often secured to tree boughs or blocks of cork bark and these have to be soaked in a bucket, when the plant has dried out. When growing in pots, the pot should be canted at an angle, as the plant naturally grows on a vertical surface and the fronds look at their best, when they can emerge horizontally. The plants will also do well in hanging baskets, which they gradually colonize, so that every orifice will have its own plant. If they are in these containers, they can be periodically lowered into a bucket, when watering becomes necessary. The classical compost for these ferns consists of equal parts of coarse peat and chopped sphagnum moss, to which a little charcoal is added. Chopped bracken seems to be an acceptable substitute for sphagnum, which is not always easy to obtain. The plants require shady conditions and a winter temperature not falling below 50°, while 55° is certainly preferable. If they are in pots, they only require potting on, when the plant has become so large that it is top-heavy. This is a remarkably unusual-looking fern and well worth the extra trouble that its habit of growth entails in the matter of watering. In old gardening books this may appear under the generic name of *Acrostichum*. Surprisingly, in view of its exotic appearance, it was recommended for room-work as long ago as 1876.

Genus PTERIS

From *pteros*, the Greek for a feather; the name was originally applied to some unidentified fern by Dioscorides. These ferns will thrive in the normal soil mixtures.

1. Pteris biaurita var. **argyraea** (Plate 84)

An attractive fern with long stipes, up to 18 inches long, while the fronds themselves range from 6 to 12 inches in length. They are bipinnate with shining green fronds with a wide silver band down the centre of each pinna, which gives the plant a very striking and attractive appearance. The plant will grow in nearly any situation, although it must be in the shade when the new fronds are unfurling, otherwise the variegation will not develop properly. Although of tropical origin, it will be quite happy with a winter temperature of 50°. *Pteris* should never be allowed to dry out at any time, although they naturally require less water in the winter and autumn.

2. Pteris cretica (Plate 85)

Although this is found in Crete, it has a very wide distribution and has proved remarkably variable. The more or less typical form has stipes about 6 inches long and long thin fronds, up to a foot in length and an inch across, while the tips of these fronds are much divided and sometimes crested. They bear both sterile and fertile fronds and the sterile fronds are broader than the more erect fertile ones. There is a variegated form known as *albo lineata*, with a broad band of creamy white in the centre of each pinna, but the form most often seen is the large vigorous *'Wimsettii'*, which has fronds up to 2 feet long, with a sort of tassel at the tip of each pinna. All these ferns are very easy of growth, which can be very rapid, so that yearly repotting is generally essential. Neither aspect nor soil seem to be of much importance in growing this satisfactorily, although *albo lineata* must have shade when the young fronds are unfurling. A winter temperature of 45° is ample and the plant survives outdoors in mild localities.

3. Pteris multifida var. major

P. multifida, the Spider fern, is not dissimilar in appearance from *P. cretica*, but the pinnules are longer and thinner, not more than ¼ inch across. The var. *major* is characterized by arching fronds that may, in well-grown mature specimens, reach a length of 30 inches. At one time there was a very robust crested form of *P. multifida* known as 'Rochfordii', but this seems to have departed with so many other selected clones, while ferns were in the doldrums. *P. multifida* needs a winter temperature of 50°, otherwise it is as undemanding as the other *Pteris* species. In older books it may be met with as *P. serrulata*. There was a variegated form of this known, although it seems to have died out in this country.

CHAPTER XI

Miscellaneous 1

I. URTICACEAE

T he Nettle family contains some 500 species, divided among forty genera, of which the Hop is the most important economically. As far as houseplants are concerned, there are two genera and eight species that are grown.

Genus PILEA

A genus of over 200 species, mostly rather weedy plants, found in all the tropics, except Australia.

1. Pilea cadierei (Plate 86)

The popular Aluminium Plant was introduced from Vietnam in 1938 and it is thought that all the plants in existence have been derived from this original introduction, which propagates very readily from cuttings. The plant throws out a number of stems from the base, bearing opposite pairs of oblong oval leaves up to 3 inches long and 1½ inches across. The leaves contain three principal veins and around these the leaves are dark green, while between them are large silver patches, which occupy most of the leaf. The original plant tended to become very straggly and needed stopping twice yearly to keep it well leafed, but fortunately a compact form has sported, to which the varietal name 'nana' has been given, and this keeps a good shape without any stopping being necessary, although it helps to nip out the growing points in April. A winter temperature of 50° appears quite sufficient for this plant, although from its provenance one would have thought that higher temperatures would have been necessary. Moderate light is required and a moist atmosphere improves all the Pileas, although they will survive in quite dry conditions without much ill effect. They will thrive in the ivy mixture or in JIP 2, but they seem to do better in this latter compost if extra peat is added.

2. Pilea involucrata

This is generally known as *P. spruceana*, but other species, including *P. mollis* are also sold under this name, so that it has become rather meaningless. The name *spruceana* commemorates Richard Spruce who botanized for many years in South America and who was responsible for bringing the Quinine tree from Ecuador to India. This is a dwarf, slow-growing plant with leaves produced four at a time, set crosswise. These leaves are oval in shape, slightly hairy and a dark bronzy green; the surface is somewhat wrinkled. The leaves reach a length of 2 inches and a width of $1\frac{1}{2}$ inches. The stems branch freely without any stopping being necessary. The plant is found in South America.

3. Pilea microphylla

The small-leaved Pilea, perhaps better known as *P. muscosa*, the Mossy Pilea. This makes a much branched little plant, not more than 6 inches tall with the stems covered with rosettes of very tiny leaves, which are a bright green. During the summer nearly invisible flowers are produced in the centre of these rosettes and these flowers, if the plants are shaken in any way, throw out clouds of pollen. This has given the plant such names as Gunpowder Plant and Artillery Plant. It needs a better lit situation than the other Pileas discussed here, which prefer a somewhat shaded situation, although preferably not too dark. Given a winter temperature of 50° the plant is very easy, although its plain green leaves and mossy appearance have militated against its popularity. With the increased interest in ferns it is perhaps due for a comeback.

4. Pilea mollis (Plate 88)

A very striking foliage plant from Mexico. The leaves are so wrinkled as to appear covered with warts, shaped like a stinging nettle leaf and capable of reaching a length of 4 inches and a width of $2\frac{1}{2}$ inches. When they first unfurl they are almost entirely maroon in colour, with an emerald green margin, but as the leaf ages the maroon tends to fade to a pure bright green. The plant should be shaded, but not dark and have a winter temperature around 55°. Abundant feeding during the summer will give exceptionally large leaves, which are very striking. We have seen this plant offered as *P. spruceana*, but it is quite distinct in its bicoloured leaves.

5. Pilea species 'Norfolk'

A plant brought from Mexico by Mr. Maurice Mason and still unnamed, although it would appear allied to the Venezuelan *P. forgetii*. The leaves are an elongated oval in shape and rounded at the tips, not pointed as are those of *P. mollis* and *P. cadierei*, up to 3 inches long and half as wide. On the upper surface they are a very dark green along the principal veins and silver grey in between, while the margins are pink. The underside of the leaf is a dull purplish red, while the stems are also reddish, covered with silvery hairs. The pink margin eventually fades from the leaves as they age. This makes a very congested plant, with a pair of leaves about every inch and sideshoots coming from the leaf axils, so that it soon makes a very bushy dwarf clump. It likes a moist atmosphere and the winter temperature should be around 60°. It likes to be shaded from direct sunlight, but should not be in a very dark position, otherwise the various colours in the leaves will not give of their best. During the winter watering must be watched, as it is rather a sappy plant and excessive wet during cold dull spells can prove fatal.

6. Pilea nummularifolia

A creeping plant, which throws out roots from the nodes, so

that it is very easy to propagate. It is much grown on the Continent, particularly for hanging baskets, but has found no favour in Great Britain. The stems and leaves are somewhat hairy; the leaves are yellowish-green, nearly circular, about ¾ inch in diameter and the plant will grow very freely with a winter temperature around 55°. The plant's greatest advantage is that it has no objection to quite heavy shade, but it is not very outstanding in itself.

Genus PELLIONIA

This genus is named in honour of Alphonse Pellion, who accompanied Admiral M. Freycinet in his voyage around the world in the early nineteenth century.

1. Pellionia daveauana

Jules Daveau was director of the Lisbon Botanical Gardens; he lived from 1852 to 1929. *P. daveauana* is a trailer from the Far East with roundish leaves of bronzy green, which may attain 2 inches in length, and which are slightly tinged with violet. This also will emit clouds of pollen when in flower. Although very attractive when young, the plant is apt to become rather bare around the centre as it grows and should therefore either be used in a mixed group or frequently re-propagated. Cuttings root quickly in warm weather, and it is not hard to replace a plant that has become too large. The centre can also be refurnished by cutting the plant back, but this is rather a slow job.

2. Pellionia pulchra (Plate 87)

Also from the Far East, this *Pellionia* has rounded leaves 1 inch long, of a beautiful iridescent silvery green with dark green markings along the veins: in newly emerged leaves these markings are a dull vermilion. It makes a more satisfactory plant than *P. daveauana*, as the centre remains green and it grows more slowly: the leaves, too, are set closer together on the stems. It requires a shady situation and should remain damp at the roots. It should be treated as slightly tender and kept on the dry side in the winter, though it must never dry out entirely.

II. PROTEACEAE

A large family of some 1,100 species in fifty genera. A hundred years ago they were very popular, but are less so today as the most spectacular species are large shrubs and require greenhouse protection, although great heat is not necessary.

Genus GREVILLEA

Named in honour of Charles Greville, a founder of the Royal Horticultural Society.

1. Grevillea robusta

Although capable of forming a tree over 100 feet high, this makes an attractive plant within 6 months of seed sowing. It has large fern-like leaves, sometimes as much as 12 inches long, bronzy green in colour and silky beneath. It is very hardy and easy to grow, the main snag being its attraction for Red Spider, which is hard to detect and which will cause leaf fall very quickly. After some years the lower leaves fall and the plant takes on a more tree-like appearance. The plant responds well to feeding. Propagation is invariably by seed.

Genus STENOCARPUS

The name comes from two Greek words meaning narrow fruit.

1. Stenocarpus sinuatus (Plate 89)

One of the most delightful and easy of houseplants, which can be grown out of doors in the Scilly Isles and so requires no more heat than is necessary to keep out frost. The plant is a native of New South Wales and Queensland, where it makes a large tree with conspicuous red flowers. It is possible that there may be two species confused under the one name, as the plant appears to have two distinct leaf forms. The form which is cultivated as a houseplant has leaves that suggest a large deeply incised oak leaf, and, in a large specimen, these can apparently reach 12 inches in length and 9 inches across. These are a pleasant green, but the young leaves emerge reddish in colour and the plant is very agreeable to look at. Plants are grown from seed and may be stopped after two years to encourage the production of side branches. A light situation is preferable and the plant will need to be potted on at fairly frequent intervals. Although it flowers when young, it is improbable that it would do this in the house, but if the plant could be grown on in a conservatory, you would eventually be rewarded by handsome scarlet flowers. The stems and young leaves are slightly silky in appearance. This plant seems little known and should, we feel, become more popular.

III. POLYGONACEAE

Although there are some 750 species in this family, which includes the Bistorts and Snakeweeds, only one is suitable for a houseplant.

Genus MUEHLENBECKIA

Named after a Swiss doctor, H. G. Muehlenbeck, who lived from 1798 to 1845.

1. Muehlenbeckia platyclados

A very curious-looking plant from the Solomon Islands, quick growing and reasonably hardy. In the young stage it is difficult to tell what parts of the plant are the leaves and what part the stems, as the latter are flat and leaf-like, while the actual leaves are very similar in appearance. As the plant matures the lower stems round out and take on the appearance of a bamboo shoot. The plant is quick growing and bushy and in its native country will reach a height of some 3 feet, though 18 inches is the normal height under cultivation. The plant is a bright middle-green in colour. It is perhaps more curious than beautiful, but is always interesting. It will thrive in the same soil mixture as is suitable for the *Peperomias*. It should be kept out of draughts, which it dislikes strongly. It is propagated by cuttings, which are not easy to root.

IV. NYCTAGINACEAE

This is a small family of only some 120 species, distributed among ten genera. Only one of these is of interest to the house-plant grower.

Genus HEIMERLIODENDRON

Into this unwieldy name has gone the plant called Pisonia in our second edition.

1. Heimerliodendron brunonianum variegatum

Although this plant turns up in a number of tropical gardens, very little seems to be known as to its origins, but probably it is native to islands of the Malaysian Archipelago. In these tropical gardens it forms a small tree, but grown in the greenhouse it tends to make a bushy plant with numerous secondary growths ascending from the base. The leaves are rounded, more or less oval in shape, set very densely on the stems and light green in colour with irregular blotches of cream and dark green. This is a very attractive plant, but very difficult as a houseplant, since it requires a moist atmosphere at all times, as well as high tem-peratures. Although plants have survived with a winter tem-perature of 55°, at least ten degrees more are required for good growth, while the summer temperature should preferably be around 75°. It requires ample light, but should be shielded from too much direct sunlight through glass, which can easily scorch the foliage. This is best treated as a greenhouse plant, which can be brought into the house for limited periods.

V. CRASSULACEAE

The *Crassulaceae* are composed of plants all characterized by their fleshy succulent leaves. As a result they are chiefly found in dry places, and are very suitable as houseplants, from the survival point of view. Most of them, however, are curious rather than beautiful. They are not a very large family, some 600 species distributed among fifteen genera. Only two are generally grown, and one of these is not a true houseplant.

Genus AICHRYSON
1. Aichryson × domesticum variegatum

A. × domesticum is a garden hybrid of which only one of the parents is known. This was *A. tortuosum*. The *Aichrysons* are natives of the Canary Islands where they grow in full sun and in very little soil. In the nursery the same mixture as that advised for *Peperomias* has been found the most satisfactory for producing a nice plant rapidly, but it will be happy in any mixture that is not too rich. In its early stages the plant produces a short stem, densely covered with leaves the shape of an oar-blade, attaining a length of 1 inch. The young leaves are a pure ivory, with but little green, but as the leaves age the centre becomes a dark olive-green and only a narrow ivory margin is left. As the plant matures the elongating stem drops its lower leaves and the resultant plant is like a Japanese tree. The plant can be kept as dry as you like, though it will grow more rapidly if kept damp in the summer. It likes fairly strong light, and, if it cannot be given this, it must be kept on the cool side, as otherwise it will become rather floppy. The plant may be regarded as very hardy. Cuttings root easily and quickly.

Genus SEDUM

The largest genus in this family, with some 300 species including our native Stonecrops.

1. Sedum sieboldii

The variety grown as a houseplant is termed *medio-variegatum*, or variegated in the middle, so called because the centre of the rounded leaves is yellow, while the margin is the blue-green that is the natural colour of the type. The type, a native of Japan, will grow out of doors, but the variegated form would probably succumb in a severe winter. This easily grown plant is not a true houseplant, as its growth is only of annual duration. At the end of October it will die down and will not start into growth again until about late February. Before dying down the plant produces heads of pink flowers that are small in size, but many-flowered. While growing the plant likes light, but little water; a very damp soil seems to inhibit root growth. When growth is completed and the shoots start to yellow, water should be withheld altogether, and the plants kept quite dry until February when they are given a good soak to restart growth. Once this soaking has been given, water should be again withheld until it is seen that growth is starting and that the soil has dried out. When growth and roots are well advanced the plant can be potted on. Propagation is by cuttings and it is most satisfactory to take every top cutting from one plant, which will then break again evenly. Six to seven cuttings placed in a 3-inch pot will soon grow into a handsome-looking potful of plants. The type plant with blue-green leaves may be considered by some to be more handsome than the variegated form. As there are certain to be a few sprays that have lost their variegation, this is easy to obtain. The plant is very hardy and blends well with other houseplants. The same soil mixture as for *Peperomias* will suit this plant, as will any rather heavy mixture made open with plenty of sharp sand.

Although difficult to obtain, many species of *Aeonium*, a genus endemic to the Canary Islands, are suitable as houseplants. These plants make rosettes of fleshy leaves, sometimes unstalked, and sometimes on stems so that they look like miniature trees. They like bright conditions and are used to being extremely dry. During the summer some of the larger species, such as *A. canariense*, which is capable of producing a rosette 3 feet across, tend to curl in on themselves and look less attractive; moving the plants to a more shaded position will help to overcome this.

VI. SAXIFRAGACEAE

The *Saxifraga* family is represented among the houseplants by that old favourite, Mother of Thousands, and its variegated form *tricolor*.

Genus SAXIFRAGA

The name is formed from two Latin words and means rock-breaker. Many of the species grow in rock crevices. (An alternative derivation is that an infusion of the leaves was believed to disperse gallstones.)

1. Saxifraga stolonifera (Plate 90)

Invariably known and sold under the name of *Saxifraga sarmentosa*. Nearly hardy out of doors, this old favourite is easy to grow and it throws runners like a strawberry, so that further stock is easily obtainable. Its London Pride-like flowers are also attractive. The short-stalked rounded leaves are marbled. This makes a very attractive plant if placed so that the runners hang down all round the plant.

The var. *tricolor* has handsome leaves variegated red, cream and green. It is more tender than the type, a much slower grower and does not throw so many runners. It is not easy to get the young plants to grow away. JIP is a satisfactory soil mixture for the *Saxifraga*.

VII. PITTOSPORACEAE

A small family of 120 species divided among ten genera. The *Pittosporum* that is sold as foliage for cut flowers is *Pittosporum tenuifolium*.

Genus PITTOSPORUM

Named from two Greek words meaning pitch and seed, because many of the seeds are coated with a tar-like resin.

1. Pittosporum eugenioides

This grows outdoors in a few favoured places in Cornwall, but it is essentially a plant for the home or cool greenhouse. Although it will eventually make a large tree it takes a very long time doing it. It is a native of New Zealand. The shiny green leaves are some 2 to 3 inches long and $\frac{3}{4}$ inch across. They are produced at intervals in groups of four around the wiry branches and make a very elegant-looking small tree, which is very hardy as a houseplant. It is not a very fast grower, but will respond well if not starved, but potted on regularly. Of course there is a limit as to how large a pot will be convenient. It would be possible to go on potting this up until it ended in a tub, by which time you would probably have a tree some 10 feet high. It is very slow to propagate by seed, and cuttings, although more satisfactory, do not root easily or quickly. There is a variegated form, which is highly spoken of.

2. Pittosporum tobira

This is occasionally offered as a houseplant, though it is not clear exactly why. The rounded leathery leaves look like those of some rhododendron of the *Neriiflorum* series (these are shorter and narrower than the majority). The plant is less hardy than *eugenioides*, though it is not particularly tender. The variegated form is not very agreeable. Under suitable conditions the shrub will produce fragrant flowers, but these are not liable to be seen in the home.

VIII. ROSACEAE

The Rose family is not well represented amongst houseplants. Indeed there are only two species and one has some disadvantages.

Genus RUBUS

This genus includes the raspberry and the blackberry.

1. Rubus reflexus var. pictus (Plate 52)

This name is probably incorrect, but we know of no other. This is a handsome trailer with lobed leaves of a bright green colour with maroon blotches along the main vein of each lobe. The number of lobes may vary from three to five and the maroon is far more conspicuous in the younger leaves. A mature leaf is 5 inches long and about 3 inches in width. The stems will elongate almost indefinitely, but if stopped, will branch in an attractive manner. The plant is extremely hardy, needing only to be kept free of frost. It likes a well-lit position. Occasionally a branch may appear without the maroon blotches. This should be cut back to the second leaf that is marked, so that future growth will be of the desired type. Propagation is by cuttings. This is an easy and handsome houseplant.

Genus ERIOBOTRYA

The name is derived from two Greek words meaning a cluster of wool, owing to the woolly appearance of the new growth.

1. Eriobotrya japonica

This is the Loquat or Nespoli tree and has been offered under the wildly incorrect name of *Ficus nespoli*. As the plant can be grown outdoors against a south wall, it has the advantage of extreme hardiness as a houseplant. The long lance-shaped leaves, from 6 to 12 inches long and 3 to 6 inches across, are not truly evergreen and seldom persist more than three years, while during their second season they tend to turn brown at the tips and have to be trimmed with nail scissors. To offset these disadvantages, the new growth is a wonderful pearly grey in colour and covered with soft down. The plant grows freely from seed and will thrive in JIP. It likes a well-lit position. It is not usually obtainable from houseplant growers, but many shrub nurseries supply it. As it ages, it tends to become leggy and unsightly and can then be planted out in a sheltered situation in the garden.

IX. RUTACEAE

The Rue family also includes the various *Citrus*. Although the ordinary Orange is too large for most rooms, there exists one reasonably small species.

1. Citrus sinensis

Since this is the name given to the majority of sweet oranges there is considerable doubt as to its being correct. This is, however, the name under which the plant is invariably sold. *Citrus sinensis* is a small slow-growing shrub, requiring cool conditions and a certain amount of light. When sufficiently developed it will produce clusters of small white flowers with the delicious orange-blossom fragrance and these will be followed by small fruits resembling lemons as much as oranges. Propagation is by cuttings, and the theory that they have to be grafted on to a bitter orange rootstock to produce flowers is a child of fantasy. They will flower and fruit on their own roots without the slightest trouble. This is an easy plant to grow, although mature specimens are rather expensive and with immature specimens you may have to wait a few years before the plant flowers. The leaves are a pleasant glossy green.[1]

2. Citrus mitis (Plate 91)

The Calamondin is a delightful dwarf orange from the Philippines. The adjective *mitis* means smooth, as most citrus species have thorns, although they are never very fierce and, in point of fact if you sow the pips of *C. mitis*, the young plants will be quite spiny, although the mature plant is unarmed. *C. mitis* makes a small bush, which starts to flower and fruit at an early age if raised from cuttings; seedlings appear to take much longer to come into bearing. The leaves are medium green, oval, about $1\frac{1}{2}$ inches long and $\frac{3}{4}$ inch across. The white flowers are usually produced about March, but can appear either earlier or later and have the typical orange blossom perfume and they are followed by a small round orange-coloured fruit, about $1\frac{1}{2}$ inches in diameter. These are edible and have a taste reminiscent of limes. During the winter the plants should be kept at a temperature of 55°, although 50° is quite acceptable and at this period they must not dry out, although the usual warnings against overwatering apply here as always. When the flower buds are seen an occasional syringeing is advisable and this is most essential to help set the fruit when the flowers are open and care must be taken that the plant never dries out while the fruits are swelling, otherwise they will drop off. At the end of June the

---

[1] This plant is always sold under the name given here, but it is in reality the Kumquat, *Fortunella japonica*.

plants should be stood out in full light, where they can receive any sunshine that is available and kept somewhat on the dry side, in order to ripen the wood. If this is not done the plant is rather unlikely to flower again, although it will continue to make growth. The leaves may get rather discoloured during this period, but when the plants are brought in again, which is towards the end of September, it is not long before they re-acquire the lustrous green they had before. Although it requires a little more trouble than many other houseplants the attractive scented flowers and the glowing orange fruits are more than a recompense for any additional labour.

X. EUPHORBIACEAE

The Spurge family contains some 4,500 species distributed among 210 genera. Although they take many different vegetative forms, from trees to small annuals, they all contain a milky juice which flows freely at the slightest wound. From the houseplant point of view this large family is not very rewarding. The showy Crotons are not ideal for room work, although perfectly possible.

Genus CODIAEUM

The name is derived from *kodiho*, the native name of the plant in Ternatea, where, presumably, it was first collected. For some reason these plants are always known as Crotons, though *Croton* is the name of another genus, whose interest is medical rather than decorative.

1. Codiaeum variegatum var. **pictum** (Plates 92 and 96)
This plant, a native of Malaya and the archipelago, is now grown all over the tropics and sub-tropics as a garden plant. It is so variable that it is not possible to give any accurate description of a typical plant. In most varieties the leaves are an oblong-oval, but the cultivar 'Van Ostensee' has long thin, almost grass-like, leaves, which are dark green, spotted with orange. Other leaf-colours range from dark scarlet to rose-pink. It is rare that the leaf is confined to one colour, and typical combinations are light

83. Hedera helix marmorata, Platycerium bifurcatum

84. Pteris biaurita

85. Pteris cretica 'Wimsettii'

86. Pilea cadierei

87. Pellionia pulchra

88. Pilea mollis

89. Stenocarpus sinuatus

90. Saxifraga stolonifera

93. Euphorbia hermentiana

94. Euphorbia milii 'Tananarive'

95. Cuphea hyssopifolia

96. Aphelandra squarrosa louisae, Cordyline terminalis,
Codiaeum variegatum pictum

97. Beloperone guttata

98. Fittonia verschaffeltii

99. Senecio macroglossus variegatus

green and pink, scarlet and orange or nearly black and orange. When grown out of doors in the tropics the plant makes a bushy shrub some 4 feet high and is often used as a low hedge; as a pot plant usually only a single stem is grown and the plant rarely exceeds 2 feet in height. Although a constant temperature of 60° is recommended, it is probable that some 5° or 10° lower would not do any damage. The important thing would appear to be keeping the temperature constant. Sudden changes of temperature tend to cause leaf drop and should be guarded against as much as possible: draughts also, quickly cause damage. For some reason the narrow-leaved forms seem hardier than the more showy broad-leaved varieties. Propagation is by cuttings and it is necessary to dip the cutting, immediately it has been taken, in powdered charcoal to stop the bleeding. In the house, stopping is not recommended, partly owing to the bleeding that will ensue and partly owing to the fact that, as a pot plant, *Codiaeum* does not make a bushy plant. It should be regarded as similar to *Ficus elastica decora* in habit. The brightest light available should be given to *Codiaeums* and during the growing season they can be fed with advantage. If, in spite of your efforts, the plant loses a lot of leaves during the winter, it is best to cut the plant down to within some 8 inches of the ground and let it start into growth again from the bottom. Even so, without some artificial heat, the result will probably not be very satisfactory.

Genus EUPHORBIA

This name was given by Dioscorides, the father of botany, in honour of the physician to King Juba of Mauretania, who was called Euphorbus and who first used the milky latex of these plants for medicinal purposes. The genus is one of the most successful of all with well over 1,000 species ranging from annual weeds (the spurges of gardens) to trees and cactus-like succulents. All the plants contain a milky latex which gushes out, whenever the surface is punctured and this must be immediately removed with cotton wool, while still liquid, as it will eventually harden and then cannot be removed without damaging the

o

plant. If cuttings are being taken they should be immediately dipped in powdered charcoal to stem the bleeding. The house-plant *Euphorbias* are succulent or semi-succulent, with one exception; this exception is probably no longer in cultivation.

1. Euphorbia bojeri

Usually sold under the name *E. splendens* var. *bojeri*. Professor Bojer was the first systematic botanist to explore Madagascar. He would send his plants to the Botanic Garden at Mauritius and from there they went to the Botanic Garden at Calcutta, whence Nathaniel Wallich would propagate and distribute them. Anyone who has been in the tropics and seen the gorgeous Flamboyant (*Delonix regia*) planted everywhere, is probably unaware that it is confined in the wild to quite a small area of Madagascar and that it is thanks in the first place to Professor Bojer that it came into cultivation.

  E. bojeri makes a small spiny shrub and what looks like the woody stem is really not woody but succulent. It is clothed quite thickly with rather leathery, triangular leaves, which are, apparently, sometimes grey-green, but are often quite a good soft green about 1½ inches long and an inch across. These are retained on the plant for most of the season. No *Euphorbias* have showy flowers, they are always green and inconspicuous, but they may be surrounded by quite showy bracts, the most notable example being the gaudy Poinsettia. In *E. bojeri* the flowers are surrounded by two semi-circular crimson bracts. They are borne on a longish stem and two more flowers will often emerge from the centre of the first formed. The flowers start in the spring and continue for most of the summer and they are very long-lasting, so that the plant is rarely without flowers. During the winter the plant can be left with practically no water at all between December and mid-February if low temperatures are being experienced; in any case it is best that they do not fall below 50°. If high temperatures are present, the plants can be restarted into growth about a fortnight earlier or can even be kept growing the whole time. When watering is restarted this should be in very small amounts until new leaves have started to unfurl, when it can gradually be increased, although the plant never requires great quantities and should be allowed to dry out between waterings. Some cultivators recommend covering the top of the pot with small pebbles, so that water does not lodge around the base of the stem. Full light is necessary at all times and the plant will not object to direct sunlight, although in that case it should not be too near glass, as it could then get scorched. Fortunately potting on is rarely needed as the plant is very slow growing and does not make much root, but when this does take place it is as well to wear rubber gloves and if you should be pierced by a thorn, apply disinfectant immediately. The flowers are smaller than those of *E. milii* var. *splendens* and a deeper crimson.

2. Euphorbia cotinioides

Cotinioides means that the leaves are shaped like those of a *Cotinus* or Smoke tree. The leaves are nearly circular, $1\frac{1}{2}$ inches across, borne on a longish petiole and a ruby-purple in colour. Unfortunately the plant tends to be rather leggy and forms a rather lanky sub-shrub. It can be kept to manageable dimensions by stopping every spring, but stopping *Euphorbias* is a laborious business in seeing that the latex does not gush out and spoil everything, so that the plant is probably no longer available. It requires a fairly well-lit situation and a winter temperature around 55° or 60°. So far as we know the flowers have not been seen.

3. Euphorbia hermentiana (Plate 93)

This is a real child of the space age and no one would be surprised to wake up one day and find that the *Hermentianas* have taken over. The plant looks like a cactus and can eventually attain tree-like proportions, but, fortunately, is not quick growing. It produces triangular, thick fleshy stems about an inch across, with scalloped edges and a pair of stout, short spines at the top of each scallop. As the stem ascends, it sends out from its lower portion branches which are held vertically, parallel to the main stem. The main part of the thick fleshy stems are dark green, but between the spines, from the depressions of the scallops, there are wavy lines of paler green, which coalesce in the centre of the stem and form a vertical line down the centre. The plant is often confused with *E. lactea*, which is probably, indeed, the same plant from a different habitat; *E. lactea* being found wild in India, while *E. hermentiana* comes from West Africa. During the spring a few pale green, obovate leaves are produced at the tips of the branches. These are up to $1\frac{1}{2}$ inches long and $\frac{1}{2}$ inch across and do not persist for long. The plant is quite happy to be kept as low as 45° during the winter, but must then be kept absolutely dry and the atmosphere must also be dry; even so 50° is preferable. Watering can be restarted in March and can be given quite copiously when signs of growth are apparent, and the plant should always receive as much light as is available, while fresh air is much appreciated. The plant, like most of the succulent *Euphorbias*, can be propagated by cuttings. Side branches are removed and allowed to remain completely dry for at least a week. They are then inserted in sand or a sand-peat mixture, which is kept just moist and will eventually produce roots, although this is sometimes a slow process. Heat is necessary to induce rooting, while if the medium is too moist the cuttings will rot. Apparently the correct name for this plant is *E. trigona*.

4. Euphorbia milii (Plate 94)

This would appear to be a rather variable plant from Madagascar, which still seems insufficiently known.

(*a*) Var. *splendens*, which is usually known as *E. splendens*, the Crown of Thorns. This is a spiny shrub, which can eventually get as high as 3 feet, but which is very slow growing and tends to increase by producing side-branches, rather than by extending its height. It produces rather few obovate leaves, up to an inch long and heads of flowers surrounded by scarlet semi-circular bracts, which are borne on scarlet stems. These stems are branched and up to eight flowers may be produced from each stem. They start in the spring and continue for some time, while the bracts may persist for six weeks or more. The leaves do not persist for long and if the temperature falls too low, the plant may be completely leafless during the winter, when it will look rather sinister with its greyish wood and long spines. Its treatment is the same as that for *E. bojeri*, but a higher winter temperature is desirable.

(*b*) Var. 'Tananarive'. Tananarive is the capital of Madagascar and presumably this form was purchased or collected in the neighbourhood. It would seem much the best form of *E. milii*, if that is what it is. It makes a more vigorous plant than *E. splendens*, with grey spiny stems which are densely leafy; the leaves being lance-shaped, up to 2 inches long and ½ inch across. The floral bracts are the same shape as those of *E. splendens*, but primrose-yellow in colour, fading to a salmon-pink as they age. Owing to its persistent leaves it should be given slightly more water during the winter months, but only enough to prevent leaf fall. The succulent stems will maintain the plant for some time, so a slight watering once a fortnight will probably prove sufficient, but this does depend on your conditions and trial and error is the only method that will eventually prove satisfactory. The plant can always produce more leaves, so it is best to err on the side of excessive drought.

XI. CELASTRACEAE

A family of some 38 genera with around 450 species, many of which are grown for their ornamental fruits, while the flowers are small and inconspicuous.

Genus EUONYMUS

A genus of about 170 species, among which are the popular Spindle Trees, which beautify the late autumn garden scene. Only one species is used as a houseplant.

1. Euonymus japonicus

An evergreen shrub, capable of reaching heights of 15 feet or more, but slow-growing. The form used as a houseplant is known as *Aureo-picta*, but there are other variegated forms known, which will be mentioned briefly. The leaves are more or less spoon-shaped, with slightly serrated edge, up to 3 inches long and an inch across and are dark green with a large yellow blotch in the centre. *Ovata aurea* has the leaves irregularly blotched with yellow, while 'Silver Pillar' has a broad white margin and a dark green centre. All these plants are capable of surviving outdoors, so that they can be put in very cool situations. On the other hand full light is essential if they are to preserve their variegation and if they receive too much heat in the winter, there will be a lot of floppy, etiolated growth, which should be removed at the end of March. Although they have not yet been tried as houseplants the compact tiny leaved forms of var. *microphylla* might might prove very useful. *Microphylla pulchella* has the leaves variegated with yellow, while *Microphylla variegata* has a silver margin to the small leaves. In these forms the leaves are about an inch long and ½ inch across and they make a slow-growing, very compact plant. *Aureo-picta* has a reputation for reverting rather rapidly to the all green leaf, so this must be looked out for and any all green shoots cut out as soon as they are noticed. The plants can be stopped with advantage in the spring and possibly again at the end of June. If they become too large, they can be planted out in the garden. Tip cuttings root fairly readily, whenever the weather is warm and can be taken at any suitable time; summer is normally the most convenient season.

XII. BALSAMINACEAE

A family containing only two genera *Hydrocera* and *Impatiens* and since there is only a single species of *Hydrocera*, the bulk of the species are in *Impatiens*, probably more than 500.

Genus IMPATIENS

The Balsams get their Latin name from the fact that the ripe seed capsules will unfurl at a touch, scattering their seeds far and wide. They are best known by the popular Busy Lizzie (*I. wallerana*).

Miscellaneous 1

1. Impatiens petersiana

Nowadays this tends to be included in *I. wallerana*, the green-leaved Busy Lizzie, but the leaves are distinct in shape as well as in colouring. These leaves are elliptic, some 4 inches long and a little over an inch across and are dark purple in colour. The large flat spurred flowers are bright scarlet and are produced through most of the spring and summer. If shoots are taken off in late spring and early summer and left in water they will soon produce roots and can be potted up and used as replacements. The plant soon gets leggy and is rarely kept for longer than 18 months. The plants can be kept through the winter with the temperature as low as 50°, but they are liable to emerge in the spring looking rather tattered and bedraggled. They can, however, be cut back and they will break anew from the base. Since fresh plants can be propagated so easily, it is probably best to do this each year, discarding the old plants when they get too leggy. Loamless composts will serve these plants very well.

XIII. TILIACEAE

The Lime-tree family includes only one species of interest to the houseplant grower.

Genus SPARRMANNIA

Named in honour of a Swede, Dr. Sparrmann, who accompanied Captain Cook on his second voyage.

1. Sparrmannia africana

This is a rather vigorous, quick-growing shrub with hairy stems and large heart-shaped leaves some 5 to 6 inches long and 3 to 4 inches across which are a vivid green in colour. These too are covered with hairs. When large enough the plant will produce a peduncular flower head bearing many white flowers 1 inch or more across, with purple-tipped stamens which make a conspicuous feature. The plant is hardy, it is a native of South Africa and adapts itself very easily to room conditions, growing

215

equally well in light or shade and tolerant of low temperatures. Owing, however, to the hairy nature of the plant, which makes sponging difficult, it has not proved as popular as its constitution would seem to warrant. It is commonly known as African Hemp.

XIV. MALVACEAE

The Mallow family has only one representative among house-plants.

Genus HIBISCUS

1. Hibiscus rosa-sinensis var. Cooperi

The China-rose *Hibiscus* is the conventional tropical shrub, with large deep red flowers, that seductive native girls place behind their ears when Frangi-pani is out of season. Cooper's variety has rather narrower leaves than the type and they are variegated with dark green, cream and crimson. The leaves are an elongated oval in shape with a toothed edge. The plant has only recently been re-introduced and is in very short supply. We do not yet know how it will respond to room conditions, but it should be regarded as delicate and during the winter it is liable to shed leaves with rather too much frequency. It can be cut back in the spring and it will then grow vigorously. *Hibiscus* does not like too much water at any time, and if overwatered, root-rot is probable. With an established shrub JIP 3 is very suitable, but for young plants something lighter, such as the *Begonia* mixture, is more appropriate. The plant shows its best colour if in a light shade; too heavy a shade will give a drawn plant and too bright light will stunt it. Propagation is by cuttings.

XV. LYTHRACEAE

The Loosestrife family is not particularly extensive, consisting of some 21 genera, none of which are particularly large. *Lythrum salicaria*, the Purple Loosestrife, is a not uncommon British wild flower, usually seen on the banks of streams.

Genus CUPHEA

Best known to gardeners by the Cigar Plant, *C. ignea*, with its curious tubular flower, which is scarlet with an ash-grey rim.

1. Cuphea hyssopifolia (Plate 95)

Since the Hyssop has not really a very distinctive leaf, it seems rather unimaginative to describe a plant as hyssop-leaved. The plant is commonly known as Barbados Heather, as it is much grown for ornament in the West Indies. There can be very few cultivated plants that remain in flower for as long as this plant does and it is this persistence in flowering that qualifies it for inclusion in this book. *C. hyssopifolia* makes a small branching, twiggy shrub, which can eventually reach a height of some 18 inches, but since young plants are the more floriferous, it is rarely allowed to do so. The twigs are covered with linear-oval leaves arranged alternately. These are not more than $\frac{3}{4}$ inch long and an eighth across and are a fairly bright green. From the leaf axils come a number of small trumpet-shaped purple flowers which wreathe the branches and are so frequently renewed that the plant is in flower for most of the year from April until November. Great heat is not required for this plant—50° in winter is ample and lower readings will cause no damage—but it does require a well-lit situation. The twigs will break naturally without any stopping, but it can do no harm to trim the plant back somewhat in March, although this is not essential. During the winter the plant is not very exciting, although it makes a pleasant enough little leafy shrub during this period. Tip cuttings of fairly firm young growths will root fairly readily in the summer and start to flower some four months after rooting. The plant has only recently been brought into cultivation over here, although one cannot imagine why it has not been popular for a long time. The only possible objection that can be levelled at it, is that the individual flowers are not very long lived and drop off as they fade, thereby slightly increasing the dusting problem. This seems a small price to pay for nine months of non-stop flowering. Altogether this seems one of the most promising of recent introductions.

217

XVI. MYRTACEAE

A fairly large family of trees and shrubs with some 70 genera and nearly 3,000 species. The Clove is a member of this family and several Myrtles in warmer climes bear fruits large enough and palatable enough to be worth growing commercially. So far as houseplants are concerned there is only one genus to interest us.

Genus EUCALYPTUS

This is a large genus, which is still not terribly well known to botanists and the number of species is still a question of argument. At least 500 have been described, but of these 100 are known to be natural hybrids and the true number has yet to be agreed. The genus is nearly confined to Australia and Tasmania, but there are a few outliers to the north as far up as New Guinea and Indonesia. They vary in size from the scrubby plants known as mallees and marlocks to *E. regnans*, which has been measured at over 370 feet, making it one of the tallest trees in the world. The species are found under very varying conditions, from the tropics to snow mountains and from deserts to steamy jungle. They can only be propagated by seed, which tends to be slow to germinate, but seedlings then grow with great rapidity. They are remarkable for the various leaf shapes that they show as the plant ages (a feature found in many antipodean plants). The juvenile leaves are usually opposite and tend to be more or less circular in outline, while the adult leaves are usually lance-shaped, rather narrow and occur alternatively on the twigs. None of the plants recommended below need much in the way of heat and many have survived outside in places like Tresco in the Scillies. They do, however, require as much light as possible at all times. They are very suited for sun parlours, where such exist. Apart from requiring ample light, the only other problem that is liable to assail the grower is that of size. The plants will grow very rapidly if left to themselves and would soon become unmanageable. This can be overcome by pruning the plants really hard back at the end of March. This has the double advantage of keeping the plants a reasonable size and also preserving the juvenile foliage, which is usually more attractive than the adult leaves. The disadvantage is that for a few weeks you are just looking at a pot with a stump in it. If you have room for two plants, this can be overcome by pruning one plant one year and the other the next year. When the new shoots are developing, the strongest upper shoots should be stopped two or three times during the summer, as otherwise they will elongate to excess and inhibit the growth of the lower shoots. A fairly rich compost, such as the Ivy mixture or JIP 2 is required for these plants and they should be kept reasonably moist at all times. A winter temperature of 45° is more than adequate and too much heat in winter is undesirable.

1. Eucalyptus cinerea

This is apparently known in New South Wales, of which state it is native, as the Argyle Apple. In nature it makes a small tree and is notable for its very glaucous grey leaves. The adjective *cinerea* means ash-grey. This is one of the Gums, which are characterized by the bark peeling off each year and leaving the trunk and branches looking creamy white. The juvenile leaves are nearly circular, 1¾ inches long and 2 inches across, while the adult leaves are also very glaucous, lanceolate and up to 6 inches long. The plant is extremely attractive with its ashy leaves and attractive bark. With the necessary pruning it is probable that only the juvenile foliage will be seen.

2. Eucalyptus citriodora

The epithet means that it smells of lemons and it is for its attractively lemon-scented foliage that this plant is grown. It is native to Queensland and so can take rather more heat than the other two species described here. The juvenile leaves are oblong-lanceolate up to 6 inches long and 3 inches across, the adult leaves are narrowly lanceolate, up to 9 inches long. Both adult and juvenile leaves are dark green.

3. Eucalyptus perriniana

Native to Victoria, New South Wales and Tasmania, with plants from the latter region proving hardy outside in many parts of southern England, known in Australia as the Round-leaved Snow Gum and also as Rodway. The juvenile leaves are particularly attractive, being an intense blue-grey in the best forms, round, egg-shaped, $2\frac{1}{4}$ inches long by 4 inches across. They have no petiole but spring directly from the stem. The adult leaves are also fairly glaucous, stalked up to 7 inches long but only $\frac{3}{4}$ inch across. In some forms the emerging leaves are purplish in colour. In nature it makes a small tree, not exceeding 20 feet in height, so it could probably be grown as a large specimen in a 7- or 9-inch pot, without proving unmanageable. If conditions allow, both *E. cinerea* and this species can with great advantage be stood out of doors, in full sun, from the end of May until September. If this is done, pruning back can be deferred until May, so that the unsightly period of the plant's existence can take place outside our rooms.

XVII. MELASTOMATACEAE

The *Melastomataceae*, named from the genus *Melastoma*, is a family of some 200 genera and 1,800 species which are found principally in the tropics. Most of the species have handsome flowers, and two genera, in particular, have very ornamental leaves. The genus *Bertolonia*, however, though handsome, is too difficult for room work, and as far as houseplants are concerned the family is represented by one genus and one species of this genus.

Genus SONERILA

The name is derived from the Malabar name of the plant.

1. Sonerila margaritacea

The specific epithet means 'pearly'. This is a low-growing plant with a red stem and oblong-oval leaves. These are dark green in colour, but are so thickly covered with silvery dots that suggest seed pearls, that the general effect is of a silver leaf. These leaves are not very large, some 3 to 4 inches long, but are produced in great abundance. In the autumn panicles of short-lived pink flowers are produced. Several forms have been given varietal status, depending on the size of the plant and the amount of silver in the leaves. The plant is a native of Java and therefore requires warm moist conditions. The winter temperature should not drop below 60°. The plant will survive at 50°, but will lose most of its leaves and look unpleasant. The plant seems to require quite a lot of water, even in winter, though the usual warnings about overwatering naturally apply. Bright sunshine causes leaf shrivel and a shady position is essential for this delicate, though delightful plant.

XVIII. MYRSINACEAE

A family of some 550 species of trees and shrubs, divided among thirty genera and restricted mainly to the tropics.

Genus ARDISIA

The name derives from the Greek word for a point. There are two species which are admirable for room work, *A. crispa* (*crispa* means with a waved margin) and *A. japonica*. *A. crispa* is the more popular, but *japonica* is more compact. Both are low-growing shrubs which will be happy with a winter temperature of 45°. The leaves of *crispa* are an oblong-lance shape, those of *japonica* are more oval. They are shiny and dark green. The fragrant flowers are produced in terminal umbels and are not particularly showy: those of *crispa* are red, those of *japonica* white. The flowers are followed by bright red berries, which provide the real reason for growing the plant. These berries will stay on the plant for a long time, and in the meantime the plant will make further growth so that the berries will move from the apex of the branches to lower down. Culture is easy, as the cooler the plants are kept the better. A well-lit situation is essential. Shrub nurseries are more liable to produce this plant than houseplant nurseries because it is a very slow subject under glass.

XIX. ASCLEPIADACEAE

This is a large family of some 1,700 species distributed among about 220 genera. Many of the plants are very attractive, but few are suitable for room work.

Genus CEROPEGIA

The name is derived from the Greek words for wax and fountain; the flowers are waxy in appearance and the plant throws many thin stems from a central point and may suggest a fountain.

1. Ceropegia woodii

This plant was named in honour of John Medley Wood, a curator of the botanic garden at Durban. The plant springs from a corm and throws a large number of stems that may twine, but appear to exhibit themselves better from a hanging basket. The small heart-shaped leaves are dark green, mottled either with white or a lighter green. The flowers, that appear in the axils of the leaves in autumn, are brownish in colour and inconspicuous. Although the stems are annual they rarely die down before the next year's growth has appeared, so that the plant is always green. This plant is a native of Natal and likes quite warm conditions, though a winter temperature of 50° is adequate. It needs plenty of water when in growth, though, if this is withheld, the plant will become quite succulent in appearance. Very little water is required when the plant is dormant (November–March). A fairly well-lit situation is required.

2. Ceropegia barklyi

Named in honour of Sir Henry Barkly, a governor of Cape Province, this *Ceropegia* is somewhat hardier than *woodii*. The stems are very slight and do not twine at all, and the leaves are oval in shape and are green, with a red edge and white veins. This plant is only suitable for a hanging basket and is quite liable to die down completely in the winter. Cultivation is easy, but the plant is not very often offered, which seems a pity.

Genus HOYA

Named in honour of Thomas Hoy, a gardener to the Duke of Northumberland at Sion House, Middlesex.

1. Hoya bella

This plant, which is delicate, is grown for its flowers. It requires to be placed in a hanging container, as the branches droop and its beauty cannot be appreciated at eye level. It forms a small shrub with small fleshy leaves about ¾ inch in length. The flowers are produced in umbels from the underside of the branches and consist of a small waxy white star with a smaller purple star in the centre. They are handsome, fragrant and long lasting, and appear in late spring and early summer. It can be propagated by cuttings, but some people recommend grafting it on to *H. carnosa* rootstock, when it will grow rather more vigorously than on its own roots. It likes a light open soil, such as that recommended for *Begonias*.

2. Hoya carnosa variegata

This is a hardier *Hoya* and will, indeed, tolerate very low temperatures, but the higher the temperature the more rapid is the growth. It has thick fleshy oblong-oval leaves that may attain 3 inches in length and 1½ inches across and the leaves are variegated cream and dark green. In young leaves the cream portion is a pale pink. *H. carnosa* is a climber, though it can be used as a trailer. Young plants are very slow growing, but they move faster as they age. *H. carnosa* has the peculiar habit of throwing up a long, apparently leafless shoot, but this should always be left as it will produce leaves in good time, and *Hoyas* resent being stopped or interfered with in any way. They will produce sideshoots in their own time. The umbels of flesh-pink waxy flowers, for which the type *H. carnosa* is grown, are rarely produced on the vareigated forms and in any case not until some 3 to 4 feet of growth is present. The leaves are long lasting and are often used in refined floral arrangements. *H. carnosa variegata aurea* has the centre of the leaf golden yellow and a dark green margin. It is in short supply at the moment.

XX. LABIATAE

The Labiates, so-called from the pronounced lip of the flowers, are a very large family, of which Sage, Mint and Thyme are probably the best-known examples, but there are at least 3,000 species and 160 genera. They are of only minor interest to the houseplant grower.

Genus GLECHOMA

Here belongs that pervasive weed the Ground Ivy, which is sometimes put in the genus *Nepeta*. It is the variegated form that is grown.

1. Glechoma hederacea var. variegata

A plant of the easiest culture, but not really a true houseplant, as it will lose most of its leaves during the winter. Best placed in a hanging container, from which it can fountain out. The leaves are kidney-shaped and about an inch across and are heavily blotched with white in their centre. Growths of up to 2 feet are made during the season and the plant should be kept reasonably moist at all times. If the winter temperature is kept around 45° the leaves will persist to a greater or lesser degree until about February, when the growths should all be cut hard back and the plant restarted. However the plants are not really going to look very attractive after the New Year. If the trails are allowed contact with the earth, they will root at the nodes, so that the plant can be propagated with the greatest ease. The plant likes shady conditions, but they should not be too dark, as this would prevent the variegation from showing up. The violet flowers are produced with little freedom in the variegated form, but this is no disadvantage.

Genus PLECTRANTHUS

There are some quite showy shrubby greenhouse plants among

the eighty species in this genus, but the houseplant grower is only concerned with a trailing plant.

1. Plectranthus oertendahlii

The wild habitat of this plant is not known for certainty, although it is thought to be South Africa. This is very popular in Scandinavia. It makes a spreading or hanging plant and the stems will root at the nodes like *Glechoma*. The leaves are nearly circular, up to 1¾ inches in each direction, dark green above with the veins marked silvery-white giving an attractive net-like effect. The underside of the leaves are purplish in colour, and this purple will be visible if the plant is grown as a hanging specimen. The stems end in a spiked inflorescence, up to 6 inches long, composed of a number of small very pale violet flowers. The plant requires a winter temperature of 50° and a reasonably well-lit situation. It is a very easy plant to keep in good condition.

XXI. GESNERIACEAE

A family of some eighty-five genera and over a thousand species found mainly in the tropics, with the greatest concentration in South America. Many have very showy flowers and to this family belong the popular African Violet (Saintpaulia) and the showy Gloxinias. Some genera, most notably *Episcia* have very attractive leaves as well as flowers, but need moister growing conditions than living rooms can provide and the houseplant grower is confined to a single species.

Genus HYPOCYRTA

A small genus of low-growing, twiggy shrubs from Brazil. The name comes from two Greek words meaning 'curved underneath' referring to the pronounced bulge in the lower part of the flowers.

1. Hypocyrta glabra

Known popularly as the Clog plant, this is also sometimes met with as *H. radicans*. The adjective *glabra* means hairless. This makes a low spreading shrub usually not more than 6 inches high, although it can spread twice this distance. The spreading twigs are thickly set with oval, bright green fleshy leaves, about an inch long and ½ inch across. The flower buds appear in the leaf axils and consist of a pale orange calyx from which the waxy orange, red-lipped flowers emerge. These darken to nearly scarlet as they age. The flower is only about the size of a holly berry, but they are produced in great quantity and over a long period, while the orange calyx keeps its colour for some six weeks. The flowers are produced on the young wood, so that the plant should be pruned lightly during the winter or early spring. The fleshy leaves indicate that the plant can tolerate reasonably dry conditions, which is an advantage in the winter, when there is always a risk of overwatering. Cold water can mark the leaves, so that it is best to have your water at room temperature and to keep it off the leaves as much as possible. A winter temperature of 55° is desirable, although the plant will survive quite well at 50°. It requires a well-lit situation in the home, although in a greenhouse some shading is necessary. This is easy enough to manage, provided that the watering is watched, as either too dry or too wet a soil will cause the flower buds to fall before opening. With its fleshy leaves it can be allowed to dry out thoroughly between waterings but these should be ample when given.

XXII. ACANTHACEAE

The Acanthus family is quite large, containing some 130 genera and over 2,000 species. It gets its name from the *Acanthus*, whose leaves inspired the builders of Corinthian columns in classical days. Most of the family are denizens of the tropics.

Genus APHELANDRA
The name derived from two Greek words for 'simple' and 'male', because the anthers are single-celled.

1. Aphelandra squarrosa var. **Louisae** (Frontispiece. Plate 96)
This has been one of the most successful new flowering plants

introduced in the last few years. Squarrose is a botanical term, indicating that the leaves overlap each other, and the varietal name commemorates the Queen of the Belgians. The plant grows an upright stem, from which the large drooping leaves spring at short intervals in pairs. These leaves are lance-shaped, some 9 inches long and 4½ inches across, of a very dark shiny green, with the midrib and the principal lateral veins picked out with a wide band of ivory. Once the plant has become pot-bound it produces a head of yellow flowers, that are protected by greeny-yellow bracts. The inflorescence is curiously shaped in a four-sided pyramid, a characteristic of the genus. The flowers emerge over a long period of two to three weeks, but when they are all over the bracts turn green, and the head should then be removed. Sideshoots will then develop in the leaf axils and these can be used as cuttings. Once the temperature has reached 60° the plant will start growing and will grow vigorously and quickly. It therefore needs a rich soil mixture. JIP 3 is excellent, but at Turnford this mixture is used (all parts by bulk):

2 parts loam
1½ parts leaf mould
1 part cow manure
½ part sharp sand
2 48-pots full of bone meal to each barrow load.

When the plant is growing vigorously it will need frequent watering, and it should not be allowed to dry out completely at any time. A winter temperature of 50° is quite high enough and even during the winter the compost must be kept moist. Very rarely the plant is attacked by a fungus, which causes a canker at the base of the plant. This fungus will be encouraged by too much water when the temperature is low and the plant is rest-ing. In the nursery, mite and scale are sometimes serious pests, but can be controlled by nicotine and white oil. The plant needs to be repotted in fresh soil every spring. Feeding should be held back, until the flower buds can be seen, as otherwise the plant will produce larger and larger leaves and no flowers at all. *A.*

Louisae likes a well-lit position and appears tolerant of gas and oil fumes.

During many years of cultivation a number of sports have arisen and where these have appeared improvements on the original typical plants, they have been named and propagated. At the moment the cultivars most in demand are 'Brockfeld' and 'Dania'. 'Brockfeld' is a very vigorous form with extra large, crinkled leaves, which may reach a length of 9 inches and the ivory around the veins is much more marked. This form is reluctant to flower and probably only does it very rarely under room conditions. It appears to have supplanted the earlier 'Silver Beauty' in which the leaves were almost more ivory than green, but equally more closely set on the stem than in the typical form. 'Dania' is a very compact form of *A. squarrosa louisae*, with smaller leaves, which are, however, set closer together and do not droop down, but are held horizontally and is the best form to obtain when a rather small compact plant is wanted.

2. Aphelandra leopoldii

Named after King Leopold I of the Belgians, this plant has sometimes been described as another variety of *A. squarrosa*. As it differs in leaf shape, leaf marking, flower shape, bract shape and flower colour, as well as in behaviour, it is clearly entitled to specific rank. *Leopoldii* is a smaller plant than *squarrosa* and tends to branch earlier. The leaves are shorter and thinner, of a light green colour with a silvery-grey zone about the midrib and a slight purple flush on the underside. The inflorescence is a pale lemon yellow with quite elaborately netted bracts. Although its temperature requirements are similar, the plant is more delicate than *Louisae* and shows considerable susceptibility to fumes of any sort. Some plants that were in a greenhouse fumigated with sulphur for begonia mildew, dropped all their leaves, though they subsequently produced fresh ones. It is thus far from ideal as a houseplant.

With the success of *A. squarrosa Louisae* it has been natural to look for further *Aphelandras*, but so far no suitable houseplant species have been found. The most promising would appear to be *A. fascinator*, which is described as having leaves similar to *A. squarrosa*, but with a purple underside, and bright scarlet flowers. The plant is found wild in Colombia but at what height is not disclosed. *Aphelandra aurantiaca* var. *Roezlii* has leaves that are not unlike *leopoldii* and a handsome spike of orange-scarlet flowers, that are not long lasting; *Aphelandra nitens* with green leaves with a purple underside and vermilion flowers is showy when in flower, but lacks interest at other times. Nothing has yet been found to compare with *A. squarrosa Louisae*.

Genus BELOPERONE

The name is derived from two Greek words for an arrow and a band. This is a small genus of some thirty species, only one of which is in general cultivation.

1. Beloperone guttata (Plate 97)

The adjective *guttata* literally means sprinkled, but applied to plants means 'covered with dots', which is only evident in this plant if you hold the leaf up to the light. This is one of the few houseplants which are grown for their flowers (or rather in-florescences) rather than their leaves. These latter are an elon-gated oval, about 2 inches long and soft green in colour. The plant makes a twiggy shrub, which need pruning back each spring, unless a large shrub is wanted. It can reach a height of 2 or 3 feet, but is generally kept between 9 and 18 inches. The twigs end in an inflorescence composed of a head of overlapping ruddy brown bracts which look rather like a prawn and have given the plant its name of Shrimp Plant. From these bracts emerge rather inconspicuous white flowers with a purple spot on the lip, which do not persist for long, while the bracts will keep their colour for a long time and while this is taking place further shoots will be elongating and forming inflorescences and this will take place continuously, so long as the temperature remains around 60°, although growth is slowed down by the short winter days, as the plant needs ample light. The plant will survive the winter with the temperature as low as 45°, but will then take longer to come into flower again and more success is obtained with the higher temperatures. If these can be maintained, February is the best month to prune the plant back and it will start flowering again towards the end of April. Propagation is by tip cuttings, which can be taken at any time between March and September, but it is often difficult to find tips without flower buds. The plants should be in the best lit situation available. Too much heat during the winter will give long spindly growths which are unsightly and will have to be removed.

There is an albino form, with pale yellow bracts, which makes a somewhat larger plant than the brown form and which is known in the U.S.A. as 'Yellow Queen', but which tends to be sold over here as *Beloperone lutea*. It is arguably more attractive than the first introduction, which took place as recently as 1936. The botanists have had a field day with this plant, which has been known as *Drejerella guttata* and has come to rest temporarily as *Justicia brandegeana*. There are few tropical acanthads which haven't been included in *Justicia* at some period in their career. The plant is native to Mexico, presumably from fairly high up as it does seem to give of its best when the temperature is neither too high nor too low.

Genus ERANTHEMUM

We have kept this heading, although none of the plants we propose discussing are now included in this genus. As, however, they are invariably spoken of and sold as *Eranthemum*, it has seemed best to keep them under this general heading.

1. Chamaeeranthemum igneum

The prefix '*Chamae*' means dwarf or prostrate and *igneum* means fire-like. This native of Peru is a dwarf spreading plant with small rounded dark green leaves, embellished with golden veins and midrib. It is invariably known as *Eranthemum igneum*. Like so many Peruvian plants, it is not a particularly easy subject. Shade, a temperature not descending below 50° (55° is preferable) and a reasonably moist atmosphere will suffice to give it the conditions it needs and given these it should not be difficult to get a thriving plant. The soil can be kept on the dry side, but it is as well not to let the plant dry out completely.

2. Pseuderanthemum albo-marginatum

Pseuderanthemum means false *Eranthemum* and *albo-marginatum* indicates that the leaves have white edges. There are several plants of this genus with ornamental leaves, borne on long stalks in pairs up a cane-like stem. The leaves are an oblong oval in shape, but none of the species, in spite of their coloured leaves, makes a very satisfactory plant. Their habit is long and leggy and no stopping seems to alter this. They like a bright light and fairly dry conditions and the temperature should not fall for long below 50°. *P. albo-marginatum* has greyish leaves with a broad white edge, *P. atropurpureum* has very dark purple leaves, and *P. tricolor*, the prettiest of the three, has green leaves blotched with pink and purple. The plants root easily from cuttings and should be grown for short periods and re-propagated. They are all natives of Polynesia.

3. Stenandrium lindenii

The generic name signifies that the plant has narrow anthers and the specific epithet commemorates J. J. Linden. This is another Peruvian plant and very similar in appearance to *Chamaeeranthemum igneum* and is generally known as *Eranthemum lindenii*. The veins are less golden than *Chamaeeranthemum igneum* and the leaves are greyish in the centre and dark green on the margin. The habit and culture are similar.

Genus FITTONIA

The name commemorates Elizabeth and Sarah Fitton who wrote an improving book called *Conversations on Botany*.

1. Fittonia argyroneura

The specific epithet means 'with silver nerves' and refers to the white veins on the leaves. This is a charming trailing plant that has oval, nearly circular, leaves some 3 to 4 inches long when fully developed. The ground colour of the leaf is a curious green, somewhat the colour of a gherkin, and every vein is marked with ivory, so that the leaf seems covered with an ivory net. *Fittonias* are only found in Peru. They require permanent shade and a moist atmosphere and must not be allowed to dry out. *F. argyroneura* is delicate and particularly susceptible to draughts. Gas fumes in moderation it seems to tolerate. This and the following species are propagated by cuttings, and will thrive in the usual houseplant mixture.

2. Fittonia verschaffeltii (Plate 98)

M. Verschaffelt was a nineteenth-century Belgian expert on Camellias, who has, curiously, had a genus of palms named after him, as well as this *Fittonia*. The leaves are more elongated than in the previous species, the ground colour is a darker green and the network of veins is coloured carmine. It is much less exigent than *argyroneura* and provided that it is kept moist and shaded it should not present any difficulty. It will not enjoy low temperatures.

Genus SANCHEZIA

This is a small genus of low-growing shrubs from South America. The genus is named in honour of Josef Sanchez, a professor of botany at Cadiz.

1. Sanchezia nobilis

A small shrub with oblong lance-shaped leaves of a deep green which attain some 6 to 8 inches in length. The midrib and principal veins are surrounded by a yellow zone, similar to the vein markings in *Aphelandra Louisae*, though different in colour. The flowers are yellow and emerge from purple bracts. Although tolerant of quite low temperatures, *Sanschezia* does not thrive very well under room conditions. It requires a fairly well-lit position and the temperature should not drop below 50°. Scale is attracted to this plant and it should frequently be examined for this tiresome pest. In appropriate districts in the tropics it is popular as a garden plant, owing to the attraction that its flowers have for humming birds.

Miscellaneous 1

XIII. RUBIACEAE

The *Rubiaceae* is a confusing family of some 350 genera and 4,500 species. In our native flora it is represented by the bedstraws, with their panicles of white or yellow flowers and thin prostrate stems; but these are not typical of the family and you will search in vain for any resemblance between them and the plants we propose to describe. Among the products of this family are madder, coffee and quinine.

Genus COFFEA

1. Coffea arabica

This is the ordinary coffee plant of commerce, but it makes a very attractive little shrub for the house. The leaves are an oblong oval ending in a long point and some 3 to 6 inches long and 2 to 3 inches across. They emerge a coppery colour, but soon turn a dark glossy green, with a pleasant shining surface. If the plant is grown on, it will eventually produce small white fragrant flowers, that spring direct from the stem and are followed by red berries, which contain the 'beans'. Unfortunately by this time the plant has become rather large for room work. Coffee requires shady, cool and airy conditions. In coffee plantations the plants are always planted under other trees and are usually found in the hills where temperatures of 45° are not uncommon. It is not, therefore, a difficult subject, as it will tolerate as much heat as you like to give it but will also put up with cool conditions. It is not too happy in a close atmosphere, but is ideal for a situation such as a hall or corridor with enough heating to prevent the temperature falling below 45°.

Genus HOFFMANNIA

This group of South American plants is named in honour of G. F. Hoffman, who was Professor of Botany at Göttingen in the opening years of the nineteenth century. They are extremely handsome foliage plants, but are not ideal as houseplants as they have wrinkled leaves, which are hard to keep dust-free and the leaves lose some of their colourful appearance in the winter.

1. Hoffmannia ghiesbreghtii

This is a branching plant, which can attain a considerable width, though it is never very tall. The oblong lance-shaped leaves may reach a length of 12 inches, though 9 inches is the usual length: they are wrinkled and a dark velvety green on the surface and a dull red-purple on the underside. Although a winter temperature of 45° will not damage the plant it will make it unattractive and it should have, ideally, a minimum of 50° to 55°.

2. Hoffmannia × roezlii

This is described as a hybrid in the *R.H.S. Dictionary of Gardening*, but no mention is made of the parents. This is a smaller and rather more delicate plant than *ghiesbreghtii*. The leaves are from 4 to 8 inches long and green and purple with a shot-silk effect on the surface. The underside of the leaf is a pale purple colour. Although very handsome, this is not an easy plant to grow: its country of origin is said to be Mexico, but it is more delicate than most Mexican plants. Both *Hoffmannias* like a shaded, but not dark, position. In the wild state they are found at the edge of woods and in clearings.

XXIV. COMPOSITAE

This is the largest family of flowering plants, with over 13,000 species distributed in some 800 genera. They are to be found in all climates and in all forms, although there are few trees among them. They are easily recognized by their flowers, which, on inspection, show themselves to be composed of a number of florets grouped together to give the impression of a single flower. These florets are usually more or less tubular in shape, but may be surrounded by a ring of so-called ray florets, which have one large elongated petal. The Daisy of our lawns shows both types of flowers, while the horrid Groundsel has only what are referred to as disk florets. These are drab and inconspicuous in the groundsel, but can be showy enough in some thistles, so that the

Miscellaneous 1

fact that a plant has only disk florets does not necessary mean that it is not showy. Although our gardens would be badly off without the *Compositae*—you have only to think of Dahlias, Pyrethrums and Chrysanthemums, they have very few members that are suited to be houseplants.

Genus GYNURA

It is rather doubtful whether we are dealing with one or two species here, as they are very similar in appearance, although differing in their habit of growth and in their places of origin.

1. Gynura aurantiaca

This plant will eventually reach a height of 2 or 3 feet and will then be rather large for a houseplant. The leaves are somewhat jagged, about 3 inches long and a very dark olive green. However the basic leaf colour is hard to see as the leaves and stems are densely covered with hairs, which are a brilliant violet when young and reddish when the leaves are fully expanded. The shining violet growing tips makes this a striking plant to look at, but very hairy plants are not altogether satisfactory as houseplants, as dust can lodge in the hairs and is then not easily removed and *Gynuras* are probably better in the greenhouse. In February they bear heads of small orange groundsel-like flowers, which are produced in some numbers and clash badly with the violet hairs. Since the flowers have a rather disagreeable scent, they are, in any case, best removed before they open. The plant comes from Java and should have a winter temperature around 55°. It requires ample water and even during the winter should be kept reasonably moist. After flowering it should be cut hard back, although it is better, if you have the facilities, to take tip cuttings during the summer and keep individual plants for twelve months only, as otherwise they may well be too large for room work.

2. Gynura sarmentosa

Sarmentosa should mean that the plant throws out runners in the same way as a strawberry does, but in this case it means that

235

the plant is a twiner. The plant in cultivation under this name is almost identical with *G. aurantiaca*, apart from its twining habit. The plant described under this name in the *R.H.S. Dictionary* has reddish hairs and unlobed leaves, so it may well be that the *G. sarmentosa* of gardens is incorrectly named. It is slower-growing and tends to confine itself to a single twining stem with occasional branches and is thus a rather more suitable plant for rooms than the bulky *G. aurantiaca*. Against this the stem must be given some support, around which it can twine. It responds to the same treatment as *G. aurantiaca*. The true *G. sarmentosa* comes from India.

Genus SENECIO

This is thought to be the largest genus in all plants with some 1,300 species, varying in size from small annuals to plants of tree-like dimensions. They are best known to gardeners by the groundsel on the one side and the showy Cineraria (*S. cruentus*) on the other. We are only concerned with two species, both from South Africa.

1. Senecio macroglossus variegatus (Plate 99)

This plant is sometimes known as German Ivy, although it is not an Ivy and does not come from Germany. It is a fairly vigorous climber, with leaves that are basically triangular, but which may be lobed as ivy leaves are. They are up to 3 inches long and wide and variegated with silver in an attractive manner, mainly around the margin of the leaf. Left to itself the plant will reach some 10–15 feet and will then produce large heads of yellow daisies in the middle of the winter. Few rooms, however, can take plants of this size, so that in the home they are stopped every spring and encouraged to make a bushy plant up to 2 or 3 feet high, which twines round sticks placed in the centre of the pot.

Great heat is not required for this plant and a winter temperature of 45° is quite tolerable, although 50° is somewhat better. The plant resents gas or oil fumes (we have no knowledge of its tolerance of North Sea gas fumes, but usually they seem to do little damage). It requires a very well-lit situation and has no objection to a somewhat dry atmosphere. Although the plant should not be allowed to dry out completely, it does not like a sodden soil and should always be kept fairly dry. Unlike the majority of houseplants its leaves should never be syringed and indeed, apart from an occasional sponging, should never come in contact with water at all, as they are covered in a waxy secretion, which too much water would remove. It is thus not a suitable recipient for foliar feeds. Cuttings of half-ripe tip growths root fairly readily in warm conditions.

2. Senecio mikanioides

Known as Cape Ivy, this plant exists only in the green-leaved form. The leaves are a little larger than those of the last species, somewhat thin and somewhat more lobed, while the flowers have no ray florets and are less showy. The plant is grown quite extensively on the Continent, but is probably not available over here. The plant requires rather shady conditions and has no objection to water on its leaves, although a dry situation will not be resented. The plant can be used either as a climber or as a hanging plant. It quickly becomes rather bare at the base and so requires to be frequently renewed by means of cuttings. It will thrive under the same conditions as *S. macroglossus*, but has no objection to more warmth in the winter.

CHAPTER XII

Miscellaneous 2

I. PINACEAE

The Pines are widespread trees, easily distinguished by their needle-like leaves and characteristic cones.

Genus ARAUCARIA

Modern systematists are rather liable to take this out of the *Pinaceae* and give it a family of its own, the *Araucariaceae*. There are not many species in the genus, between eight and ten have been described, and they have a very odd distribution from southern Brazil to Chile and thence to Australia and the South Pacific islands. The genus is best known in Britain by the Monkey Puzzle, *A. araucana*, a native of Chile. None of the other species can be grown out of doors with much hope of success.

1. Araucaria excelsa (Plate 100)

Known as the Norfolk Island Pine, this plant is endemic to Norfolk Island, between Australia and New Zealand, where it can make trees up to 200 feet in height. The plant is not a rapid grower and the form grown as a house plant is *A. excelsa* var. *compacta*. This makes a very elegant pyramidal shaped bush which increases about 6 inches in all directions each year. The branches emerge horizontally in whorls of four up the central stem and from them side branches elongate, also horizontally so

238

that the plant is composed of a number of horizontal tiers. The plant does not require much winter heat and plants have survived outside for many years in Cornwall, although they tend to succumb during very severe winters. The branches are covered with awl-shaped, bright green needles, up to $\frac{1}{2}$ inch long and very narrow. The plant requires a well-lit situation and should be turned slightly at weekly intervals during the spring and summer, so as to maintain its symmetrical growth. Were it left unturned, all growths would tend to grow towards the light. It can, with great advantage, be stood out of doors in a somewhat shady situation between the beginning of June and the end of September. Once it has got into a 6-inch pot it will only require potting on about every three years, so that a good mixture such as JIP 3 or the Ivy compost is required and soilless composts would be no good. The plant will take ample water in the summer and must never be allowed to dry out completely at any time. It appears to be tolerant of gas and oil fumes. At one time there was a cultivar 'Silver Star' in which the tips of the branches were silvery-white. It looks marvellous in old photographs, but it has been lost and until a plant sports again, we are not likely to know whether it was as handsome in green and white as it appears in black and white.

It would seem that there are two species in commerce under this name: *A. excelsa* and *A. columnaris* and they are by no means easy to distinguish. In *A. excelsa* the branchlets are sometimes somewhat pendent, while those of *A. columnaris* remain rigid. The other main differences are that the needles of *A. columnaris* are a deeper green than those of *A. excelsa*. Moreover the young needles of *A. excelsa* are soft to the touch, while those of *A. columnaris* are much firmer. Mature trees differ markedly in habit and are not easily confused, but young plants are extremely difficult to differentiate. *A. columnaris* is native to New Caledonia and the New Hebrides and can therefore be expected to be slightly more tender than the true *A. excelsa*. Both species are invariably sold as *A. excelsa*.

II. TAXACEAE

The Yew family all tend to resemble each other in their distinctive, rather broad needles and the fleshy surround to their seeds.

Genus PODOCARPUS

The name comes from two Greek words meaning 'foot' and 'fruit' as the footstalk of the seed is pulpy like a fruit and is often edible. The plants have male flowers that are borne in catkins and female flowers which are small and inconspicuous. Some species have both sexes on the same plant; others are unisexual.

1. Podocarpus macrophyllus (Plate 101)

Macrophyllus means that it has large leaves. This is a native of China and Japan and is known in the latter country as Kusamaki. It is a small shrub, some forms not exceeding 2 feet in height, while others can reach as high as 20 feet. The plant has spreading branches which bear a very large number of side branches, all of which are densely leafy. The leaves are long, from 5 to 7 inches, but not more than $\frac{1}{2}$ inch across and are arranged spirally all along the branches. The leaves are somewhat leathery, yellowish-green on the surface and blue-green beneath. Young plants grow quite rapidly, but soon slow down and after that growth is slow. Plants have survived outside in Britain in sheltered places, so that it is of the easiest cultivation requiring cool conditions in the winter. Here again it can be stood outside with advantage during the summer. It will tolerate quite shady conditions, so long as they are not dark. It should only require potting on about every three years, but should be fed during the summer in the intervening periods. This is not a brilliant plant, but one that can give distinction to large groups.

III. PANDANACEAE

This is a small family of monocotyledons containing only three

100. Araucaria excelsa

101. Podocarpus macrophyllus

102. Tradescantia 'Rochford's Quicksilver'

111. Sansevieria hahnii

112. Philodendron verrucosum

113. Dioscorea discolor

114. Elettaria cardamomum

115. A mixed arrangement of Houseplants

116. A mixed arrangement of Houseplants

genera and some 220 species. The species of the principal genus, *Pandanus*, are known as Screw Pines as they develop corkscrew-like trunks as they age. The 'Pine' refers to the leaves, which are not unlike those of the pineapple. The leaves are serrated at the edge and have a rough texture, so that handling should be done with care. The plants require plenty of water in the growing season, but can be kept on the dry side during the winter. They require a warm atmosphere, though it seems probable that as low as 50° would cause no harm to a well-rooted plant. In their native lands they are usually found by the coast.

Genus PANDANUS

The name is derived from *Pandang*, the Malayan name for the plant.

1. Pandanus candelabrum variegatum

One of the largest species, capable, in its native West Africa, of making a tree some 30 feet high. The leaves are from 3 to 6 feet long, though only a few inches across, and are bright green with white bands running lengthwise. The leaves are somewhat spiny and are arranged, like all the species, in a large rosette. Propagation is by the suckers that arise from the roots.

2. Pandanus sanderi

One of the many variegated plants found in Polynesia and named after the orchid grower Sander. This is a much smaller plant than *candelabrum*. Even so, the leaves can reach some 2 feet long. They are slightly spiny along the edges. The plant does not make a trunk. The leaves are banded with yellow stripes.

3. Pandanus veitchii

This is about the same size as the last species, but with dark green leaves bordered with silver. It is named in honour of Robert Veitch, the famous nineteenth-century Chelsea nursery-man.

IV. GRAMINEAE

There are over 5,000 species of grasses, but only one is used as a houseplant intentionally.

Genus OPLISMENUS

1. Oplismenus hirtellus variegatus

Although officially a grass, *Oplismenus* looks like a very delicate variegated *Tradescantia* and needs identical treatment. It has a trailing stem set with lance-shaped leaves that reach 2 inches in length, but only ½ inch in width. These leaves are striped ivory and green, but if kept in a bright light much of the ivory will darken to pink. The plant roots easily at leaf joints and makes a splendid trailer. There is another variety, *albidus*, with the leaf almost entirely ivory, but it appears to be temporarily out of cultivation. Although a native of the West Indies, the plant is very hardy and is handsome either on its own or in a group.

V. CYPERACEAE

The Sedge family is one of the largest, 2,600 species in sixty-five genera, and their successful identification is one of the nightmares of amateur botanists. However, the houseplant grower need not worry as he is only concerned with two species.

Genus CYPERUS

1. Cyperus diffusus

Most native species of *Cyperus* are called Wood Rushes. *C. diffusus* has grass-like leaves and an inflorescence like the ribs of a sunshade. It is hardy, easily increased by division and will grow in practically any soil. It likes to be kept moist and shaded. It has very few vices, and also few virtues, and is at its best in a mixed group.

Genus CAREX

These are the Sedges, which are so infuriating to botanists and of which some 600 have been described.

242

1. Carex morrowii variegata (Plate 17)

Carex morrowii makes a tuft of grassy leaves, which are quite wide for a sedge, often as much as ¼ inch across, and may be a foot high, although rather less is more usual. The variegated form has green margins and a white central zone. In commerce it has been thoroughly confused with

2. Carex foliosissima variegata

This is usually offered as though it were *C. morrowii*. It has much narrower leaves than the last species, probably less than an eighth of an inch across and the leaves have silver margins and a green centre. It is also rather less tall. Both plants are native to Japan and will survive outside for some time, although they tend to succumb in really severe winters. It follows therefore that they need cool treatment, with the winter temperature not exceeding 45°. They should always be kept reasonably moist and the variegation shows up best if the plants are in a well-lit situation. They are easily propagated by division. Both these plants are at their best in a mixed group as a variegated grass on its own looks rather austere.

VI. COMMELINACEAE

The *Commelinaceae* are not a large family. There are some 300 species divided among twenty-five genera, but they contain some of the easiest and most popular houseplants. The majority are always sold under the name of *Tradescantia* though, as will be seen, the botanists have divided the plants among several other genera. For the most part they are very hardy and indifferent as regards soil, provided the texture is kept sufficiently open to prevent it becoming waterlogged. They are for the most part marsh plants and like to be kept damp. Many of them are trailers and are displayed best when put in hanging containers. Propagation is easy and rapid. Many of the *Tradescantias* will produce roots if stood in water, and all that is necessary to produce fresh plants is to break off bits of the original plant, remove the bottom leaves, and insert the cuttings around a flower pot. A satisfactory method is to put seven cuttings in a 3-inch pot: five around the edge and two in the centre. The soil should be fairly loose, and care must be taken not to break the cuttings, which are very brittle. It is advisable to water the cuttings in with a rose, or, if that is not practicable, by immersing the pot in water, as watering from the can will tend to wash some of the soil out. It is best to continue watering in this way until the cuttings are rooted and the soil has firmed naturally. Sometimes a *Tradescantia* will produce fine trails but become rather bare in the centre. Under these circumstances a few cuttings inserted in the centre of the pot will soon provide a nice bushy centre. Growth is extremely rapid during warm weather and a potful of cuttings will look respectable in three weeks. Once a plant has been chopped up for cuttings it is of little use decoratively, and in the nursery special stock plants are used for propagation while the resultant plants are sold untouched. The genera *Rhoeo* and *Setcreasea* form exceptions to this rule as propagation is by sideshoots arising from the base of the plant.

Genus TRADESCANTIA

Named after Charles I's gardener, John Tradescant.

There are a number of trailing plants with oval leaves of the easiest cultivation, known popularly as Wandering Jew. To assign them to their correct species is by no means easy and it is to be hoped that the following are more or less correct.

1. Tradescantia albiflora

The best way to distinguish this plant from the very similar *T. fluminensis* is to bear in mind that the leaves of the latter species have a very short stalk, while those of *T. albiflora* spring directly from the stem. Here probably belongs the Silver Tradescantia, with oval leaves about 2 inches long with longitudinal white streaks that vary in width from mere threads to covering most of the surface. This requires rather moist soil and a fairly moist atmosphere and plenty of light to bring out the variegation. If placed in bright sunlight, the silver will acquire a pinkish tinge, which will be enhanced if the plant is kept on the dry side, although you will pay for this by reduced growth and smaller leaves. The plant is very easy to grow, requiring only to be kept free of frost during the winter. Care must be taken to remove immediately it is seen any unvariegated growth, as otherwise this will take the plant over and you will be left with a wholly green plant.

2. Tradescantia blossfeldiana

Named in honour of Robert Blossfeld, who had a famous nursery at Potsdam at the end of the last century and early in this one. This plant is popular in Germany. The leaves are quite large, up to 3 inches long and $1\frac{1}{2}$ inches across, oval in shape, dark green on the upper surface, purple below, the upper surface and the purple stems covered with fine white hairs. It is less hardy than either *T. albiflora* or *T. fluminensis*, although it will tolerate a winter temperature of 45°. It will grow under rather more shady conditions and is best propagated in warm weather.

3. Tradescantia fluminensis

Fluminensis means that the plant grows by rivers and it may therefore be expected to like rather moist conditions. Here probably belong the Golden Tradescantia and the plant known as *Tricolor*. The Golden Tradescantia has dark green leaves, which are slightly larger than those of *T. albiflora* and these are variegated with comparatively narrow stripes of yellow, which is really too pale to be called golden. This does best in a shady situation and likes to be kept moist. 'Tricolor' has the leaves striped green, white and pink and often the underside is quite a vivid pink. The white variegated *Tradescantias* always seem to require rather more light than the cream coloured forms.

4. Tradescantia elongata 'Rochford's Quicksilver' (Plate 102)

The variegation in this plant appears to be part of its normal pattern, so there is no risk of it reverting to plain green leaves. This is a more compact plant than the two Wandering Jews, but even so it should be stopped once or twice in the summer. The leaves are larger than in the other species we have been discussing, up to 3 inches in length, but only about an inch across and are a bright green with longitudinal silver stripes. The flowers, which are rarely produced, are pink in colour, while those of *T. albiflora* and *T. fluminensis* are white. The plant should be in a well-lit situation, but should not be exposed to too much direct sunlight. A winter temperature of 45° is necessary, but no harm will accrue should it be higher. This is arguably the best of the *Tradescantias*.

Genus ZEBRINA

This genus is named from the Zebra-like stripes on the leaves of *Zebrina pendula*. It is very similar in appearance to *Tradescantia*, from which it differs only in the shape of the flowers.

1. Zebrina pendula (Plates 49 and 103)

One of the most beautiful and cheapest of houseplants. The leaves are similar in shape to the *Tradescantias*, but have a short stalk, as opposed to springing directly from the stem. They are up to 3 inches long and half as wide, and have as the main colour a silvery grey-green. The edges of the leaf are dark green and there is a large purple stripe in the centre. The underside of the leaf is green and rosy purple. Keeping the plant on the dry side will emphasize the purple colour, but it should not be exposed to too much light as that tends to turn it an unpleasant rusty-brown colour. Few plants more reward the trouble of producing a large specimen plant. If room allows, a 6-inch pot full of *Zebrina* is a joy for ever. In its early stages it grows upright, but after a time, as the stems elongate, they turn down and the plant is seen at its best if it is in a hanging container or high up on the wall.

The variety *quadricolor* (four-coloured) is very spectacular. The upper side of the leaves is striped with white, rosy purple, dark green and silvery green, with the rosy purple predominating. The underside is composed of varying shades of purple. It is less vigorous than the type and needs keeping on the dry side, otherwise it is liable to rot. It requires to be placed in the brightest light available, as, if shaded, it is liable to revert to the type. This is, in any case, liable to happen during the winter, but with the coming of spring the more brilliant leaves will reappear. It does not appear to be a very stable variety; the variegation seems very dependent on warmth and light.

2. Zebrina purpusii

This has long been known and is still sold as *Tradescantia purpurea*. This is another beautiful and easy member of the family. It is even more pendulous than *pendula* and needs to be placed so that both the upper and underside of the leaf are visible. The upper side is a rather dull purple, while the underside is much more vivid. It is happiest in a light airy situation and is very suitable for hanging in front of a window. It produces small purple-pink flowers from time to time. It is extremely hardy and trouble-free, but do not overwater or it will lose its purple colouring.

Genus COMMELINA

This genus was named in honour of two Dutch botanists of the seventeenth century, Kaspar and Johann Commelin. Only one species is a houseplant.

1. Commelina benghalensis variegata

Similar in appearance to *Tradescantia fluminensis* but with slightly smaller leaves with a cream margin. It is more tender than the plants we have considered hitherto and is chiefly grown on account of its small bright gentian-blue flowers. These are attractive, but last only for a day. However, they are produced in some quantity.

Genus CYANOTIS

1. Cyanotis moluccensis

Similar in appearance to other *Tradescantias*, but with much smaller leaves, usually under an inch in length. However, if the plant is grown under warm, moist conditions, the leaves will become as long as $1\frac{1}{2}$ inches. The leaves are slightly hairy and bright green with a purple fleck in the centre, which fades out as the leaves age. The plant produces quite large panicles of minute white flowers, which are produced very freely if the plant is put in a well-lit airy position. The plant is not showy, but it has charm.

Genus SETCREASEA

No explanation for this name has yet been given.

1. Setcreasea striata

This is similar in appearance to the other *Tradescantias*, though the leaves are set rather closer together. They attain a length of 2 inches and a width of 1 inch, and are a rather dark green striped along the veins with ivory. The underside is green shading to purple. The leaves and stem are downy.

2. Setcreasea purpurea

The 'Purple Heart'. In appearance this is completely different from any of the other *Commelinaceae* we have been considering. It does not have a trailing stem, but erect, oblong-oval leaves, which may be as much as 6 inches long, though only 1½ inches across. During the summer it will throw up tall flowering stems, as much as a foot high, which will produce, if allowed, magenta-coloured flowers that clash most horribly with the leaves. The leaves and stems are a charming Tyrian purple, and, as the plant is very hardy and easy to propagate, there seems no reason why it should not be better known than it is. Its one disadvantage is that it tends to become leggy, but this can be overcome by cutting down or cutting out any growths that spoil the appearance of the plant. All stopped growths will break at a joint. The stems are very brittle, so it is best to purchase the plant in a young stage before the stems have grown. It is a quick grower and will need potting on in its first season. It seems to do best if not too heavily shaded, though it will probably not appreciate too much direct sunlight. If the plant is allowed to flower it is advisable to cut out the stems when flowering is finished.

Miscellaneous 2

Genus DICHORISANDRA

Named from its two valved anthers.

1. Dichorisandra mosaica

This plant is known in the United States as the Seersucker Plant and has only recently been re-introduced in this country. It throws longish stems which carry oval leaves of a dark green colour covered all over with thin white lines, and with a purple underside. The plant eventually produces a handsome head of bright blue flowers. The plant is a native of Brazil and is somewhat delicate. The variety *undata* (waved), which is sometimes given separate specific rank, is perhaps more satisfactory as a houseplant, as it is far more compact and has larger leaves. These are banded longitudinally with silver-green and a blackish green and the surface of the leaf is undulated. The underside of the leaf is purple.

2. Dichorisandra reginae (Plate 104)

Reginae means the queen's, but it is not clear if any particular queen is referred to. Until recently this Peruvian plant was known as *Tradescantia reginae*. It is more tender than the other plants we have been discussing and much slower growing. In appearance it is not unlike a large *Tradescantia*, but the stems grow upright and do not trail. The leaves are said to attain 6 inches in length, although $4\frac{1}{2}$ inches is more usual; they are about $1\frac{3}{4}$ inches across. The centre of the leaf is blackish purple in the new leaves, fading to dark green as the leaf ages. On either side is a silvery zone and the margin of the leaf is dark green. The underside of the leaf is dark purple. This is a very striking plant.

Genus RHOEO

1. Rhoeo discolor (Plate 104)

The only species of this genus. Its appearance is quite different to any other member of the family. It has long thin fleshy leaves that come from a central stem, like an aloe. These may be as much as 9 inches long, though only 1¾ inches across, and are dark green on the upper side and rosy purple underneath. The inconspicuous flowers are produced in curious little purple purses at the base of the stem. The plant likes shady, but not too shady, conditions. It is not outstandingly hardy and wants watching in the winter to see that it does not get too wet. The variety *vittatum* (Plate 105) has vivid cream stripes on the upper side of the leaf. *Rhoeo* is a striking and unusual-looking plant that is happiest on its own. It can become in time quite tall. It produces offshoots from the base of the stem that can be used for cuttings.

VII. LILIACEAE

The lily family is extremely large, containing some 200 genera and over 2,000 species. As far as houseplants are concerned their resemblance to the lily is not very apparent. Indeed it would not surprise us if *Dracaena* and *Cordyline* were given a family of their own.

Genus ASPARAGUS

It would seem the wildest folly on the part of the botanists to assert that *Asparagus* is related to the lilies, but if you take the trouble to examine the flower of an asparagus through a magnifying glass, you will see that it is almost identical with the flower of a bluebell. It is not, however, for their flowers that *Asparagus* are grown but for their finely cut foliage.

1. Asparagus meyeri (Plate 106)

This may be only a form of *A. sprengeri*, but it appears so distinct in habit and foliage as to warrant treatment as a separate species. It has the same cluster of tuberous roots as *A. sprengeri*, but there the resemblance ends. The stems are erect and not more than a foot high, generally somewhat less and are densely branched, with the branches, which are about an inch long, clothed with soft linear phylloclades about ½ inch long. The whole plant is a soft green and gives the impression of a lot of miniature cypresses arising from the root. A minimum of 50°

during the winter is more than adequate, probably 45° would be tolerated, and temperatures around 60° are quite high enough in the spring and summer, although higher temperatures are not unwelcome. All these South African *Asparagus* like plenty of light and ample water while they are making their new growths, although, with their tuberous roots, they can be kept very dry during the winter.

2. Asparagus plumosus var. compactus nanus

Asparagus plumosus, the feathery asparagus, is the plant well known as asparagus fern, which is used a lot in cut flower work particularly as backing for buttonholes and corsages. It is naturally a twining plant and the variety used as a houseplant has lost this climbing habit and makes a bushy plant about 18 inches high. The stems are rather stiff and wiry and bear occasional prickles. The branches emerge horizontally and are densely covered with hair-like leaves, which are, strictly, not leaves at all but phylloclades, or flattened leaf-like twigs. The plant is native to South Africa and does not require much heat at any time. 45° in the winter is adequate, although slightly higher readings are better. *Asparagus* plants are unisexual, some plants bearing only male flowers with stamens, while others bear female flowers with a pistil and ovary, which, when fertilized, will produce a red berry. Plants come readily from seed, but they can also be increased by division, which is best done about the end of March. The plant should be kept moderately wet at all times and prefers shade, although this must not be too dark.

3. Asparagus sprengeri var. compactus

This has the branches covered with rather wiry phylloclades, unlike the soft ones of *A. plumosus* and the stem tends to get rather woody and to bear hooked prickles. The phylloclades are also much longer, about an inch as opposed to the $\frac{1}{4}$ inch of the last species. The stems have a slight tendency to flop and the plant is often seen as a hanging plant. It needs treatment similar to that recommended for *A. plumosus*, although it comes from a rather warmer region of South Africa. A variegated form turned up at one time but appears to have been lost.

Genus ASPIDISTRA

A genus of some eight species from the Eastern Himalayas, China and Japan.

1. Aspidistra elatior

This well-known plant arrived in cultivation from Japan in the 1830's and soon superseded *A. lurida*, from China as a room-plant of cast-iron hardiness, which would put up with the most intolerable conditions. It bears single leaves on short stalks that spring straight from the rhizome. They are an oblong lance-shape and may be up to 20 inches long and 5 or 6 inches across. They are a dark green in the type and striped with ivory in the var. *variegata*, which has become quite scarce recently, after being extremely common. During the summer small, starry inconspicuous purple-maroon flowers appear at ground level, and their appearance is usually a sign that the plant needs potting-on. Otherwise they are left to become pot-bound and should never be in too large a pot, until they become very large. If this does happen they can easily be divided. They like a fairly rich compost originally and some feeding during the summer, but they do require a restricted root-run. Too much heat in winter is resented and it should not exceed 50°. Shady situations are perfectly satisfactory, as the plant will grow practically anywhere.

Genus CHLOROPHYTUM

The name is derived from two Greek words, *chloros* meaning green, and *phyton* a plant, which does not suggest much inventiveness on the part of the botanist who named it. As only two species are in general cultivation one would have thought that the chance of their being misnamed was remote, but in point of fact the plant that is sold universally under the name of *Chlorophytum capense*, should be correctly referred to as *C. comosum*. This is one of the oldest houseplants and in 1828 was presented to the great German writer, Goethe. He was so impressed by its habit of producing young plants at the end of the flowering scape that he distributed it widely amongst his friends and the plant has maintained its popularity ever since.

1. Chlorophytum comosum var. variegatum (Plate 107)

This plant is a native of South Africa and is, in consequence, extremely hardy. It produces long narrow blue bell-like leaves, striped with cream. On what, in any other plant, would be the flower spike it produces tufts of leaves, which will quickly root when they touch soil. These very young plants require to be kept on the dry side until they are well rooted. A mature plant will take quite a bit of water. This plant is rarely displayed to its full advantage. A well-grown specimen in a 5- or 6-inch pot, placed by itself with the leafy inflorescences left on, looks most impressive: a small plant in a group looks like a rather unpleasant grass. As we said above, it is invariably sold under the name of *C. capense*, from which it differs by its habit of throwing these tufted flower spikes.

2. Chlorophytum orchidiastrum

The resemblance of this plant to an orchid is confined to its flower spike, which appears from the side of the plant in a fashion more usual with orchids than with other plants. The plant makes a large rosette of leaves about a foot across and the individual leaves are some 2 inches wide. They are a dark bronzy green with copper-coloured stems and this colour is preserved in about two-thirds of the midrib. As the leaves age this copper shade disappears and it is not very prominent in the new leaves, so that the whole plant shades from dark green through copper to a lighter green, and is very attractive in a subtle rather than spectacular fashion. The plant, which is probably incorrectly named, is found on hillsides in Tanganyika. It therefore requires warmer treatment than *C. comosum*, although it will probably thrive so long as the temperature does not fall below 45°. As the leaves are somewhat fleshy, it can tolerate long periods of dryness without ill-effect. The plant does not produce many offsets and propagation is generally by seed.

Genus CORDYLINE

This is named from the Greek word for a club. These plants are very similar to the next genus *Dracaena* and are usually sold under that name. They have the reputation of being somewhat delicate, but have in practice turned out to be hardier than their reputation warrants. One species, *Cordyline indivisa*, though less showy than the varieties of *terminalis*, is extremely hardy and can be grown out of doors in mild districts. Most *Cordylines* and *Dracaenas* are palm-like plants, and as they age and the bottom leaves die off, a central trunk can be observed. If this centre stem is cut into sections and put into a propagating bed kept at a high temperature (70° to 75°), a shoot will appear from each leaf joint. Most *Cordylines* and *Dracaenas* like a rich soil such as:

6 parts loam
5 parts peat
4 parts leaf mould
2 parts sand
1 48-pot full of bone meal per barrow load.

They should be kept moist when growing. Apart from Red Spider they do not attract pests.

1. Cordyline indivisa (Plate 108)

A native of New Zealand that can be grown out of doors in very mild places. This is a palm-like shrub, capable of reaching a height of 25 feet in its native land. The leaves are long and spiky at the end and some 2 to 4 inches across. The central midrib is usually red in colour and the general effect is of bronze-coloured leaves.

2. Cordyline terminalis (Colour Plate III. Plate 96)

Although in theory these plants can reach a height of 5 to 12 feet, in practice they rarely exceed 18 inches. The type has plain green leaves, but the numerous varieties contain some of the most brilliant colours of all leaves. The leaf may be as much as 12 inches in length and some 4 inches across and is shaped in an

III. Cordyline terminalis

elongated oval. A bare description of the plants can do little to suggest their remarkable beauty. They are unfortunately rather expensive, as young plants do not show the brilliant colours and the plants have, as a result, to be grown on for some years in the nursery before they can be offered for sale. Some of the varieties have been given cultivar names and some varietal names, and no attempt has been made here to sort them out.

(*a*) 'Juno'. The centre leaves are cerise-pink which fade slowly to a purplish brown, flecked with red.

(*b*) 'Prince Albert'. This is similar to Juno, but the leaves are somewhat redder and the plant is taller with a more upright habit.

(*c*) 'Firebrand'. The young leaves are a bright cerise fading rather quickly to a dark purple with cerise margin.

(*d*) 'Smetana'. The young leaves are pink and age to a dark green with a red edge.

(*e*) 'Margaret Story'. The young leaves are pale cream flushed with pink; the mature leaves are a medium green with a pink edge.

(*f*) *Baptistii*. The young leaves are cream with pink and green streaks, fading to a dark green with a cream edge.

(*g*) *Guilfoylei*. The lower half of the leaves is white and the upper half striped with red, pink and white.

(*h*) *Volckaertii*. This is, presumably, the typical wild form of the plant and does not deserve a cultivar name at all. It has dark green leaves without any trace of variegation.

It is interesting that most of the coloured leaved forms of *C. terminalis* were brought back from the South Sea Islands by James Gould Veitch in 1866. One wonders if there was some sort of gardening tradition in these islands.

3. Rededge

This seems to be the most appropriate place to insert the plant that is sold under the name *Dracaena* 'Rededge'. This is a mysterious plant and it is not known whether it is a *Cordyline* or a *Dracaena*. It has much the habit of *C. terminalis* and the

255

young leaves are margined and blotched with cerise, which, however, soon fades leaving a rather bronze blade with a cerise margin. The leaves are much smaller than those of *C. terminalis*, being elliptic in shape, about 5 inches long and 1½ inches across. If it were possible to hybridize *C. terminalis* and *Dracaena marginata* one might expect the resultant plant to be something like this. At the moment its origin is a mystery. It could, possibly, be just a dwarf form of *C. terminalis*. In any case it needs similar treatment, with a winter temperature around 60° or 65° and good light, but not direct sunlight. They should also have a fairly moist atmosphere, which can be supplied either by syringeing or by standing the pots in some moist medium. Although the cerise soon fades from the leaves, the leaf-stalks remain pink all the time, so that the plant is rather brilliant at all times. The tips of the leaves are rather liable to brown during the winter and it may be necessary to trim them with nail scissors. This plant may be a form of *Dracaena concinna*, a plant from Mauritius, with dark green, purple-edged leaves and a greenish purple stalk. It would be satisfactory to know its true genus and specific identity.

In the Turnford collection there are several other *terminalis* cultivars whose names have been lost. One seems near *Mayi* with the older leaves green edged with red, and the younger leaves entirely red.

Genus DRACAENA

This genus is named from the Greek word for a dragon, the dye known as dragon's blood is obtained from one species.

Dracaenas come mainly from Africa and represent the main contribution of that continent to houseplants. Although most of the species are a little more tender than the *Cordylines*, they require less tropical conditions than most text-books would suggest. A minimum of 50° is quite sufficient, though they will enjoy warmer conditions if they are available.

1. Dracaena deremensis (Plate 109)

A palm-like plant with dark green edges to the leaves, which are then decorated with two silver stripes, while the central portion of the leaf is greyish in colour: a beautiful plant. The variety *Bausei* has the whole of the centre of the leaf silver and the stem is also silvery.

2. Dracaena fragrans

This has very broad leaves some 4 inches across. The type is not in cultivation, but there are two varieties which are very desirable, (*a*) var. *Lindenii* which has wide gold edges to the leaf and a narrow green and gold centre band, and (*b*) var. *Massangeana* (Plate 107), which reverses the coloration, with a gold centre to the leaf and an emerald-green edge.

3. Dracaena goldieana

Named in honour of the Reverend Hugh Goldie, an American missionary in W. Africa in the 1870s. This has leaves up to 8 inches long and 4 to 5 inches across. The midrib is golden in colour and the leaf is glossy green with wide bands of silver-grey. The young leaves have a pinkish tinge.

4. Dracaena godseffiana

This species is named in honour of Joseph Godseff, a famous gardener and collector, who died in 1921. This is different in appearance and habit to all the other *Dracaenas*. It is a low, branching shrub with leaves either opposite, or in whorls of three, at close intervals. The leaves are oval, some 3 inches long and 1½ to 2 inches across, and are dark green, thickly spotted with small cream spots. A cultivar, known as 'Florida Beauty' (Plate 109), has the leaves much more thickly spotted with cream and is altogether more showy than the type.

5. Dracaena marginata

This native of Madagascar has the same long, sword-shaped leaves as those of *Cordyline indivisa*. They may be as long as 15 inches, but are little more than an inch across. The leaves are dark green with a distinct red margin, hence its name *marginata*, and also reddish veins. Eventually the plant will get a trunk, which in mature specimens will reach a height of 4 or 5 feet, but this trunk elongates very slowly and the plant remains reasonably short for a long time. The plant will be quite happy with a winter temperature of 50° and appreciates a certain amount of light, which will enhance the red margin.

6. Dracaena parrii

This is one of the most hardy types of *Dracaenas* and can be used outside in the summer time. One sees it used to great effect in many municipal parks. It is best when grown as a large plant and has a sturdy trunk. From the top of this trunk grow, in palm-like fashion, the narrow spiky leaves, which are of olive-green, with vivid pink markings on the underside rib which show up well because of the extremely erect habit of the leaves.

7. Dracaena reflexa

Under this rather dubious name we are putting the plant which is always known as *Pleomele reflexa* 'Song of India'. Salisbury's name *Pleomele* has been taken into *Dracaena* and our plant seems to agree fairly well with the plant known as *Dracaena marmorata*, a Malayan plant. 'Song of India' was brought from Ceylon, but presumably from cultivated plants, as a plain green-leaved form is known. This is an attractive plant with strap-shaped leaves, that rise and then fall back, about 6 inches long and $1\frac{1}{2}$ inches across, with wide yellow margins and a narrower dark green centre. The plant branches freely as it ages and so makes a plant different in shape from most other *Dracaenas*, which may be the reason why it retained its name of *Pleomele*. It is a somewhat delicate plant, requiring a winter temperature of 55° and a moist atmosphere during the growing season. This entails syringeing the leaves in hot, dry weather and standing the plant in some container which will hold moisture. Although the variegated 'Song of India' is perhaps the more attractive, the plain green form has its own charm and is easier to keep in good condition. Like most plants from monsoon districts it will require very large quantities of water, while it is making its growth, but can tolerate dry conditions during the autumn and winter.

8. Dracaena sanderi (Plate 110)

This *Dracaena* was named after Henry Sander, who founded the well-known orchid nurseries at Bruges and St. Albans. This has proved remarkably hardy. The leaves are thin, barely 1 inch across, and are slightly wavy. The edges are ivory and the centre of the leaf is a greyish green with a few thin lines of ivory. This is a smaller plant than the majority of *Dracaenas*. A mature plant will branch at the base.

Genus SANSEVIERIA

This genus was named in honour of the eighteenth-century Prince of Sanseviero, Raimond de Sansgrio. The plants have thick fleshy leaves and can tolerate long periods of drought. What they will not tolerate is excessive watering, particularly in the winter when the plants are dormant: in this case they are liable to rot. The most popular species, *Sansevieria trifasciata Laurentii* (Plate 110), can grow equally happily in sun or shade. During the growing season they can be watered reasonably frequently, though once a fortnight may prove sufficient. During the winter, unless your room is very warm, a watering a month is ample. The plant has a creeping rhizome and will throw up sideshoots with remarkable persistence. Indeed, the way to propagate them on a commercial scale is to plant stock plants out in a bed in the greenhouse and leave them there. It will be two years before much will be obtained in the way of results, but after that numerous new plants will appear. These are best severed from the parent plant when the leaf has reached a height of some 8 inches. The rhizome will not be very heavily rooted, and after potting up they must be kept warm and close until a good root system has developed. As only one or two new leaves are produced each year it is best to put two or three plants into one pot. Leaf cuttings will root satisfactorily, but the chromosome which causes the yellow bands in the leaves seems to exist only in the rhizome and the resultant plant will be the type

Sansevieria trifasciata with mottled green leaves and will lack the two yellow bands, which characterize the variety *Laurentii*. Most of the *Sansevierias* like a heavy soil such as:

2 parts loam
1 part leaf mould
¾ part sharp sand.

In time, and given the right conditions, *Sansevieria trifasciata Laurentii* can reach a height of 4 feet, but in pots it rarely exceeds 18 inches. The leaf is rarely more than 2 or 3 inches across and is erect with a slightly undulating edge. The two yellow stripes look as if they are marginal, but a close inspection will show a very thin green edge to the leaf. In the U.S.A. they have *Sansevieria trifasciata Craigii* which has very much more yellow in the leaf.

There are other varieties of *Sansevierias*, but none are so attractive as *Laurentii*.

2. Sansevieria hahnii (Plate 111)

This has a dense rosette of mottled dark and grey-green leaves and is not unlike a small Aloe in appearance. There is said to be a variegated form of this, but it does not appear to be in commerce.

3. Sansevieria arborea

S. arborea is an epiphyte with a creeping rhizome and requires to be grown on a block of wood or bark. The leaves are long and pointed, but it does not seem very suitable for a houseplant.

4. Sansevieria herckii

S. herckii has a long thin solid leaf and a somewhat strange appearance, as though it were a cactus.

5. Sansevieria cylindrica

S. cylindrica also has long cylindrical pointed leaves in two shades of green. The leaves are not quite so solid-looking as in the preceding species, and eventually open slightly.

6. Sansevieria grandis

S. grandis has thick fleshy flat leaves like elephant's ears.

Of these only *S. hahnii* is generally offered. With the exception of *S. arborea* they will respond to the same treatment as *trifasciata*.

VIII. AMARYLLIDACEAE

The Amaryllis family consists principally of bulbous plants, such as the daffodil. It is not really represented among house-plants, but some people like to grow some of the aloes (*Agave* spp.) in the room. These have the advantage of a great hardi-ness and tolerance of drought, so that they can be left for a month at a time without watering. Their disadvantages are that they require very bright light, and so can only be grown on window ledges, and the fact that the leaves are armed with stout spines and prickles, sufficient to cause an injury. In the opinion of most growers these disadvantages are too marked to warrant their cultivation as houseplants.

IX. DIOSCOREACEAE

The *Dioscoreaceae* or Yam family is small, containing nine genera and some 220 species. It is represented among English wild flowers by the Black Bryony and also provides the Yam of the tropics.

Genus DIOSCOREA

Named after the father of botany, Dioscorides.

1. Dioscorea discolor (Plate 113)

Like *Cissus discolor,* this is not a true houseplant at all, but it is so beautiful that it cannot be overlooked. Unlike the *Cissus* it is easy to grow. It is a twining plant (when training it, it is worth remembering that it twines to the left) with large heart-shaped leaves, 8 inches long and 6 inches across when fully expanded, and mottled with contrasting shades of green, and with an irregular greyish zone around the midrib. The underside of the leaf is a vivid matt purple. The plant gives a most striking effect. When growth is completed the plant dies down. All water should then be withheld and the pot laid on its side and stored away in a warm situation. Towards the end of March or early April the soil should be shaken out and the potato-like yams should be put in a moist mixture of two-thirds peat and one-third sand, and kept in a warm position until they sprout. They should then be potted up, using a soil mixture similar to that given for the Ivies (or JIP 2) and three sticks should be inserted in the pot, between which the shoots are trained. The plant grows very rapidly once it starts, and when it has reached a suitable size will take large quantities of water. To make a shapely plant attention must be paid to training the shoots whose instinct is to go straight up.

There are two other species of *Dioscorea*, *illustrata* and *multicolor*, which are very similar to *discolor* and since they are all natives of Brazil may be local varieties. *Dioscorea vittata* with red and white leaves sounds interesting, but is not in cultivation.

X. ZINGIBERACEAE

The Ginger family contains forty genera and some 800 species. Until quite recently its members were included in the family *Scitamineae*, which no longer exists. As far as houseplants are concerned they are represented at the moment by one species.

Genus ELETTARIA

1. Elettaria cardamomum (Plate 114)

This is the source of the Cardamom seed, which is a feature of curries and other Oriental dishes. Although it is said to reach a height of 9 feet in its native land, it rarely exceeds a foot as a houseplant. The plant has a creeping rhizome from which, in time, many shoots arise. The shoots show the typical habit of the Ginger family; not unlike a bamboo in appearance, with an erect almost woody stem from which the long oblong-oval leaves spring at intervals of about 1½ inches. The leaves are about 6 inches long and 1½ inches across and are dark green in colour: when handled they give off a strong perfume of cinnamon. *Elettaria* grows happily in the usual houseplant mixture and is hardy and easy. It does not like strong light, which discolours the leaves, and should be kept on the dry side in the winter.

Another possible houseplant of the Ginger family is *Alpinia rafflesiana* var. *Sanderae*, usually called *A. sanderae*. (The genus is named after an Italian botanist, Prosper Alpino; none of the plants are alpines.) This has the typical ginger habit, but the leaves are a shiny green, striped with silver, and look most striking. This rather scarce plant is usually placed in the hottest greenhouse and is not evergreen, but is so striking that if it proves suitable for a houseplant, its brief resting period will not militate against it.

XI. ORCHIDACEAE

The Orchid family is one of the largest, with over 15,000 species in more than 600 genera. Although there are certain genera with very ornamental leaves, they have neither been tried nor offered as houseplants. There would appear to be no reason, however, why some of the Japanese *Goodyeras*, such as *G. japonica* and *G. macrantha* and the North American *G. menziesii*, should not be grown as houseplants with great ease, if they can be obtained. They require cool, shady, moist conditions and not only have handsome leaves, but *G. macrantha* also produces quite showy flowers. They should be potted in a mixture of peat and leaf mould, made open by the addition of sharp sand. Far more spectacular are the various species of *Anoectochilus*, which have some of the most handsome of all leaves. These are difficult to grow in the greenhouse and might well prove easier in the house, if a sufficiently moist atmosphere could be provided. The main essential would appear to be shade and temperatures rarely dropping below 50°. As in so many plants it does not seem to be the actual temperature that is so important, as that this temperature should remain fairly constant. *Anoecto-chilus* are found from the Himalayas to the south-east, usually at some height and in shady situations. Those who have had a tropical aquarium and got tired of it, can use the tank as a Wardian case, and in this *Anoectochilus* would probably thrive. They are usually grown in a mixture of chopped Osmunda fibre and sphagnum moss, as though they were epiphytic orchids, but might well be better in a mixture of leaf mould and woodland mosses. *A. discolor* from Hong Kong is one of the handsomest and is comparatively easy. *A. regalis* from Ceylon is more easily obtainable, but is not so easy as *discolor*. The word 'easy' is in any case only relative. This genus has always been regarded as one of the most difficult of cultivation; but it does not seem unlikely that the room might be a better place for it than the greenhouse.

Another ornamental-leaved genus of orchids is *Microstylis*. One of the best, *M. discolor* from Ceylon, has deep red-purple leaves with a green edge and is very ornamental. It is, however, a deciduous species, forming a new pseudobulb each year. *M. lowii* and *M. macrochila* from Borneo and Malaya are evergreen. They require a moist atmosphere, shade and reasonably high temperatures; 55° should be an acceptable minimum, though, like so many plants, they would probably survive happily enough at 50°. The usual orchid mixture of chopped Osmunda and sphagnum is usually prescribed for these orchids, but they might well do better in a mixture of leaf mould and sand topped with a layer of sphagnum.

We have no experience of the culture of orchids in the home and they are not, at the moment, offered by any houseplant growers. Orchid nurseries could probably produce some *Anoecto-chilus* and *Microstylis* and others can be obtained from Indian nurserymen; the *Goodyeras* would presumably have to be imported from Japan. Although most orchids are tenacious of life and easy to grow, the terrestrial species (i.e. those that root in the soil, as opposed to most tropical orchids which are epiphytes) have always been found more difficult. Most terrestrial orchids are dependent on a fungus in the soil (*Rhizoctonia*) which infects the roots and helps them to take in nourishment. If the soil is sterilized, the fungus will be destroyed and this may account for many failures. It is also probable that the *Rhizoctonia* of our soils are not those met with in the tropics, but the fact that these orchids can be grown successfully suggests that this is not of critical importance. Most orchid growers concentrate on those species with large showy flowers and little work has been done on the ornamental-leaved species. They can be seen in the principal botanical gardens, but in small quantities, and some research into their reaction to different soil mixtures might solve the difficulty of growing so many of these fascinating plants.

CHAPTER XIII

Pests

I t is impossible to grow a large number of plants without attracting the attention of various insects and fungi. Fortunately, plants in the home do not attract pests with quite the same abandon as when they are grown in a nursery.

Control measures on a nursery are simple, but they often consist of lethal poisons. It cannot be too strongly emphasized that the most rigorous care must be taken when handling preparations such as Systox or Malathion and these should be kept under lock and key when not in use.

When handling the concentrate it is essential to wear rubber gloves, but when used in diluted form, gloves are not necessary. Systox makes the plant toxic, which means that insects living on the plant will eventually die even if they missed the actual spray when it was applied.

Systemic sprays are only advocated for nurseries where all safety precautions can be taken. They are not advised for use in the home where there could be danger to children and animals.

For the home, white oil preparations are recommended as being safe and having the advantage of being non-poisonous. White oils have no systemic value, and therefore it is a hit-to-kill spray. If a plant is badly affected it is better to dip the whole plant, but do not let the soil become saturated; hold the plant upside down when it is being immersed.

When mixing up any insecticide do not be tempted to add more than is recommended, if you have a heavy infestation. You will not kill more insects and you may do damage to the plant.

Pests

In greenhouses and the open air the insecticides are usually applied by means of a spray, but as this is inconvenient in the house it is better, as already stated, to mix your insecticide in a bucket and immerse the aerial portion of the plant in the mixture by holding the pot upside down. If the plant is too big for this operation, it should be stood in a shed where it can be syringed. It is advisable to drench the plant, making sure that the spray goes on the undersides as well as on the tops of the leaves.

Now let us consider the most common individual pests.

Aphis

Greenfly and Blackfly are comparatively rare pests of house-plants, and can easily be controlled by the application of some non-poisonous spray such as Sybol. It seems unlikely that there is anyone who has not met these pests at some time in his life, but, for such fortunate people, it may be mentioned that Aphides are small green or black insects, usually wingless, which congregate in great numbers on the growing points or on the undersides of the leaves. The former will cause distortion and prevent normal growth taking place; the latter will cause yellowing and leaf drop. Routine examination of the plants will bring any infestation to your notice, and control measures can be taken before any harm is done.

White Fly

The adult, as its name implies, is a small white winged creature, but the damage is caused by the larvae known as 'scales' which look like a very small grey scale insect. They excrete honey-dew on which a fungus called Sooty Mould soon appears, covering the leaves with a black soot-like substance. Spraying is not very effective, except with a systemic insecticide. Derris if applied at three weekly intervals to the undersides of the leaves gives a certain amount of control, but would probably not be 100 per cent effective.

Red Spider

This is not a spider and is not always red. It makes its presence known by mottled or yellowed patches on the leaves. If these leaves are handled they will be found to feel rough, and if the underside is examined it is just possible to see the tiny spider-like mites. The appearance of Red Spider is a clear indication that the atmosphere is too dry and it is advisable to rectify this, before the trouble spreads to other plants. Nothing will obliterate the damage already done but the mites can be killed by an application of one of the systemic insecticides. It must be borne in mind, as we have said above, that they are *extremely poisonous*, and every precaution must be taken. White oil sprays are less effective, but safe to use in the home as they are non-poisonous. If you catch the infection early enough it is possible to sponge the mites off with cold water, but it is rare that one becomes aware of Red Spider until there is quite heavy infestation.

Scale

This is one of the more likely pests to occur in the home, but, unlike Red Spider, fails to make its presence felt for some time. It is therefore advisable to make periodical inspections of the plants. Scale insects are small, though they may be as much as $\frac{1}{8}$ of an inch long, and do not move. They are of different colours, but the soft Scale, which is the one most frequently met with, is brownish. They usually make their first appearance on the underside of the leaf; in the case of large-leaved plants, such as *Dieffenbachias*, they tend to congregate along the main veins of the leaves. With a light infestation no damage is noticeable, but they breed rapidly and will soon cover the plant, causing the leaves to fall off. Although the adults do not move, the nymphs, which are all but invisible, are active. Regular examination of the plants is a standard recommendation. If only a few Scale are present they can be removed with a matchstick tipped with cotton wool and dipped in methylated spirit. In heavy infestations only systemic insecticides are effective.

Thrips

You should never have Thrips on your houseplants, and if you do, they have probably come from the nursery and should be reported. Thrips are minute winged insects, which lay their eggs in the tissues of the leaves or young stems of the plant and the larva lives in the tissues, sucking the plant's vital juices. Yellowing of a section of the leaf or distortion of the growing point should lead one to suspect Thrips, if no more obvious pest is present. Control is simple by means of a Derris spray.

Slugs and *Snails* may sometimes arrive in the bottoms of flower pots, but they can usually be sought out and destroyed.

Most insect pests can be controlled, but we are not so fortunate with fungal and bacterial pests. Root-rot caused by overwatering is generally fatal to the plant, and some plants, such as *Aphelandra*, occasionally get a canker, which girdles the stem and causes the plant to die. In these cases there is no cure, and it is necessary to prevent conditions arising which will cause these diseases. Overwatering is the usual cause and if this is looked after, fungus diseases are unlikely. There is, however, one fungal infection which may arise and can be treated. This is Begonia Mildew, which attacks the leaves of begonias, covering them with a unsightly white mould. This attacks plants that are unhappy owing to low temperature and excessive moisture. Spraying at regular intervals with Captan will prevent the fungus spreading, but it may not cure the infected leaves, in which case they should be removed and destroyed.[1]

It is often observed that insects and fungus do not attack plants that are healthy and growing well. It seems as if there has to be some weakness present before a bad infestation results. Though this is evidently not completely true, it does indicate that the best way to prevent pests is to buy healthy plants and keep them healthy. To say that prevention is better than cure may be a platitude, but is none the less true.

However, if in spite of all your efforts, pests arrive, treat them promptly. Most of them reproduce at a prodigious rate and it is not a question of a stitch in time saving nine, but of saving 900.

On the whole, houseplants do not attract pests, and although it is advisable to examine them weekly it will probably turn out to be nothing but a routine measure.

[1] A new non-poisonous systemic fungicide has just been introduced and will cope well with all mildews.

The Range of Houseplants

I n this appendix we are listing all the houseplants that have been described, according to their temperature requirements. We have divided them into four categories, which for purposes of convenience may be described as 'very hardy', 'hardy', 'delicate' and 'tender' and the operative factor that we have selected is their minimum temperature requirements.

In this respect various factors should be borne in mind. Well-rooted healthy plants will not object to an occasional drop of 5° below the minimum that we have given. On the other hand this might well prove fatal to plants that are not well-rooted or that are overwatered. Plants that have just been purchased, need acclimatizing and should not be plunged into too cold an environment at once. It should also be noted that the temperatures given are those recommended for survival purposes when the plants are in a relatively dormant state. They will require higher temperatures to make growth; in the ordinary way seasonal change will give this, but plants in the 'delicate' category should be thought of as requiring a minimum of 70° for growth. To a large extent plants can move from one category to another, but plants that are 'very hardy' will not enjoy too much warmth, particularly during their resting period. It is always safe for plants to move up one category and usually they can move up two, but some 'hardy' plants will not thrive under 'delicate' conditions. There are exceptions such as *Philodendron scandens*, which will tolerate cool or warm conditions.

Appendix 1

1. 'Very hardy' plants suitable for rooms that are frost-proof but otherwise unheated.

Chapter IV   *Acorus gramineus*

Chapter V   All *Hedera helix* cvs
             H. canariensis is possible, but better in warmer conditions
             Fatsia japonica
             × *Fatshedera lizei*

Chapter VI   *Ficus pumila*

Chapter VII *Cissus antartica*
             Cissus striata

Chapter IX   *Billbergia nutans*

Chapter X   *Chamaerops humilis*
             Phoenix canariensis
             Rhapis excelsa
             Cyrtomium falcatum
             Davallia canariensis
             Pteris cretica

Chapter XI   *Grevillea robusta*
             Stenocarpus sinuatus
             Aichryson × *domesticum*
             Sedum sieboldii
             Saxifraga stolonifera
             Pittosporum eugenioides
             Rubus reflexus
             Eriobotrya japonica
             Euonymus japonicus
             Eucalyptus cinerea and *perriniana*
             Glechoma hederacea variegata
             Senecio mikanioides

Chapter XII *Araucaria excelsa*
             Podocarpus macrophyllus
             Cyperus diffusus
             Carex morrowii and *C. foliosissima*
             Tradescantia albiflora and *fluminensis*
             Zebrina pendula and *Z. purpusii*
             Setcreasea purpurea

Appendix 1

Aspidistra elatior
Chlorophytum comosum
Cordyline indivisa

2. 'Hardy' plants, requiring a minimum temperature of 45°–50°.

Chapter IV   *Philodendron scandens*
                  P. bipinnatifidum
                  P. hastatum
                  P. lacerum
                  P. × *rubris nervis*
                  P. selloum
                  P. 'Tuxla'
                  Monstera pertusa
                  Syngonium podophyllum and *vellozianum*

Chapter V   *Hedera canariensis*
                  Cussonia spicata

Chapter VI   *Ficus elastica decora*
                  F. benghalensis
                  F. indica
                  F. lucida
                  F. macrophylla
                  F. cyathistipula (*panduriformis*)

Chapter VII   *Cissus capensis*
                  C. sicyoides
                  Rhoicissus rhomboidea
                  Many Begonia spp. will survive under these conditions although they prefer the next category

Chapter IX   Most Bromeliads will survive under these conditions, although a minimum of 50° is to be preferred

Chapter X   *Collinia elegans*
                  Livistona chinensis
                  Asplenium bulbiferum
                  Davallia bullata
                  Pteris biaurita argyraea
                  Pteris multifida

Chapter XI	*Pilea microphylla*
	Pittosporum tobira
	Citrus sinensis
	Euphorbia hermentiana
	Impatiens petersiana
	Cuphea hyssopifolia
	Eucalyptus citriodora
	Ardisia crispa and *A. japonica*
	Hoya carnosa variegata
	Beloperone guttata
	Coffea arabica
	Senecio macroglossus variegatus
Chapter XII	*Tradescantia blossfeldiana*
	T. elongata 'Rochford's Quicksilver'
	Asparagus spp.
	Dracaena parrii
	Sansevieria trifasciata laurentii
	S. hahnii
	Elettaria cardamomum

3. 'Delicate' plants, requiring a minimum temperature of 50° to 55°.

Chapter IV	*Philodendron cordatum*
	P. × *corsonianum*
	P. erubescens and *P.* 'Red Emerald'
	P. elegans
	P. fenzlii
	P. gloriosum
	P. ilsemannii
	P. imbe
	P. laciniatum
	P. mamei
	P. melanochryson
	P. micans
	P. radiatum
	P. sagittifolium
	P. squamiferum

Appendix 1

P. verrucosum
P. wendlandii
Anthurium scherzerianum
Dieffenbachia arvida
Monstera deliciosa
Scindapsus aureus
Spathiphyllum wallisii and *S.* 'Mauna Loa'

Chapter V *Dizygotheca elegantissima*
Schefflera actinophylla

Chapter VI *Ficus elastica*, variegated forms
F. benjamina
F. diversifolia and *F. triangularis*
F. infectoria
F. lyrata
F. nekbudu
F. australis variegata

Chapter VII *Tetrastigma voinerianum*
All Begonias except *B. rajah* will thrive under these conditions

Chapter VIII All *Peperomia* spp. will do well here
Ctenanthe lubbersiana and *oppenheimiana*
Maranta leuconeura vars.

Chapter IX All Bromeliads will do well here, although *Vriesia fenestralis* and *hieroglyphica* will enjoy more warmth

Chapter X *Howea* spp.
Adiantum cuneatum
Asplenium nidus
Nephrolepis spp.
Platycerium bifurcatum

Chapter XI All *Pilea* spp. will survive here, although more warmth is appreciated
Muehlenbeckia platyclados
Citrus mitis
Euphorbia bojeri
Euphorbia milii and vars.
Ceropegia spp.

274

Appendix 1

Hoya bella
Plectranthus oertendahlii
Hypocyrta glabra
Aphelandra squarrosa and *A. leopoldii*
Fittonia verschaffeltii
Sanchezia nobilis
Hoffmannia spp.
Gynura spp.

Chapter XII   *Pandanus* spp.
Commelina benghalensis variegata
Cyanotis moluccensis
Setcreasca striata
Rhoeo discolor
Chlorophytum orchidiastrum
Cordyline terminalis cvs.
Cordyline 'Rededge'
Dracaena spp., but they are happier in the next category
Sansevieria spp. other than *trifasciata* and *hahnii*
Dioscorea discolor

4. **'Tender' plants requiring a minimum temperature of 60°.**

Chapter IV   *Philodendron leichtlinii*
P. sodiroi
Aglaonema spp.
Anthurium crystallinum
Caladium spp.
Dieffenbachia spp.
Scindapsus pictus

Chapter VI   *Ficus radicans variegata*
Ficus religiosa

Chapter VII   *Cissus discolor*
Begonia rajah

Chapter VIII   All *Calathea* spp. do best at this range, although many will survive if given 'delicate' treatment
Piper ornatum

Appendix 1

Chapter IX   *Vriesia fenestralis*
                        V. hieroglyphica
Chapter X   *Phoenix roebelinii*
                        Reinhardtia gracilis
                        Adiantum tenerum
Chapter XI   *Pilea 'Norfolk'*
                        Pellionia spp.
                        Heimerliodendron brunonianum
                        Codiaeum variegatum cvs.
                        Euphorbia cotinioides
                        Hibiscus rosa-sinensis var. *Cooperi*
                        Sonerila margaritacea
                        Chamaeeranthemum igneum
                        Psuederanthemum albo-marginatum
                        Stenandrium lindenii
                        Fittonia argyroneura
                        Oplismenus hirtellus
                        Dichorisandra mosaica
                        D. reginae
                        Dracaena reflexa

The Arrangement of Different Houseplants in One Container

A bowl, or some other container, planted up with a selection of houseplants can be very attractive, but the different plants must be selected with some care. It is clear that you should select plants that require similar conditions of light, soil and temperature; that their rate of growth should be comparable, and that the plants should look better together than they do separately.

The ideal container is one provided with drainage holes and a plate on which to stand it. If this is not obtainable, a false bottom of perforated zinc will help to prevent root-rot from water-logging. A good handful of granulated charcoal placed at the bottom of the bowl will help to prevent the soil from getting sour. The soil mixture should be of a coarse open texture, such as a mixture of one part loam, two parts peat and one part sharp sand. Leaf mould should be avoided as it pans down quickly and causes sour conditions. A rich compost is not required at the outset; feeding can be applied after the plants have rooted into the compost.

The surface of the soil can be decorated with moss, or with pieces of cork bark or with granite chippings. Very attractive results can be obtained by using pebbles painted with transparent varnish; this gives the effect of stones at the edge of the sea, translucent and shining.

In planting up a bowl it is necessary to think ahead. A small *Rhoicissus* and two *Peperomias* would look handsome when planted, but the *Rhoicissus* is a far more vigorous grower than the *Peperomias*, and, if left to itself, would swamp the other plants. Of course it is possible to prune a vigorous plant back, so as to preserve the proportions of the bowl, but vigorous growth denotes vigorous root action and the less active plants may get starved. However, a little forethought will prevent any difficulties and the number of possible combinations is enormous. All we can do here is to suggest a few, grouped round one main plant. One plant that looks better in a bowl than on its own is *Sansevieria Laurentii*. This requires to be kept dry in the winter so it is clear that we are creating difficulties if we try to combine it with plants requiring a fair amount of winter watering. Now among plants that like dry conditions are most of the *Peperomias* which would be ideal. All the Bromeliads are another family that require to be dry especially in the winter: *Cryptanthus*, in particular, is seen to best advantage in a bowl, where its starfish shape can be contrasted with other leaf forms. The *Tradescantias* all fit in very well, and they are so vigorous that they need frequent cutting back, unless they are placed at the edge of the bowl and made to trail over it. These will combine happily with such plants as *Saxifraga stolonifera tricolor*, *Acorus gramineus* and *Marantas*. It is possible to combine one plant with others liking different conditions, so long as the exception is kept in its pot (which will be concealed under the soil) so that it can be given individual treatment.

The large-leaved *Ficus* are generally better on their own, but the smaller-leaved species such as *benjamina*, and *pumila*, are most useful and will combine happily with small-leaved *Hederas* and the various *Pileas*.

All *Dracaenas* look splendid in a bowl, especially *terminalis*, which, being brightly coloured, makes its best effect when combined with plants of quiet colours. *Elettaria*, though it may grow rather too tall, makes a good foil and so do the small-leaved green *Hederas*. *Philodendron scandens* and *Scindapsus* trained on bark make excellent subjects, but, if they thrive, they will eventually cover the whole bowl, and the other plants should be regarded as temporary fill-ups. If you have a really warm room the combination of *Begonia rex* and *Dieffenbachia* is superb.

Pittosporum eugenioides is a splendid centrepiece for a bowl, and *Chlorophytum* is equally effective in a bowl or by itself. For a shady situation, × *Fatshedera* or the variegated *Hedera canariensis* are very suitable and will combine well with *Ficus pumila*, *Neanthe bella* or *Philodendron scandens*.

During the Christmas season many bowls of houseplants are made up and offered for sale as gifts. These invariably look most attractive, especially when a small Cyclamen has been added. One must be prepared for the foliage plants to outlive the Cyclamen which in due course should be removed and another houseplant put in its place.

A Note on Houseplants as Cut Foliage

———————◆◆◆◆◆◆◆◆◆◆◆◆◆◆◆◆◆◆◆◆————————

With the prevalent interest in unconventional flower arrangements there is a great demand for the leaves and sprays of foliage houseplants. It must be borne in mind that taking the leaves and stems will weaken the plant and spoil the shape and symmetry. It is advisable to cut the leaves or trails twelve hours before they are used and for this period float them in cold water.

Some flowers and leaves that prove to be more difficult than others will last longer if put in warm water in which sugar has been dissolved; the proportion should be a tablespoon to a pint of water.

The reason for floating leaves for an overnight period is that the stalks draw up extra moisture and all the tiny cells which make up the leaf structure are filled to capacity. The stalk alone in water can never take up enough to compete with this total saturation.

Some flowers are the same; the *Hydrangeas* are a good example which give little trouble if immersed in water.

Some leaves will not survive satisfactorily whatever you do and it is best to avoid *Aphelandras, Calatheas, Maranta* (except *Kerchoveana*), *Ctenanthes, Fittonias, Pellionias, Rhoeo,* and *Ficus radicans.* Most other leaves are satisfactory and there are a great number to choose from with great variation for shape, size and colour.

All the *Ficus* leaves or stems require to have the tips burned, or plunged momentarily in hot water or in powdered charcoal to stop the flow of latex.

Some of the most sought-after leaves are those of the *Begonia rex*. There are many varieties giving an endless choice of pattern and colour. To cut and use one of these at once may cause trouble, so float it as already recommended.

If you are making a very big arrangement and you want to be certain of your *Begonia rex*, the surest method is to knock a whole plant out of its pot, wash all the soil away, leaving the roots clean. Cut away any of the unwanted leaves and make sure when placed in its final position that the washed roots are well down in the water of your container: a costly way of avoiding trouble but justified if the arrangement is of great importance to the occasion.

Sanseveria leaves can be used with great effect and are excellent in their lasting capacity. They can be used over and over again and will last many months. If they are constantly used give the leaves a wash each time. If wire is being used in the container the thick flat base of leaf may be difficult to fix. Cut the leaf in spear-shape form and this will fit comfortably in the wire. No damage will be done to the leaf.

Another good-shaped leaf is the *Dracaena* (*Cordyline terminalis*). A good laster and a range of wonderful colours of reds, pinks and creams.

Mature trails of *Cissus discolor* and *Dioscorea discolor* will last well, but the very young tip growth is best cut off as this will wilt quickly. Trails of many varieties of Ivies are seen in many decorations. One of the best is the cream and green variegated *Hedera canariensis*. Sometimes the tips of the trails will have leaves of pure cream. These are good to cut because when the leaves turn to all cream the growth will make little headway. The new shoot, that will grow from where it has been cut back, will grow with its true variegation. When using single leaves make sure they are really mature. A young fresh leaf may look tempting, but, when cut, it will not last: the older and really mature leaves are the ones to use.

Appendix 3

When using sprays and stems of the more hard wooded types of plants hammer the ends before placing them in water.

Tradescantia and *Zebrina* are some of the best subjects for cutting. The plant will benefit by being cut back and the pieces used will outlive the whole arrangement, and, when removed, will probably have rooted while in the water. These can be potted up and your stock will be increased.

APPENDIX 4

Houseplants from Pips

———————————————

Some of the seeds from fruit brought into the house, if sown, will produce houseplants, which are less handsome than those commercially grown but are capable of giving the grower considerable amusement.

The Avocado Pear (*Persea gratissima*) is a member of the *Lauraceae*, the laurel family. In nature it makes a large tree. The large pear-shaped stone should be planted like a bulb with the pointed end pointing towards the surface. It can be planted in a 5-inch pot. In reasonably warm conditions, it will produce a small trunk topped with a rosette of elliptical-shaped dark green leaves some 6 inches long. The winter temperature should be about 50°. As time goes on the tree will increase in size and when tall enough may sometimes be induced to branch by stopping. It resembles a rather dingy *Ficus* and the leaves are liable to brown at the edges.

The Lychee (*Litchi chinensis*), a member of the *Sapindaceae*, is a grape-like fruit, covered with a hard husk and containing a stone about 1 inch long. Though rather slow to germinate, the stone will produce a small tree with attractive glossy green pinnate leaves, not unlike the acacia. It does not appear to thrive for long in a pot and needs warmer winter conditions than one would expect from a native of China.

The various citrus fruits, oranges, tangerines, lemons, grape-fruit, etc., usually germinate easily. From the foliage point of view the most attractive is the tangerine, with dark green shining leaves. They are hardy, provided that they are not exposed to frost, and require a well-lit situation. They are rather slow grow-ing, and three to four years is necessary before a well-shaped bush is produced. They will not, of course, produce blossom or fruit until they are considerably older and far too large to be accommodated in a room.

The Pomegranate (*Punica granatum*), which belongs to a family all its own, the *Punicaceae*, is not suitable for a houseplant as it sheds its leaves in winter. It is, however, a handsome plant for a south wall, with leaves the colour of a copper beech, and after eight to ten years, handsome scarlet flowers.

The Custard Apple (*Annona reticulata*) is not very attractive nor easy to grow, though the reddish downy new growth is quite pleasant. It should be given warm conditions.

APPENDIX 5

TEMPERATURE CONVERSION TABLE

°F.	°C.	°F.	°C.	°F.	°C.	°F.	°C.
100	37·8	82	27·8	65	18·3	48	8·9
99	37·2	81	27·2	64	17·8	47	8·3
98	36·7	80	26·7	63	17·2	46	7·8
97	36·1	79	26·1	62	16·7	45	7·2
96	35·6	78	25·6	61	16·1	44	6·7
95	35·0	77	25·0	60	15·6	43	6·1
94	34·4	76	24·4	59	15·0	42	5·6
93	33·9	75	23·9	58	14·4	41	5·0
92	33·3	74	23·3	57	13·9	40	4·4
91	32·8	73	22·8	56	13·3	39	3·9
90	32·2	72	22·2	55	12·8	38	3·3
89	31·7	71	21·7	54	12·2	37	2·8
88	31·1	70	21·1	53	11·7	36	2·2
87	30·6	69	20·6	52	11·1	35	1·7
86	30·0	68	20·0	51	10·6	34	1·1
85	29·4	67	19·4	50	10·0	33	0·6
84	28·9	66	18·9	49	9·4	32	0·0
83	28·3						

Bibliography

The R.H.S. Dictionary of Gardening. 4 vols. Oxford 1951.
Supplement, 1 vol., Oxford 1956.

The Tropics. Aubert de la Rüe, F. Bourlière and J. P. Harroy.
Harrap, 1957.

Das Pflanzenreich. Ed. A. Engler.

Heft 60. *Philodendrinae* by H. Krause, 1913; reprinted 1957.

Heft 64. *Aglaonemas and Dieffenbachias* by A. Engler, 1915;
reprinted 1957.

Heft. 71. *Caladium.* Engler and Krause, 1920, 1957.

Heft 11. *Marantaceae* by K. Schumann, 1902; reprinted
1959.

Exotica. Alfred Byrd Graf, 1957.

New and Rare Beautiful-Leaved Plants. Shirley Hibberd, 1870.

Choice Stove and Greenhouse Ornamental-leaved Plants. B. S.
Williams, 1876.

Beautiful-Leaved Plants. E. J. Lowe and W. Howard, 1861.

Handboek Der Bloemisterij. D. Van Raalte, 1957.

Tropical Plants. L. Bruggeman, 1957.

Index to Text

287

Index to Text

Index to Plates

Index to Plates

DATE DUE			